Arvi

HELSINKI
ESPOO · KAUNIAINEN · VANTAA

AN ARCHITECTURAL GUIDE

Helsinki, Otava Publishing Company

OTAVA
1890

© Arvi Ilonen 1990
Layout and photo research Pia Ilonen

English translation Lauri Siilasvuo

Otava Publishing Company Printing Works
Keuruu 1990

ISBN 951-1-10762-3

CONTENTS

To Mörri and Kirmo

FOREWORD

In 1963 the Museum of Finnish Architecture published an architectural guide to Helsinki, and the present volume is a revised and updated version of that book. A committee headed by Professor Aarno Ruusuvuori selected the new buildings, and architect Arvi Ilonen was chosen to rewrite the book.

This guide is a continuation of a tradition of cooperation between the Museum of Finnish Architecture and the Otava Publishing Company.

Helsinki, March 1, 1989

Marja-Riitta Norri
Director of the Museum of Finnish Architecture

PREFACE

This architectural guide is more detailed and comprehensive than the ones that came out in the 1960s and 1970s. The guide presents short written descriptions of 310 architectural objects and milieus, with additional references to some 140 objects. The description facts date from January 1989.

Some important objects have been left out of the guide due to difficult access. On the other hand, important interiors have been included, although they are closed to the public. The number of villas and private residences that have retained their original use is small. The fact that they appear in this publication does not justify any breach of privacy.

Although a chronological guide would be more practical from the point of view of architectural development, this guide has been grouped geographically in order to facilitate its use. A chronological index and indexes of planners and building types add to the usefulness of the book.

The metropolitan area has been divided into thirteen partial maps. Most of the objects in Helsinki are on the downtown area map and the extended downtown area map. The other four maps depict areas along the Ring I road. Two of the Espoo maps depict areas on both sides of the Western Highway, and the two others areas along the Turku Highway. The three Vantaa maps depict areas along the Ring III road.

It is in the nature of architectural guides that they tend to become out-of-date fairly rapidly. The division of this guide to thirteen areas will facilitate the addition of new objects in future editions. The author is grateful for corrections, and subscribes to the remark of the English architectural critic Sir Nikolaus Pevsner, that architectural guides ought to be evaluated only after their second edition.

Arvi Ilonen

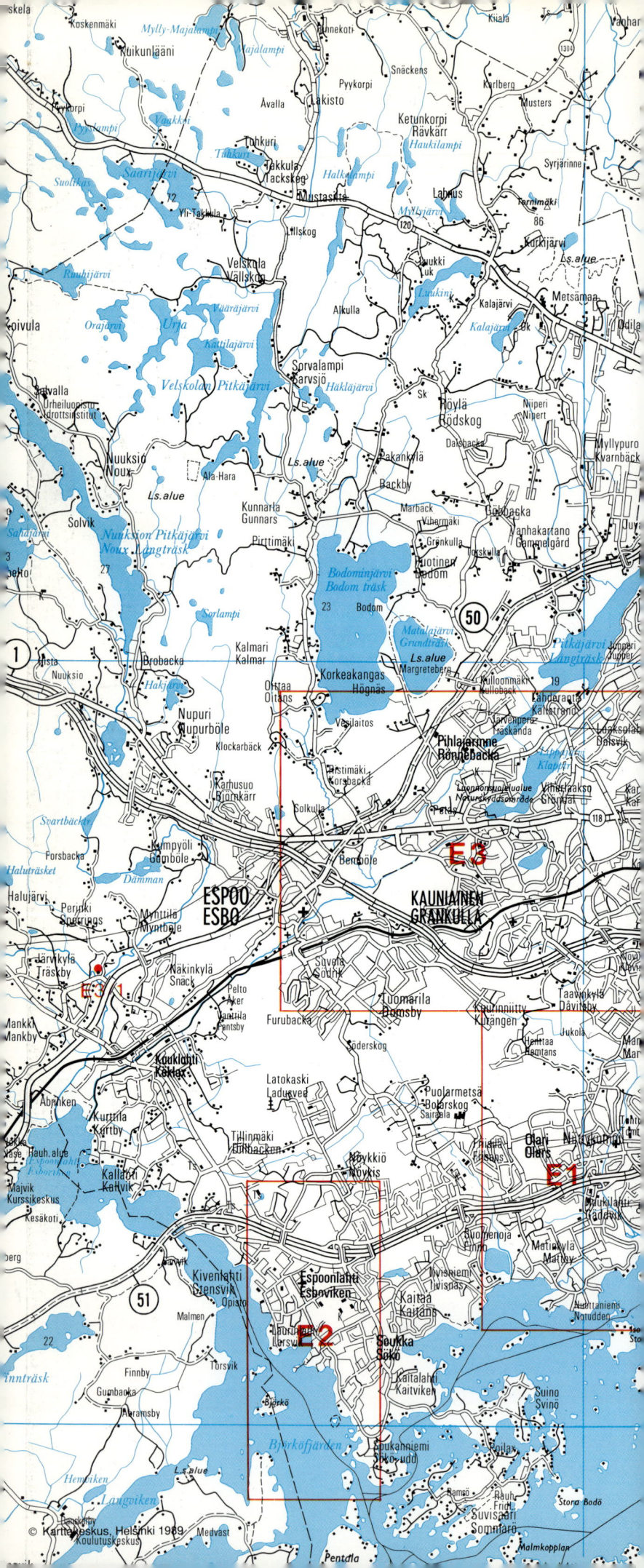

skela
Koskenmäki
Ruikunlääni
Mylly-Majalampi
Majalampi
Hennekoti
Kiiala
Vanhar
1304

Pykorpi
Pyykorpi
Vaakki
Tähkäri
Saarijärvi
Tohkuri
Takkula
Tackskog
Halkalampi
Mustasilta
Avalla
Lakisto
Pyykorpi
Snäckens
Ketunkorpi
Rävkärr
Haukilampi
Karlberg
Musters
Syrjärinne
Tärnimäki
120
Myllyjärvi
Lahnus
86
Kurkijärvi
Ls.alue

Yli-Takkula
72
Lillskog
Nuukki
uk
Luukini
Metsämaa
Odila

Koivula
Ruuhijärvi
Velskola
Vällskog
Alkulla
Kalajärvi
Kalajärvi Bk
19

Orajärvi
Urja
Vääräjärvi
Kattilajärvi
Myllypuro
Kvarnbäck

Salvalla
Urheiluopisto
Idrottsinstitut
Velskolan Pitkäjärvi
Sorvalampi
Järvsjö
Haklajärvi
Sk
Röylä
Rödskog
Niperi
Nipert
Duy

Nuuksio
Noux
Ls.alue
Ala-Hara
Ls.alue
Pakankylä
Marback
Vihermäki
Grönkulla
Toxskulla
Vanhakartano
Gammelgård

Sahajärvi
Solvik
Nuuksion Pitkäjärvi
Noux Långträsk
27
Kunnarla
Gunnars
Pirttimäki
Backby
Bodom
Klotinen
Bodom
Dalsbacka
Golbacka

3
Jeho
Sorlampi
Bodominjärvi
Bodom träsk
23
Bodom
Matalajärvi
Grundträsk
Ls.alue
Margreteberg
Pitkäjärvi
Långträsk
Jupperi
Juppert

1
Nsta
Nuuksio
Hakjärvi
Brobacka
Kalmari
Kalmar
Korkeakangas
Högnäs
50
Kulloonmäki
Kulloback
Lähderanta
Kallstrand
Lognsolahti
Dalsvik

Ohtaa
Oitans
Karvasperä
Maskanda
Klapp
Kaf

Nupuri
Nupurböle
Vesilaitos
Pihlajarinne
Rönnebacka
118

Klockarbäck
Ristimäki
Korsbacka
Luonnonsuojelualue
Naturskyddsområde
Viherlaakso
Gröndal

Karhusuo
Björkärr
Solkulla
Pellas
E3

Svartbäcken
Kåmpyöli
Gobböle
Bemböle

Forsbacka
Dämman
KAUNIAINEN
GRANKULLA

Halutäsket
Halujärvi
Periaki
Sogenäs
Myntilä
Myntböle
ESPOO
ESBO

Järvikylä
Träskby
Näkinkylä
Snack
Suvela
Sodnk
Taawinkylä
Dåvitsby

E3 1
Pelto
Äker
Vantila
Fantsby
Tuomarila
Domsby
Kaurinniitty
Kilrängen
Jukola
Mar

Mankki
Mankby
Furubacka
Söderskog
Henttaa
Hemtans

Åbränken
Kurttila
Kurtby
Kouklahti
Käklax
Latokaski
Laduvee
Puolarmetsä
Bolarskog
Sairaala
Triala
Fsans
Olari
Olars
Nahaumaa

Vase
Rauh.alue
Esborvik
Tillinmäki
Gilbacken
Nöykkiö
Nöykis
Finno
Suomenoja
Haukilaht
Haddvik

Majvik
Kurssikeskus
Kesäkoti
Kallahti
Kallvik
Ivisniemi
Iwisnas
Matinkylä
Mattby

berg
Järvik
Kivenlahti
Stensvik
Opisto
Espoonlahti
Esboviken
Kaitaa
Kaitans
Nuottaniemi
Notudden

51
Malmen
Laurinlahti
Larsvik
E2
Soukka
Sökö
Suino
Svino

22
Finnby
Torsvik
Björkö
Kaitalahti
Kaitviken
Rauh.
Frid-
område

innträsk
Gumbacka
Abramsby
Spukaniemi
Spokudd
Ramso
Suvisaaristo
Somnarö
Stora Bodö

Hennikén
Langviken
Björköfjärden
Ls.alue
Koulutuskeskus
Medvast
Pentala
Malmkopplan

© Karttakeskus, Helsinki 1989

A. Ehrenström's plan for Helsinki, 1817.

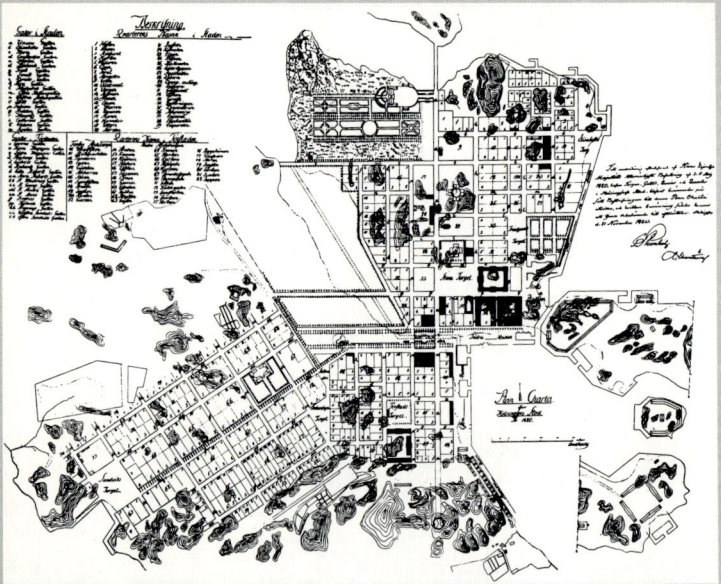

Suomenlinna

HELSINKI
A HISTORICAL AND
ARCHITECTURAL SURVEY

Finland constituted a part of the Swedish realm from the middle of the twelfth century until 1809, when it was incorporated into Russia as an autonomous Grand Duchy. During this period of history, the monarch's duties included the establishing of towns, and the granting of their privileges. Thus in 1550, King Gustavus Vasa decided to found a city on the northern coast of the Gulf of Finland, to compete for the trade with Russia carried out by Tallin, a town on the opposite coast under control of the Hanseatic League. To achieve his plans, he commanded the inhabitants of Rauma, Ulvila, Ekenäs and Porvoo to move to Helsinki, the chosen site for which was at the mouth of the Vantaa River. The measure met with scant success, and a few years later he had to permit the settlers to return. As it was located unsuitably at the head of a shallow bay a fresh site was soon considered. Finally Vironniemi, known today as Kruunun-haka, was selected, and in 1640 it was decreed that the town be moved there.

But even in Vironniemi, Helsinki remained a languishing small town, which grew in a somewhat erratic fashion due to the rocky terrain. During the Great Northern War, Viipuri, a fortress town on the eastern border, fell to the Russians. The retaliatory war of 1742 proved unsuccessful, bringing a further diminution of the realm, and new defensive fortifications became necessary. Count Augustin Ehrensvärd was commissioned to plan and construct a mighty fortress, Suomenlinna, on the islands lying off Helsinki. Construction began in 1748, and on the death of Ehrensvärd in 1772 the fortifications were almost completed, although supple-mentary work continued for a few decades.

Suomenlinna brought new life to the small country town. Helsinki would nevertheless have remained a very insignificant place had not the War of 1808–1809 changed the course of history. During this war the Russians occupied Helsinki and in 1808 the town was destroyed by fire. Reconstruction commenced and Lieutenant Anders Kocke drafted a new town plan. Accord-ing to his plan the burnt part of the town would have resumed its earlier appearance, with narrow streets skirting the hills, and only the planned new extensions would have been rectilinear.

Before this plan could be put into full effect, Emperor Alexan-der I, Conqueror of Finland, confirmed the old law of the land to the Grand Duchy of Finland, guaranteeing its autonomy, but he decided, however, to move the capital further away from Swe-den. In 1812 he decreed that Helsinki should replace Turku, which had been the capital for several centuries. At the same time he wanted to make the new capital worthy of its standing, and thus express his magnanimity and enlightenment to his new subjects and the world at large. Therefore a new town plan, which was given its final form in 1817, was drafted according to the instructions of the statesman Johan Albrecht Ehrenström.

Ehrenström's Neo-Classical town plan, except for being exceptionally broad in scope, was typical of its time. The old marketplace was to be enlarged to a forum bordered by government buildings and dominated by the principal church in town, and the old town would be separated from the new part by a broad esplanade, which incidentally is still the backbone of the Helsinki town plan.

But no town plan alone could have made this part of Helsinki into the fine Neo-Classical town it is today had not Carl Ludvig Engel (1778–1840) become the leading architect. Born in Germany, he got to know Russian Neo-Classical architecture in St. Petersburg, and later gave Helsinki that transparent quality which has earned the city the sobriquet »The White City of the North». Though Engel had no marble at his disposal and had to make do with bricks and wood, he created here in the far North a town with a Hellenic impression, and which was unusually homogenous and harmonious for its time.

Engel's town was open and low. In the centre the buildings had three stories, and on the outskirts he built one-story wooden houses with large gardens. Amidst them the present cathedral dominated the whole composition. It stood on a massive terrace, the front of which originally consisted of a Doric-style guardhouse soon to be replaced by the present enormous flight of steps. When the University was moved to Helsinki after the great fire of Turku in 1827, the Senate on the other side of the Senate Square was counterbalanced by the University Building. The University Library, one of the finest works of the designer, stands at the north-west corner of the square. The southern edge of the square was lined in part by private houses, which formed an unobtrusive wall for this dignified square and acted as a foil to the public buildings. Something of the old Helsinki still remains here. In the south-east corner the Sederholm House with its mansard roof represents 18th-century architecture, and the small sites in the block remind of the days when Helsinki was a small rural town.

Engel planned a succession of monumental buildings, a few churches, three barracks, three hospitals and much more; in addition, he and his Finnish assistants planned a number of private residences. This was a giant undertaking in those days: upon Engel's arrival Helsinki had only 4,000 inhabitants, the population had risen to some 18,000 when he died.

Most of the monumental buildings by Engel remain, but the ideal Neo-Classical town with its differentiated scale disappeared when the garden-city-type residential areas were replaced by brick and mortar. The change is so complete that Helsinki can no longer show one single example of the unique, sophisticated wooden architecture of the Empire style.

Quiet times followed Engel. Life in Finland was sedate, partly

The Senate Square, lithograph by F. Tengström, 1838.

Carl Theodor Höijer: The Grönqvist Building, 1883.

due to a reactionary political climate, partly to the Crimean War, which was felt as far as the shores of Finland. In 1867–68 years of famine sowed death throughout the country. But an era of greater political liberty was dawning, and its outcome was a period of general prosperity. From 1862 onwards the railway reached the remotest parts of Finland, and industrialization was taking its first steps. The 1870s initiated lively building activity. Four- and five-story buildings replaced the low wooden houses in the town centre. The foremost exponents of the Neo-Renaissance school were Frans Sjöström and Theodor Höijer, who had been trained in Sweden. Höijer in particular left his mark upon the centre of the capital.

His work can be seen in Helsinki's most important street, Pohjoisesplanadi. The most typical examples are the former Hotel Kämp, and its neighbor, the Grönqvist Building. The latter occupies a whole block, no mean accomplishment in a small town of that time. A third example is the building in Erottaja now occupied by the State Board of Forestry. Gustaf Nyström, designer of the House of the Estates and the National Archives, was a representative of the last stage of this development.

The last years of the 19th century saw the births of the Art Nouveau and Jugendstil, reactions against imitations of the old. Their goal was to mold architecture into a language of form in keeping with the ideas of the period. In Finland they awakened interest in the use of domestic building materials, and granite and wood were once again taken up. But in the 1890s a vigorous interest in the national inheritance had also been aroused; the old styles were rejected and a National Romanticism gained foothold: it was first recognized in international circles when a gifted trio of architects, Gesellius, Lindgren and Saarinen, built the Finnish Exhibition Pavilion at the World Exhibition in Paris in 1900. These architects built their home and studio, a magnificent log structure, near Helsinki on a rugged cliff overlooking Lake Vitträsk. The talented architect Lars Sonck (1870–1956) created massive log houses influenced by the old vernacular architecture. He planned Tampere Cathedral, which draws influences from the medieval stone churches and castles of Finland.

The following buildings in Helsinki date from this period: the Pohjola Insurance Company and the National Museum by Gesellius–Lindgren–Saarinen, the Telephone Company Building by Sonck, and the Polytechnic Student Union Building by Thomé and Lindahl.

The National Romantic school was short-lived; a style that had been appropriate for the vernacular buildings of a forest people could not satisfy the demands modern man made of his surroundings. Around 1905 a change took place and a style of building better in harmony with the times was sought, with inspiration especially from Austria and Germany.

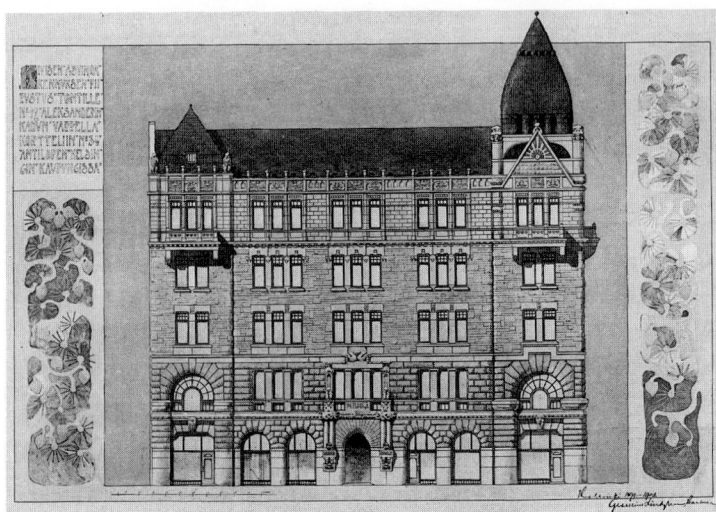

Gesellius, Lindgren, Saarinen: The Pohjola Insurance Company, 1901.

International Jugendstil architects, such as Selim Lindqvist, had concentrated on constructivism from the outset. Early on the astute architect-philosopher Sigurd Frosterus (d. 1956) pointed the way to the present. In his Helsinki Railway Station the great architect Eliel Saarinen (1873–1950) indicated the future of Finnish architecture. A new era in town planning was also dawning. It no longer was merely a question of terrain and traffic; towns themselves were to be works of art – this was the theme of a book by Gustaf Strengell. Bertel Jung and Eliel Saarinen were among these pioneers of town planning. Saarinen not only achieved fame as an expert abroad, with his second prize in the Canberra International Competition, but also in Helsinki, with his great Munkkiniemi–Haaga plan, published in 1915. In 1918 Saarinen and Jung drafted a master plan for metropolitan Helsinki which anticipated the present-day suburban structure.

Historic Romanticism reappeared at the close of the First World War, but the dominant style of the next decade was a form of concrete Classicism with roots in the historical architecture of Italy. J.S. Sirén's granite Parliament Building, standing proud on its rock foundation, is an example of the monumental buildings of this period. Its effect is, however, partly muted by the railway yards immediately opposite, at least for the time being.

Functionalism became popular in the 1920s, freeing Finnish architecture from all historical influences. The writings of Pauli Blomstedt, who died young, were particularly successful in convincing Finnish architects of the need for architecture to be in harmony with the spirit of the new age.

Erik Bryggman (d. 1955) and Alvar Aalto (d. 1976) guided the Finns along the new path. Since then Aalto has become the standard-bearer of Finnish architecture; he has brought it worldwide fame. Bryggman was active in Turku all his life. His Resurrection Chapel in Turku cemetery bears witness to the sensitivity and high level of his conceptions. Aalto built many works all over Finland. Helsinki boasts only a few of them, such as the Social Insurance Institute Building and the Enso Gutzeit Building, which harmonizes with the Neo-Classical Market Square. One of his earliest monumental buildings, the Viipuri Library, was damaged in the Second World War, and in the peace treaty Viipuri was ceded to Russia. Also worth mentioning is Yrjö Lindegren (d.1952), who together with T. Jäntti planned the Helsinki Olympic Stadium.

With the inspiration of Aalto to guide them, a number of talented architects have emerged. Some of their works are described below.

By the turn of the century the southern part of the Helsinki Peninsula had been almost completely built up, and at Pitkäsilta Bridge the town plan had already been extended to the area

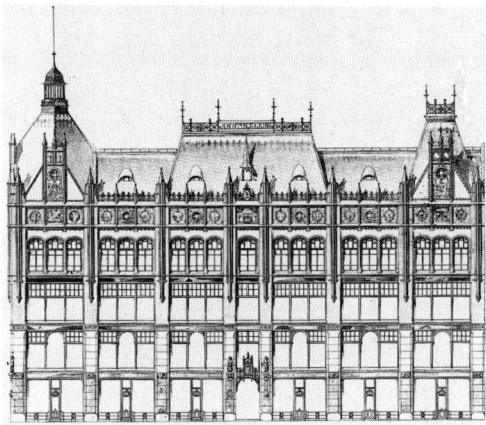

Selim A. Lindqvist: The Lundqvist Building, 1900.

Bertel Jung, Eliel Saarinen: Plan for Greater Helsinki, 1918.

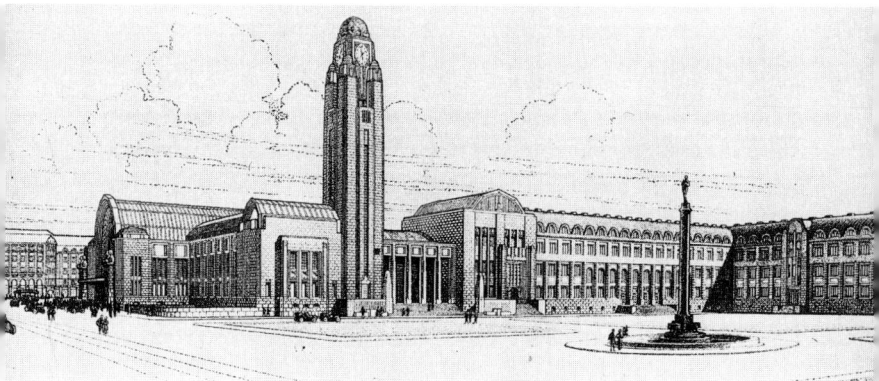

Eliel Saarinen: The Railway Station, 1914.

J.S. Sirén: The Parliament Building, 1931.

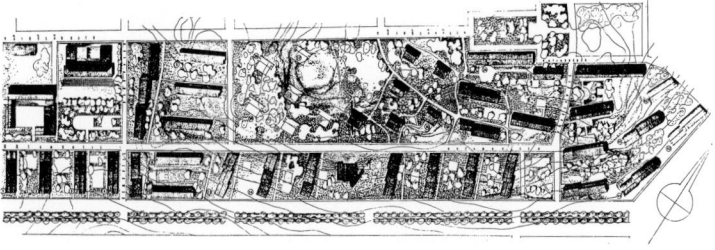

Hilding Ekelund, Martti Välikangas: The Olympic Village, 1940.

north of the inlet. As the town grew, the railway yard and the Töölö inlet forced the expansion in a V-shaped area along the edges of the peninsula, with an open parkland bisected by the railway.

At almost the same time separate residential areas began to emerge outside the town proper. The Kulosaari Villa Town was founded as early as 1907, Munkkiniemi during the First World War and Käpylä soon after, in the northeastern part of the peninsula. Particular attention should be given to Käpylä, which was built in 1921–24. While adapting to modern times, it reflects our traditional way of using wood in building, and exemplifies a garden city erected in a typically Finnish landscape.

The essential question stated by Eliel Saarinen in his Greater Helsinki plan – adapting the core of the capital to the demands of modern life – was left unresolved in the period preceding the Second World War. At the turn of the century Helsinki had only 91,000 inhabitants, but at the outbreak of the war the population numbered 317,000. At that time the area of the town was less than 3,000 hectares, and only after the incorporation of some 16,000 hectares from adjacent areas could Helsinki breathe more freely. Even this enlarged area has become inadequate for the needs of a growing capital city of half a million inhabitants.

After the Second World War the expanding metropolis needed a commercial centre appropriate to its scale and outlying neighborhood areas. In the latter half of the 1950s unprecedented urbanization made an even more extensive general plan inevitable. The task was left to a new generation.

Otto-I. Meurman

POST-WAR CONSTRUCTION IN HELSINKI

Planning and Housing

Planning in Greater Helsinki after the Second World War follow-ed the outlines proposed in Eliel Saarinen's plan of 1918, which were reinforced by the »neighborhood theory» which by that time had reached Finland. Migration from rural districts to Helsinki and recently initiated state-supported housing transferred the emphasis of new construction in the 1950s to the suburbs. However, the small garden-city units proposed by Saarinen were not realized, with scattered housing developments built instead. Neither was public transport given the same attention as in Saarinen's plans. When the plans for the metro were begun in the 1960s, a comprehensive overview was still lacking.

An exception to this piecemeal planning is the Tapiola Garden City, sponsored by the Housing Foundation (a consortium of several civic organizations and trade unions), where determined objectives were set regarding the variety of services, traffic differ-entiation, and architectural quality. In addition, new forms of housing and methods of construction were experimented with. Owing to its experimental nature, the townscape has remained somewhat incoherent, though relieved by low density and care-ful landscaping.

Some of the most successful areas in Tapiola are the main centre, by Aarne Ervi, and the eastern area by Ervi, Aulis Blomstedt, Viljo Revell and Kaija and Heikki Siren. One of the late additions is Reima and Raili Pietilä's interesting Suvikumpu Residential Area in the western quarter. Compared to Tapiola, Otaniemi, based on a town plan by Alvar Aalto and built around his Technical University buildings, is a more cohesive environ-ment. The sensitive Chapel and the residential buildings by the Sirens contribute to the successful character of the whole, with the Pietilä's Student Union Building, Dipoli, as a special feature.

In the 1950s very few projects comparable in quality to Tapiola or Otaniemi were built in Helsinki. Some successful achievements can, however, be mentioned, such as Hilding Ekelund's charming area in eastern Maunula and Viljo Revell's and Keijo Petäjä's municipal housing development in northern Maunula. Ahti and Esko Korhonen grouped three residential buildings in Lauttasaari around a friendly courtyard. Aalto built a high-standard housing group for Social Insurance Institution staff in Munkkiniemi, and Yrjö Lindegren created an exceptionally original plan for a municipal apartment building in Käpylä (the Serpentine House).

In the beginning of the 1960s a new phase in Finnish housing began with the construction of the Pihlajamäki housing area. It was planned and constructed in collaboration between the muni-cipal authorities and two developers, and for the first time prefabrication was used on a large scale. Pihlajamäki still reflect-ed the architectural goals of its times, but during the 1960s

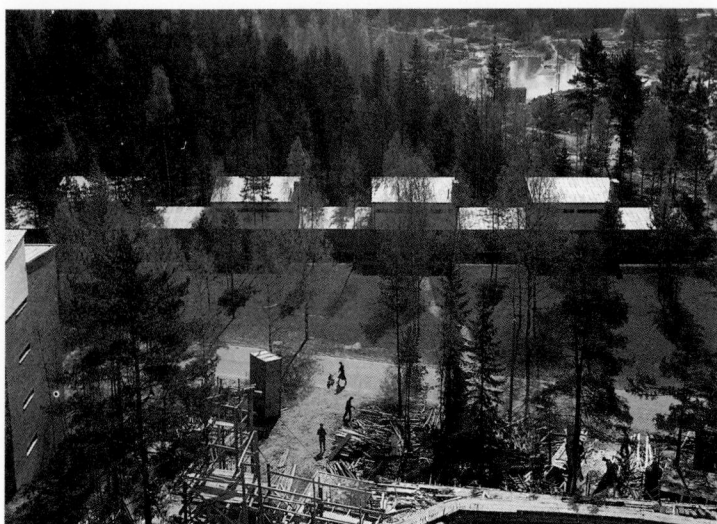
Tapiola under construction, 1954.

planners gradually lost control of the situation. The development of architecture was dictated by large-scale concrete panel systems to which architects did not contribute, and the crucial decisions in environmental quality were left to politicians and construction companies. This was partly due to the architects' primary interest in personal expression and public buildings at the time industrialized prefabrication was in its formative stage, although the deeper reasons are undoubtedly linked to economic developments.

In the mid-1960s there was a tendency in Finland toward systematic architecture, which directed the architect's attention once more to town planning and housing. This has not, however, resulted in high quality residential environments, apart from a few exceptions. One such exception in the Helsinki area is the centre of Olari in Espoo, as are Bengt Lundsten's plans for terraced housing in Hakunila. The new housing areas in Kannel-mäki, part of what is known as the Haaga-Vantaa operation, will also probably be considerably above average. Usually, however, the municipalities and contractors have used systematic means of planning and building merely to achieve excessive density without a concomitant concern for the quality of the environment.

In Helsinki in particular the lack of sites and the continuing migration of tax-payers to surrounding municipalities has led to extreme exploitation of land and put strong pressure on existing open spaces. The latest development reached a climax in the recently completed Itä-Pasila. Of the original megastructure principle, only excessive density and a partly forced multi-level transport system remain. The application of normal building types in high-rise construction has led to a clumsy scale and indeterminate space structure. The mediocre architectural level dictated by the prefabrication systems emphasizes the dreariness of the environment.

The Old City
Until the beginning of the 1960s changes in the Centre were slow, and new buildings harmonized with their surroundings. The Palace Hotel by Revell and Petäjä, completed for the Helsinki Olympic Games – an important turning point in the transition from the romanticism of the 1940s back to the functionalistic tradition – added a valuable element to the South Harbor milieu. Ervi took great care to link his Porthania Building to the adjoining Empire Centre, although due to this functionalistic approach he abandoned the traditional closed-block system. The finest downtown building to go up in the 1950s is beyond doubt Alvar Aalto's Rautatalo (Iron Building), adapted with a master's skill to the demanding milieu of Keskuskatu. The Marble Court was a welcome addition to the few public interiors in Helsinki.

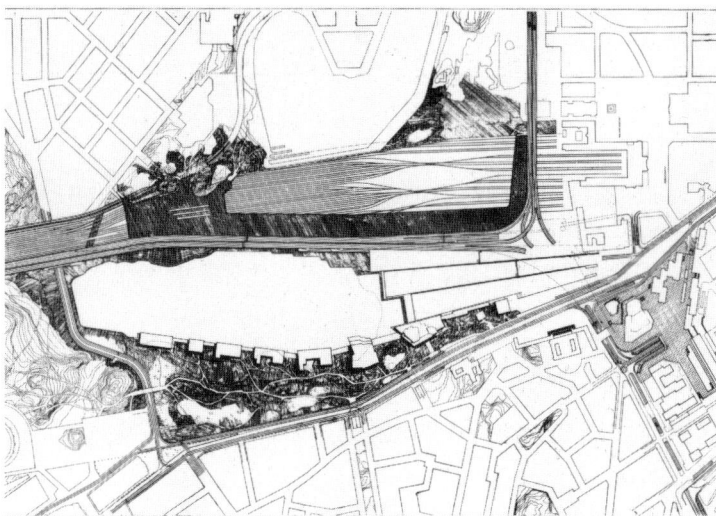

Alvar Aalto: Plan for Helsinki New Centre, 1964.

Aalto also composed with remarkable skill the huge volume of the Social Insurance Institution in the midst of the Taka-Töölö residential district.

During the 1960s business began to tighten its grip on the downtown area. In the beginning of the decade the unified Neo-Renaissance façade of the western side of Mannerheimintie was sacrificed to new buildings which, however, did not destroy the old block layout. A few years later there ensued an impassioned struggle to save Pohjoisesplanadi. Destructive renewal of the block opposite the Railway Station finally caused a larger public to realize the value of the inherited townscape.

Unchecked traffic growth has already invaded the squares and parks; cinemas and cafés have been converted to commercial premises; small shops have been unable to compete with the vast supermarkets built on the outskirts of the city and offices have infiltrated old residential blocks. All this has essentially reduced the attraction of the downtown area. A return to the old environmental qualities appears rather difficult due to current planning and legislative policies. However, increasing awareness among city-dwellers and especially the changed attitudes among the younger generation of planners have, over the past few years, somewhat retarded destructive developments.

The New Civic Centre
Ever since the times of Eliel Saarinen the question of extending downtown Helsinki to the inner bay area had been considered, but had remained unresolved. The competition of 1948 produced inconclusive results, and Yrjö Lindegren and Erik Kråkström were commissioned to prepare a plan, which was completed in 1954. Partly on the basis of this general plan, Alvar Aalto eventually developed, at the end of the decade his centre plan, which drew considerable attention. In both plans the area chosen for the extension of commercial activities was Kamppi. Detailed planning began in the early 1970s.

Of the monumental buildings proposed in Aalto's plan for the shores of Töölönlahti Bay, the congress and concert hall was immediately constructed. However, the compact building up of Hesperia Park provoked strong resistance and consequently the City asked Aalto to reconsider his plan. In the latest proposal the continuous row of public buildings has been abandoned, and the buildings are situated freely around a central park.

In this respect the plan approaches P.E. Blomstedt's proposal in the early 1930s, on which Lindegren and Kråkström's plan in many respects was also based. Timo Penttilä's Municipal Theatre, completed in 1967, fits naturally into this freer siting principle, which also provides greater equality in the distribution of cultural services to Helsinki's inhabitants.

Alvar Aalto, Elissa Aalto: Finlandia Hall, 1971, 1975.

Since the war few cultural buildings have been built, compared to the number of commercial and residential premises constructed. The Sirens' extension of the National Theatre and Aalto's House of Culture represent the restrained high quality architecture of the 1950s as does Blomstedt's refined extension of the Workers' Institute. The City Theatre and Finlandia Hall represent prestige orientated planning in the spirit of the 1960s. The only public buildings in the new housing developments were schools and churches. This provoked criticism of the excessive centralization of cultural activities.

Renewal and Conservation

Building conservation and restoration issues began to arouse general interest in the 1960s. The important stimulus was the compiling of a list by the Museum of Finnish Architecture of the most valuable buildings of architectural and historical interest. The renewal plans for the Town Hall block, by Aarno Ruusuvuori, proposed the construction of completely modern administrative and office premises behind the old façades. After completion of the first stage this method was, however, strongly criticized, and in the ensuing debate general opinion swung toward the conservation of old buildings and their re-use with minimal changes. During the 1960s there began a new appraisal of the turn-of-the-century Jugendstil quarters (e.g., Katajanokka, Eira and parts of Ullanlinna), which had earlier been considered merely examples of unprofessional design.

A notable achievement of contemporary trends is the preservation of the Käpylä garden suburb. Active criticism of both environmental and economic aspects resulted in the rejection of an already completed rebuilding plan. Instead of completely rebuilding the area, it was decided to renovate and repair the old buildings. A similar debate ensued later about the future of the Vallila area, also consisting of wooden houses for workers. Some of the most recent achievements of this conservation policy are the Suomenlinna Restoration and Re-use Plan and the Comprehensive Plan for Katajanokka.

Although the post-war years have in many respects shown negative development, one can still view the future of Helsinki with a certain optimism. The old centre is not yet as badly damaged as in many other European cities. Recently the authorities have been urged to reconsider exaggerated growth projections which have resulted in negligence toward environmental quality. The increasing eagerness of planners and inhabitants to participate in decision-making on planning issues is a potential hindrance to fateful mistakes.

Kirmo Mikkola

CONSTRUCTION IN METROPOLITAN HELSINKI IN THE 1970S AND 1980S

The Quantity and Quality of Habitation

Metropolitan Helsinki in the 1970s concentrated on solving the quantitative problem. Due to extensive migration a substantial segment of the population in predominantly agricultural areas moved to the industrialized south. This was the starting point for suburban construction in Helsinki, Espoo and Vantaa. The suburbs were built on a tight schedule, with inflexible production techniques and under considerable financial strain, and as a result it is difficult to pinpoint a positive example of suburban construction from the period. Olari in Espoo is among the few qualitatively high-standard projects from the 1970s. Also above the norm are certain parts of Kivenlahti in Espoo, the construction of which has continued in the 1980s.

The dreary environments provoked a lively debate about the significance of quality and ways and means of achieving it. The results are visible in several residential construction projects of the early 1980s, although they are more modest in their extent than were the earlier ones. Helsinki has resolutely attempted to regulate prices and see to that qualitative goals are attained in the what is known as the »hitas» regulated price-controlled construction.

A notable residential area from the 1980s is in the tip of Kataja-nokka, where residential blocks were constructed in a former docks area in downtown Helsinki; Malminkartano in northern Helsinki; Kumpula at the border of Helsinki proper; and some single-family housing developments, such as Torpparinmäki, where the planning incorporated urban forms of individualized habitation and economical energy solutions.

Improved Services

A focal point of development in the 1980s has been the services in residential areas, which resulted in several new area centers. They diversify the functions of the suburbs and deter commercial construction in the downtown area. Itäkeskus in Helsinki was the first new area centre, and it represents both architecturally and functionally balanced planning. The whole consists of linked cultural and commercial services and residential blocks. The other area centres constructed on the same principles are located far from the downtown area, with the exception of Pasila, which has the special function of balancing activities in the downtown area. Länsi-Pasila, constructed in the 1980s, reflects a rather different approach to planning than eastern Itä-Pasila, which was constructed during the previous decade.

The density in Tapiola, the well-known garden city in Espoo, has become more concentrated in the last few years with the construction of new commercial buildings which, however, have in part spoiled the original open character of the centre. The large commercial building projects in Vantaa are for the time being in the planning stage.

Diversified residential areas have also meant the construction of new public buildings – schools, churches, and cultural centres. The recently completed Finnish Science Centre, Heureka, in Vantaa, is worth special mention.

The largest transportation project in Metropolitan Helsinki has been the construction of the Metro subway system, which began in the early 1980s.

The Old Town Structure Changes

The emphasis of construction in the end of the 1980s has been on commercial buildings, as the several completed or planned office buildings indicate. There have been vast construction and renovation projects in the downtown business area. In these projects the preservation of the old buildings has often been limited to the façade fronting the street, which for the sake of the townscape is of course a better alternative than complete destruction. The expansion of the Stockmann Department Store, the Forum and the City Passage have been completed, and several commercial blocks in the downtown area are under construction or in the planning stage, some based on invitational competitions. The starting point for planning in these projects is usually a large, glazed pedestrian area, surrounded by commercial services on different levels. At the same time, new passageways are opened through the downtown blocks.

The furious destruction of old buildings that was characteristic of the 1960s left several irreplaceable gaps in downtown Helsinki. Today more attention is paid to the preservation of the townscape. Public buildings of national importance – the Parliament Building, the University, the Atheneum Art Museum, and the Council of State Building – have undergone renovations and repairs. The renovations of the Helsinki City Hall block have been completed, and repairs and renovations continue in Suomenlinna.

The Development of Downtown Helsinki

A considerable portion of the most central area in Helsinki is taken up by the railway freight yard and the temporary bus station. The interim use of the area has continued as long as it has been a part of the city centre. Since the beginning of the century a number of urban architectural and functional visions have been developed, among them the Pro Helsingfors plan by Saarinen (1918), and Alvar Aalto's plan for the city centre (1959-64). The practical effects have been scant: the only part of Aalto's plan to be completed is Finlandia House. Neither have three planning competitions for the area, the most recent one in 1986, led to any visible results, although a component master plan based on the competition is being drafted. Because the first prize was shared by three entries of equal quality, it is not possible to predict what forms the planning process or its results will take. According to a general functional composition, Kamppi will predominantly contain office and commercial buildings, and the public buildings will be concentrated in the Töölönlahti area.

Ruoholahti, one of the last industrial areas in downtown Helsinki, is gradually changing to a residential area. Changes will also take place in other industrial blocks, as the original activities move away from the centre of the city. The scarcity of reasonably priced apartments is a special problem, and new housing is a primary goal in the planning of the whole city, whether by conversions of existing blocks or by planning completely new areas.

Marja-Riitta Norri

J.S. Sirén: The Parliament Building, 1931. (H1/61)

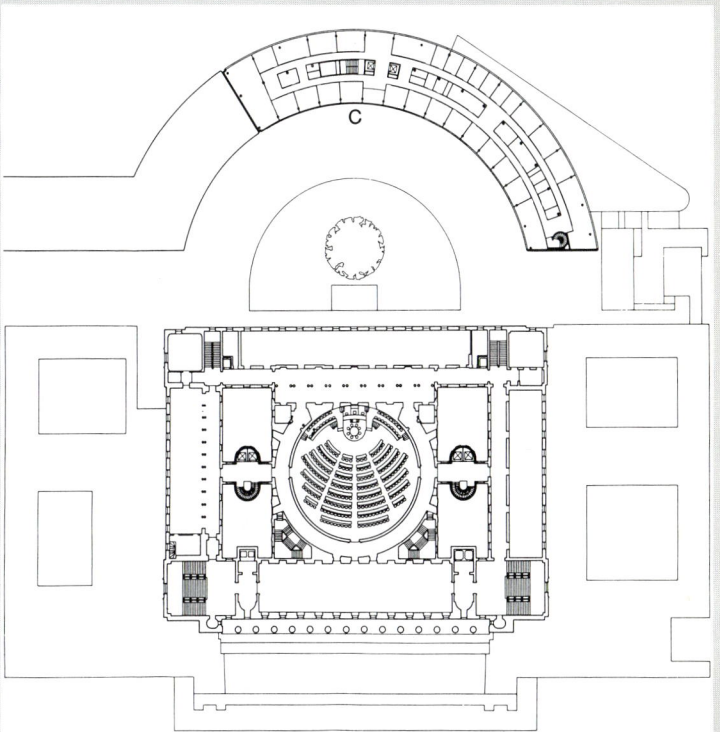

The Senate Square – Senaatintori

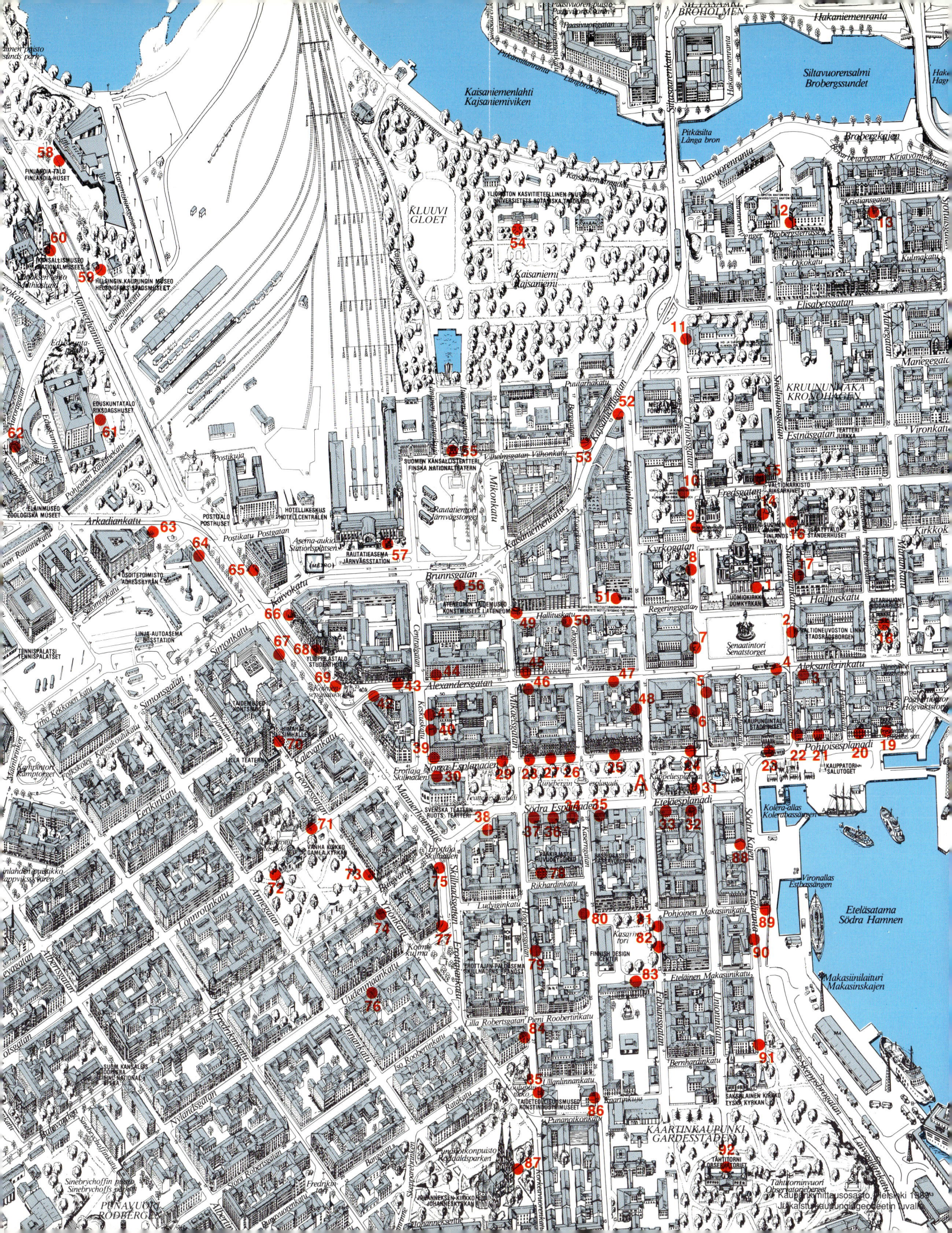

BROHOLMEN
Hakaniemenranta

Siltavuorensalmi
Brobergssundet

Haka
Hagr

Kaisaniemenlahti
Kaisaniemiviken

Pitkäsilta
Långa bron

Brobergskajen

58 FINLANDIA-TALO
FINLANDIA-HUSET

YLIOPISTON KASVITIETEELLINEN PUUTARHA
UNIVERSITETETS BOTANISKA TRÄDGÅRD

KLUUVI
GLOET

54

12
13

Kristiansgatan

60 KANSALLISMUSEO
NATIONALMUSEET

59 HELSINGIN KAUPUNGIN MUSEO
HELSINGFORS STADSMUSEET

Kaisaniemi

Elisabetsgatan

Okokatu

11

KRUUNUNHAKA
KRONOHAGEN

62

EDUSKUNTATALO
RIKSDAGSHUSET

61

Estnäsgatan Jutka
Vironkatu

Manegegatan

Postikuja

Hotellikeskus
HOTELCENTRALEN

10

15 VALTIONARKISTO
RIKSARKIVET

52

53

9

14

ELÄINMUSEO
ZOOLOGISKA MUSEET

Arkadiankatu

POSTITALO
POSTHUSET

Postikatu Postgatan

SUOMEN KANSALLISTEATTERI
FINSKA NATIONALTEATERN

8 FINLANDS BANK

16 STÄNDERHUSET

Kyrkogatan

Kirkkok

63

64

Asema-aukio
Stationsplatsen
(METRO)

RAUTATIEASEMA
JÄRNVÄGSSTATION

57

Rautatientori
Järnvägstorget

51

Hallituskatu

Regeringsgatan

TUOMIOKIRKKO
DOMKYRKAN

1

17

Halituskatu

2 VALTIONEUVOSTON LINNA
STADSRÅDSBORGEN

65

Brunnsgatan

56

49

50

7

18

66

ATENEUMIN TAIDEMUSEO
KONSTMUSEET ATENEUM

KAUPUNGINTALO
STADSHUSET

Aleksanterinkatu

Pohjoisesplanadi

4

Simonkatu

67 68

44

45

Alexandersgatan

46

47

5

KAUPUNGINTALO
STADSHUSET

TENNISPALATSI
TENNISPALATSET

LINJA-AUTOASEMA
BUSSTATION

69

43

48

6

19

20

LASTENLINNA
KONSTMUSEE

41
40

99

Norra Esplanaden

29 28 27 26

25

23 22 21

KAUPPATORI
SALUTORGET

70

LILLA TEATERN

30

Kluuvikatu

A

Södra Esplanaden

31

Eteläesplanadi

Kolera-allas
Kolerabassängen

71

Georgsgatan

38

Svenska Teatern
SVER. TEATER

35

33 32

88

Vironallas
Estbassängen

VANHA KIRKKO
GAMLA KYRKAN

Eroottaja
Skillnaden

37 36

Rikhardinkatu

ETELÄSATAMA
SÖDRA HAMNEN

72

73

75

78

80

81

Pohjoinen Makasiinikatu

89

74

Ludviginkatu

79

82

90

77

Kaivopiha

FINNISH DESIGN

83

76

Eteläinen Makasiinikatu

Makasiinilaituri
Makasinskajen

84

91

Lilla Robertsgatan Pieni Roobertinkatu

Bernhardinkatu

95

TAIDETEOLLISUUSMUSEO
KONSTINDUSTRIMUSEET

86

SAKSALAINEN KIRKKO
TYSKA KYRKAN

KAARTINKAUPUNKI
GARDESSTADEN

87

92 TÄHTITORNI
OBSERVATORIET

PUNAVUORI
RÖDBERG

Sinebrychoffin puisto
Sinebrychoffs park

JOHANNEKSEN KIRKKO
JOHANNESKYRKAN

Tähtitorninvuori
Observatoriebergen

Kaupunkimittausosasto, Helsinki 1989
Jäljistä kaupungingeodeetin luvalla.

H1

C.L. Engel: The Cathedral, 1852. (H1/1)

C.L. Engel: The Helsinki University Library, 1840. (H1/8)

1

2

The Cathedral 1852
The Senate Square – Senaatintori

Carl Ludvig Engel

When, in 1818, C.L. Engel drafted his first plans for a Lutheran church to be located on the north side of the Senate Square, they involved the present form of the church – a Greek cross with a central tower. Construction of the Nicholas Church, later renamed the Cathedral, began in 1830, but the church was not consecrated until 1852, twelve years after Engel's death. The exterior of the church is dominated by a central tower and Corinthian columns and triangular gables at the ends of the arms of the cross.

A guard house from 1818, originally intended as a foundation for the church, was demolished before construction began and replaced by a monumental flight of steps facing the Senate Square. After Engel's death the church and its environs were changed and given an appearance at variance with the original plans. E.B. Lohrmann added four smaller side towers to the church, and two pavilions were erected on the Senate Square side of the terrace, one as a belfry and the other for congregational activities.

During construction of the church a lofty cruciform crypt took shape beneath it. When the church was renovated in the 1960s the crypt was converted into storage space, and in the early 1970s it was remodelled to a plan by Tarja Salmio-Toiviainen to accommodate exhibitions, concerts and meetings.

The Palace of the Council of State 1822
Snellmaninkatu 1

Carl Ludvig Engel

The Senate was the first of Engel's monumental buildings on the square. The building is rectangular, measuring 83 by 110 meters, and it encloses a yard. The main building fronting the Senate Square was built in 1818–20. There is a domed central projection and side projections at both ends of the façade facing the square. The most important interior features in the main building are the staircase and the Senate Chamber, today the Presidential Chamber.

A two story wing on the Aleksanterinkatu side, with an adjacent corner pavilion, both by Engel, were completed in 1824. The two-story wing on Ritarikatu and four-story pavilion on the corner of Ritarikatu and Hallituskatu were built in 1826–28. The most impressive interior in the east wing was the library, which was destroyed when the low wing was replaced by a four-story structure in 1911–13. The north wing, by E.B. Lohrmann and built in 1853, was also razed and replaced by a building by C.R. Björnberg in 1900. A six-phase renovation was completed in the 1980s.

4

3

The Old Town Hall 1819
Aleksanterinkatu 20

Carl Ludvig Engel

The Old Town Hall, or the Bock House, together with two other merchants' houses, form the Senate Square side of the City Hall block, which was renovated in the 1980s.

The merchant Gustaf Bock's house was completed in 1763. Originally of two stories with a mansard roof, it was in private use until 1801, when it became the office and residence of the Helsinki District Major. In 1816–19 the Bock House was renovated according to a plan by C.L. Engel as the Governor General's residence: a further story was added and the façade was given a projecting central addition, massive on the ground floor with four freestanding Ionic columns supporting a triangular gable incorporated into the two upper stories. A barrel-vaulted assembly hall was built in the annex.

The house came into civic use in 1837, first as Town Hall, and from 1882 as City Hall. When the City Hall was relocated in the former Society House, the Municipal Court moved in to the Bock House.

The Old Town Hall, along with the adjacent Burtz and Hellenius Houses, was restored in 1985–88 according to a plan by Aarno Ruusuvuori. A new building within the block houses the Town Council Chamber and, below it, a civil servants' dining room.

The Sederholm House 1757
Aleksanterinkatu 18

Samuel Berner

The oldest stone house in mainland Helsinki was commissioned by the merchant Johan Sederholm, who later became a member of Parliament and the most prominent shipper in Helsinki. The architect was probably Samuel Berner, who had planned, for example, the City's old Ulrika Eleonora Church. The house has two stories and a mansard roof, originally of tarred board. Throughout history the façade and interiors have seen many changes, but basically the house has retained its original character. In 1866, when architect Konstantin Kiseleff owned the house, extensive renovations were carried out. The windows were enlarged and those on the second story were embellished with wooden balustrades. The roof was set with black sheet metal and the walls were painted yellow to match the other buildings fronting the Senate Square. The City of Helsinki acquired the house in 1949 and it is administered by the Helsinki City Museum, which will establish a merchant museum there once renovations are completed in 1991. After considerable controversy and doctrinal dispute the house is to return to its original 18th-century form.

5

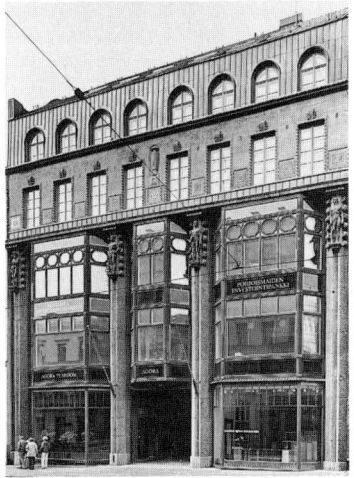

6

5

The Kiseleff House 1818
Unioninkatu 27

Carl Ludvig Engel

The Kiseleff House, as well as the Sunni House – its neighbor on the Senate Square – was originally a merchant's dwelling from the end of the 18th century. It was built for Johan Sederholm in 1772–78. The house has three stories, and originally a pitched roof. The current exterior dates from 1818, when the wing facing Unioninkatu (by C. L. Engel) was also built. The main façade, with rich ornamentation and a five-window central projection and Tuscan pilasters, faces Unioninkatu. Kiseleff's sugar factory operated in the house from 1806 to 1821. The merchant G.F. Stockmann bought the house from Kiseleff's heirs in 1879. A bazaar-like two story department store with skylights, designed by Lars Sonck, was built in the interior of the lot in 1911–12. The building on the Sofiankatu side, from the same period, was connected to the department store, which operated in these premises until the present Stockmann Department Store was completed. After the city acquired the house it was used, for example, by the Police Department, until it was restored as a department store in 1984–85. The exhibition rooms of the City Planning Department are in the »Sonck's Hall» of the building on the Sofiankatu side. The renovation work was planned by Timo and Tuomo Suomalainen.

6

The Former Wuorio Commercial Building 1909
Unioninkatu 13

Herman Gesellius

Built for Salomo Wuorio, the proprietor of a house-painting company which undertook most of the ornamental painting of public buildings in Helsinki, the building reflected continental solutions, with large faceted glass surfaces between visible granite pillars. The façade is more daring and refined in its details than the lower façade of the Lundqvist Building, which was completed ten years earlier. The added fourth floor (Armas Lindgren, 1914) has a natural stone façade, and the two top ones form a mansard roof. Lindgren's and B. Liljeqvist's office was in the sixth-floor gable, with a view towards the Havis Amanda statue. The Nordic Investment Bank bought the house in the 1970s, and renovations by Eric Adlercreutz were completed in 1981. The original roof style and highly visible southern tympanum were restored and a glass-covered gallery was built in the courtyard.

7

7

Helsinki University – Main Building 1832
Unioninkatu 34

Carl Ludvig Engel

The University was built on the west side of the Senate Square to pair symmetrically with the Senate Building (today the Palace of the Council of State) opposite. The University echoes the principal features of the Senate's façade, but differs from it in detail. The Senate's sumptuous Corinthian style was replaced by Ionic columns in the University's central projection, and the side projections have Tuscan pilasters.

The Main Building comprises an auditorium, assembly hall and lecture halls. The staircase and auditorium are architecturally significant interiors. The spacious staircase is built around a central space three stories high, with landings opening onto it through gallery corridors supported by Doric columns. The auditorium, which was originally semicircular with ascending rows of benches, was damaged during World War Two, and was slightly expanded during reconstruction. J.S. Sirén's plan, awarded the shared second prize in an open competition for the expansion of the Main Building in 1931, served as the basis for the construction of the annex, built in 1934– 37.

Renovation work now under way and to be completed in 1990 was planned by Ola Laiho, Ilpo Raunio and Mikko Pulkkinen.

8

The Helsinki University Library 1840
Unioninkatu 36

Carl Ludvig Engel

The Library was built in 1836– 40, and the interiors were completed in 1845. The building forms the centerpiece of a line of classical facades over 300 meters in length. It was built with careful consideration to the height of its neighbors, and the composition of its facade also harmonizes with that of the Nicholas Church, which was under construction when the library was completed. The layout of the library comprises three main halls which form a broad letter H. The middle hall has a necked dome with semicircular windows. The sides of the H are barrel-vaulted halls with side lighting. Freestanding columns support two galleries in each hall. The interior of the University Library is without doubt the most magnificent secular interior in the history of Finnish architecture, and on an even broader scale is one of the highlights of classical European spatial art.

The book storage room, designed by Gustaf Nyström and built in 1902–06, is a rotunda-shaped six-story annex behind the Library, with a steel structure and radial bookshelves. A public planning competition for an extension to the University Library was held in 1937, and a further competition in 1938. The winning entry, by Aarne Ervi, was not realized due to the Second World War. Renovation of the library by Olof Hansson was carried out in 1977–82.

10

8

9

9

The Church of the Holy Trinity 1826
Unioninkatu 31

Carl Ludvig Engel

The Church of the Holy Trinity was planned as a temporary Orthodox temple until the Uspenski Cathedral in Katajanokka was completed. The church is rectangular, the tower on the western end, resembling that of Engel's cathedral in Oulu and the freestanding bell tower of the Old Church in Tampere. The first story of the three-story belfry is smooth while the top two are pilastered. Originally the staircase on Unioninkatu was framed by two pavilions, but these have been demolished.

10

The Clinic for Internal Medicine 1823
Unioninkatu 38

Carl Ludvig Engel

The buildings facing Unioninkatu were originally built for a Russian Cantonist school. The grouping resembles the Naval barracks in Katajanokka, where the main building is joined to two adjacent wings with walls and portals. The façade of the main building and the gables of the wings are articulated with Ionic columns and pilasters. The portals are framed with thick Tuscan double columns. Originally the attics were covered with palm frond ornaments, wreaths and winged geni, but today they are smooth. The building was converted into a Russian military hospital in 1831, and the wings were connected to one another with the building facing Fabianinkatu. The buildings have been in use by several University Hospital clinics since Finland's independence in 1918.

29

11

12

11

The Old Clinic 1833
Unioninkatu 37

Carl Ludvig Engel

The Old Clinic, which was built as a University hospital or Clinical Institute, consisted at first of the main building on Unioninkatu, two one-story annexes bordering the yard, and a maternity hospital opposite the main building, on the Snellmaninkatu side. In 1838 the annexes were connected with the main building by a two-story structure, giving the yard its present shape and park-like character. The main building is ascetic and unadorned; only the simple frames around the windows on the main floor and the staggered attic over the central projection enliven the smooth façades. The building rests on a high plinth wall, which continues on both sides of the façade and on the Liisankatu side forms the retaining wall of the yard.

12

The Institute of Anatomy 1928
Siltavuorenpenger 20 A

Jussi and Toivo Paatela

The University Institute of Anatomy was built in 1926–1928 on the Siltavuori heights near the Institute of Physiology and the Institute of Physics. The three- story main mass of the building encloses a rectangular courtyard, with two wings extending from the north side. The most important space in the Institute, the anatomy lecture hall, is in a semicircular part of the building adjacent the main entrance. The large anatomy hall is in the second story of a separate wing.

The shallow arched windows in the base of the Institute of Anatomy, its main entrance portal, various other details, and the purplish color of the façades recall 1920s classicism.

In 1969 the University Institute of Nuclear Physics, designed by Olof Hansson, was constructed between the east wings of the Institute of Anatomy and the Institute of Physics (Gustaf Nyström, 1910).

13

Burgher's House 1818
Kristianinkatu 12

Burgher's House, also known as the Pumpmaster's House, is the oldest extant wooden house in the original old town; it was built in 1817–18, soon after the great fire, for the seaman's widow Christina Wörtin. In 1859 the house was bought by pumpmaster Alexander Wickholm, who later became town bailiff. The house was owned by his descendants until 1974, when the City of Helsinki purchased it. The building facing the street has retained its original character with the exception of the hip roof, which was rebuilt as a pitched roof in the 1860s. The building in the courtyard was brought to the site from elsewhere. The Helsinki City Museum renovated and restored the house in 1978–80 according to a plan by Aino Tandefelt-Laurila. It was renovated as a petit bourgeois dwelling from the 1860s and is today a museum at its original site.

14

13

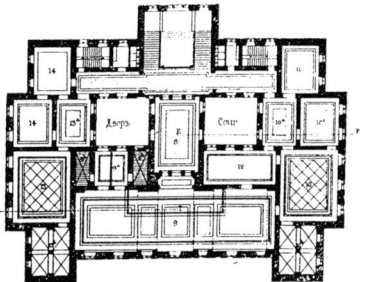

14

The Bank of Finland 1883

Snellmaninkatu 6

Ludwig Bohnstedt

A boom in timber exports during the 1870s brought added income to the Bank of Finland and spurred a building project.

After seeing the recently completed Bank of Denmark in Copenhagen, A.H. Dalström, Director General of the Directorate of Public Buildings, drafted a plan, but it met with so much adverse criticism that in 1876 an international planning competition for the bank was organized, thus breaking with the tradition that the highest ranking official of the buildings administration was allowed to plan all significant government buildings. The winning entry was submitted by the German architect Ludwig Bohnstedt, who had worked in St. Petersburg and four years previously had won the competition for the Reichstags building in Berlin. The bank was completed in 1883, by and large in accordance with the winning entry. F.A. Sjöström drafted the working drawings and was in charge of construction.

The symbolic significance of the Bank of Finland was enhanced by the completion of adjacent buildings: the National Archives in 1890, and the House of the Estates in the following year. The Post Office by Lohrmann already stood on the square. A statue of J.V. Snellman by Emil Wikström was unveiled in front of the bank in 1923. Later a banknote printing works was built behind the bank. It was replaced with an annex to the bank, by Harry Schreck, in the early 1960s.

15

15

The National Archives 1890
Rauhankatu 17

Gustaf Nyström

The National Archive was the first major public building by Gustaf Nyström, and its architectonic merit is generally acknowledged. Its façade blends naturally with the surrounding Empire-style buildings, particularly the University Library. The Rauhankatu façade is dominated by a two-story pilasterade topped by a smooth fascia but without a tympanum.

In its original form the building consisted of archive storage space along Rauhankatu, a parallel reading room, and a gallery that joined these two spaces. The entrance hall, gallery and reading room form a significant architectonic entity. The annex on Snellmaninkatu (1928) was planned by Magnus Schjerfbeck.

In 1968–1972 a new annex was built to the north and west of the original building. The new entrance to the reading rooms is behind the old archive storage rooms. The old and new reading rooms are connected by the catalogue room. The offices of the archive are in the structure terraced on the bedrock. The majority of the new storage rooms are in a wing set back on the site parallel with Snellmaninkatu. The ventilation channels extend from the façade and accentuate the closed granite surface. The annex and alterations were planned by Olof Hansson.

16

The House of the Estates 1891
Snellmaninkatu 9

Gustaf Nyström

The House of the Estates, in all its details, is considered the best preserved late 19th-century public building in Finland. F.A. Sjöström submitted the winning entry in an international planning competition for the building held in 1881, but its location could not be resolved. Sjöström died before he could complete the plans. A competition by invitation between four architects was held in 1887 to determine the building's placement on the present site. Nyström's winning entry bears some resemblance to Sjöström's, planned for Tähtitorninmäki Hill. Other models can be found in Vienna, especially in the »Greek Renaissance style» of Theophilus Hansen.

The building was an assembly hall for the three commoner estates: the clergy, the burgesses and the peasantry. The building served its original function for fifteen years, until the constitutional reform of 1906. It was not large enough for the new 200 member parliament, but several parliamentary committees met here and the building housed the library of Parliament until 1931. Various scientific societies have used the house after that.

After a magnificent entrance hall, the interior is dominated by a monumental staircase illuminated by a colored skylight. The sculpture »Lex» by Walter Runeberg surmounts the landing. The assembly rooms on the main floor contain rich illustrations depicting the life of the respective estates. An allegorical group of sculptures by Emil Wikström adorns the tympanum in the façade.

The renovated House of the Estates awaits its centennial in 1991; in addition to the current use it will serve as a space for official functions. The renovations were planned by Vilhelm Helander and Juha Leiviskä.

16

17

18

17

18

The Arppeanum – the Former University Chemistry Laboratory 1869
Snellmaninkatu 3–5

Carl Albert Edelfelt

The laboratory building is located on the north-east corner of the Senate Square. Originally it housed the University's chemistry laboratory and museum, and was the most notable post-Engel university building. It has a simple mass and the façade has groups of two, three or four arched windows with rectangular casements. The first story is rusticated, and the other stories are divided with horizontal fillets on a plaster surface.

The most impressive interior feature is the rare cast-iron structure of the main staircase. The building is currently used by the University Department of Geology.

The House of Nobility 1862
Hallituskatu 2

Georg Th. Chiewitz

The House of Nobility, planned by Th. Chiewitz at the end of the 1850s, is considered Helsinki's most notable example of the neo-gothic style. While the Gothic idiom is apparent in the details, the façade is laid out in the Renaissance manner. A new and unusual feature is the use in a public building of an unplastered brick surface.

The symmetric façade of the House of Nobility externalizes the division of its interiors. The street level story was originally intended to be rented out, and the façade is modest. The main-floor windows in the assembly hall for the knights and nobility are exceptionally large, with small round windows in the gallery. Due to instability, the ceiling of the auditorium was subsequently reinforced with a steel construction by Gustaf Nyström.

The Department of Architectural History of the National Board of Antiquities and Historical Monuments has its offices here. The auditorium is a popular chamber music venue.

A The Esplanade

The Market Square, Pohjoisesplanadi and Eteläesplanadi, and the Esplanade Park form one of the two uniform architectural entities in the historical centre of Helsinki, the other being the Senate Square. The Esplanade appears for the first time in the 1812 plan for the reconstruction of Helsinki, which was drafted by Johan Albrecht Ehrenström. In his plan the Esplanade forms an unbuilt zone between the brick-and-mortar town around the Senate Square and the wooden suburbs. The Market Square and the Esplanade were given their final architectural structure in a draft plan made a few years later. When Carl Ludvig Engel was planning a theatre building in 1826, he suggested that the Esplanade Park be composed of three parts, which were later called the Chapel, Runeberg, and Theatre Esplanades. The planting of the park planned by Engel commenced at the end of the 1820s, and later on the lindens, which even today are a central element of the Esplanade, entered the picture. The hollow left in the Runeberg Esplanade by Kluuvinlahti Bay was filled in the 1880s, when the ground level was raised by more than a meter, and a statue of Runeberg erected in the park cut off the street from Kluuvikatu to Kasarmikatu.

Pohjoisesplanadi in the north was reserved for the brick-and-mortar buildings of Helsinki's commercial burghers, whereas Eteläesplanadi in the south was given over to the wooden dwellings of civil servants. The original spirit of the plan was followed only partly, as in the early phase several wooden residential houses were built on Pohjoisesplanadi. Several public buildings were built among the dwellings in both Esplanades. The original difference of character and the leading role of commerce in Pohjoisesplanadi are still evident. The only architecture left from Engel's era are the Smolna, and the row of former residential buildings that fronts the Market Square, and the Seurahuone-cum-City Hall. The style that began as Gustavian Classicism and developed into St. Petersburg Empire characterizes the buildings along the Market Square and the Chapel Esplanade. The rest of Pohjoisesplanadi dates mostly from the 1880s. The difference in scale between the low burghers' houses along the Market Square and business and residential buildings worthy of a continental city is striking.

The Neo-Renaissance adopted by a new generation of architects is at its best along this stretch, especially in the unbroken series of buildings by Höijer. The architectural character of Eteläesplanadi is different. It is characterized by a stylistic diversity and the architecture of a period of transition, with elements from early and late Jugendstil, early Classicism and Classical Functionalism.

SCULPTURES IN THE ESPLANADE:
Tale and Truth (Zacharias Topelius), by Gunnar Finne, 1932
Eino Leino, by Lauri Leppänen, 1953
Johan Ludvig Runeberg, by Walter Runeberg, 1885

SCULPTURES IN THE MARKET SQUARE
The Mermaid (Havis Amanda), by Ville Vallgren, 1908
The Empress's Stone, by Carl Ludvig Engel, 1835

19

The Presidential Palace 1820
Pohjoisesplanadi 1

Pehr Granstedt

Originally planned for commercial councilor J.H. Heidenstrauch, the building was unusually large for a burgher's residence. It was modelled after the palaces of nobility in Paris, with the main building set back from the street, two wings toward the street, and a fenced forecourt. The main building has three stories, with Ionic columns articulating a projecting gable, the first of its kind in Helsinki. Pehr Granstedt's plans were inspected by Jacopo Quarenghi and C.L. Engel.

The state bought the private residence in 1837 and C.L. Engel drafted a plan for converting it into an imperial palace. Engel planned, among other things, the dining room, the mirrored hall, the Gothic hall and the chapel, currently the library. The renovation was completed in 1843 under the direction on Carl Alexander Engel, who took over after the death of his father.

In Governor General Bobrikov's time an extensive renovation planned by Jac. Ahrenberg was carried out, and the Hall of State, Round Hall, and kitchen were created. The entrance facing Mariankatu was added in 1938. The most recent extensive renovation was undertaken in 1969–73 to a plan by Sirkka Tarumaa.

20

The Supreme Court 1816
Pohjoisesplanadi 3

Pehr Granstedt

Built originally for sea captain Castegren, the house was a two-story corner building, with shops and storerooms on the ground floor and two apartments above. Originally Gustavian Neo-Classical in motif, it was given its present Neo-Renaissance guise in 1883, when a further story was added and the façade and interior were altered extensively. The alterations, characterized by rich ornamentation of the façade, were designed by F.A. Sjöström. The entrance axis of the main wing fronting the Esplanade has been accentuated with a pilastered central projection, a balcony and a dome.

The state purchased the house in 1933 for the Supreme Court and Supreme Administrative Court. In the 1930s some changes were made in the interiors and annexes. When the Supreme Administrative Court moved, the building was renovated for the Supreme Court. The renovations, completed in 1986, were planned by Timo Jokinen.

21

The Swedish Embassy 1924
Pohjoisesplanadi 7

Torben Grut

J.H. Heidenstrauch bought the site of the present Swedish Embassy in 1837 after he sold his building in the next block for use as an Imperial Palace. In 1814 C.L. Engel had drafted a plan for the Stock Exchange on this site. The symmetric structure of the block comes from Engel's plan, which Pehr Granstedt followed when he laid out the corner buildings as a symmetric pair. In 1839–1843 the grand patrician Heidenstrauch Building by Anders Fredrik Granstedt was built between the corner buildings.

The main floor of the two-story stone building contained Heidenstrauch's luxurious bachelor apartment. It is said that he was the first in town to have a bathroom adjacent to his bedroom. Commercial Councilor Jakob Tschernischeff bought the building in 1883, and converted it into rental apartments according to a conversion and extension plan by Konstantin Kiseleff. The facade conversion, however, was planned by W. Reiss. The pompous Baroque-style facade was in great contrast with the adjacent buildings. The Swedish government bought the building in 1921 and Torben Grut drafted the alteration plans for the embassy building. The facades facing the street underwent once again a complete change. The embassy building has often been called a miniature copy of the Royal Palace in Stockholm because of its Tessinian Baroque character.

22

23

22

The Former Kleineh's Hotel 1819
Pohjoisesplanadi 9

Pehr Granstedt

Pehr Granstedt was the leading residential planner in Helsinki in the 1810s. He originally planned this building for commercial councilor Henrik Jakob Govinius. Set on a corner lot, it represents what is known as the »try-square» or corner building. The rounded corner, the central projection and gable triangle of the façade are highly characteristic of the period.

The house was known, after subsequent owners, as the Tigerstedt House and Kleineh's Hotel. The City of Helsinki obtained it in 1935. The group of buildings at Pohjoisesplanadi 9, Aleksanterinkatu 16–18 and Katariinankatu 1–3, was renovated according to a plan by Aarno Ruusuvuori for the Helsinki City real estate office. The White Hall by Walter Jung (1923) in the annex of the Remander House is a valuable addition to this whole.

23

The City Hall 1833
Pohjoisesplanadi 11–13

Carl Ludvig Engel

The building facing the Esplanade in the City Hall block was originally built to plans by C.L. Engel as the Seurahuone club. The ground floor of the three- story building contained shops, the second story banqueting rooms, and there were hotel rooms on the top floor. By the 1860s the hotel was already out of date and too small. Extensive alterations planned by Carl Albert Edelfelt were made in 1861–62, and the new auditorium, by Axel Hampus Dalström, was built in 1863–65. In 1887 the hall was extended to almost its present form by Bruno F. Granholm, and a balcony by Hugo E. Sauren was built over the main entrance. The city bought the building in 1901, but it continued functioning as a hotel until 1913, when the city organized a public competition for a new City Hall, which was to have been located on the present City Hall block and part of the block to the west of it. None of the entries saw the light, and the Seurahuone building was made the new City Hall virtually as it stood. The same blocks were the object of another competition in 1960. The winning entry was by Aarno Ruusuvuori, and the southern part of the block was renovated according to his plan in 1965–70. The radical manner in which he combined new and old was at the time the subject of considerable debate.

24

The Former Privatbanken Bank 1904
Pohjoisesplanadi 19

Lars Sonck

The Privatbanken (currently the Helsinki City Jugend Hall) was built as an annex to the house of merchant Jegor Uschakoff (1816, by Pehr Granstedt), and a portal was opened in the façade facing the Esplanade. Due to its location the only way to provide the building with natural lighting was with skylights. The bank hall has three aisles separated by two arched colonnades. The impression is distinctly sacral, an allusion to the Finnish medieval church. The skylights are above the tall central aisle. The furnishings and ornaments were designed by Walter Jung. The hall was long in use for a purpose out of keeping with its character, until it was restored by Aarno Ruusuvuori in 1968.

The Jugend Hall, and the Unioninkatu staircase and façades of the Uschakoff House, were retained when the structure was renovated as the Kluuvi Office Building.

26   25

24   26

25

The Grönqvist Building 1883
Pohjoisesplanadi 25–27

Carl Theodor Höijer

The Grönqvist Building was once the largest residential structure in the Nordic countries, and also the first building in Helsinki in which the entire ground floor was originally given over to shops. »The Grönqvist Stone Wall,» as it was called, initially comprised 193 rental apartments. It was built for financier and developer F.W. Grönqvist, who also built the Catani and Kämp buildings in the next block.

The five-story structure had two elevators, kitchens with running water, and in the larger apartments bedrooms with baths. With its 90-meter-wide façade, broad central projection and corner towers, it overwhelmed the contemporary buildings adjoining it. Each story is different and very rich in detail. The Grönqvist Building was the first of Höijer's apartment houses to have plaster ornamentation, which in his previous buildings had been limited largely to colonnades and rustication. The ornamental character of the building is enhanced by a rich roofscape of arched windows and towers.

26

The Former Hotel Kämp 1887
Pohjoisesplanadi 29

Carl Theodor Höijer

The industrialist F.W.Grönqvist built a five-story hotel adjoining the large residential building he constructed earlier; in the corner of the Esplanade and Kluuvikatu, and master cellarer Carl Kämp secured a twenty-year lease on the property. On the ground floor there was, in addition to the lobby and handsome main staircase, a large café and two shops. The best rooms were on the second story facing the Esplanade; and a large sectioned restaurant, with a transverse two-story high ballroom, faced Kluuvikatu. The upper stories contained hotel rooms.

The basic level on the façade was a brick surface with raised mortar seams, extensively covered with plaster and plaster ornamentation. The angled corner has been accentuated with an appendage. The Esplanade side façade is dominated by a central projection capped by a dome motif. The original French-style roof was lost in 1914, when a story by Lars Sonck was added.

As the foundation was laid on mud the building began to sink; and, following considerable controversy, it was demolished in 1966. The Kansallis-Osakepankki

28   27   26

Bank, owners of the building since 1917, replaced the hotel in 1969 with an office building, by Antero Pernaja and Nils-Henrik Sandell. The façade fronting the Esplanade, part of the Kluuvikatu façade, and some valuable interiors are reconstructions of the original Hotel Kämp.

27

The Catani Building 1890
Pohjoisesplanadi 31

Carl Theodor Höijer

The-five story residential and business building commissioned by the confectioner Florio Catani was completed in 1890 next door to the Hotel Kämp. Catani's famous confectionery, with its decorative Rococo rooms, took up the entire ground floor, the kitchens and ancillary area faced the yard, and the upper stories contained apartments, two to a floor. The façade has horizontal ornamentation in harmony with the façade of the Hotel Kämp. The wall surface is dominated by gradually decreasing rustication and alternating framed windows. The original arched shop windows on the ground floor have been replaced with rectangular windows.

The main sales rooms of Marimekko in the ground floor and cellars (1985) were planned by Juhani Pallasmaa.

28

The Merkurius Building 1890
Pohjoisesplanadi 33

Selim A. Lindqvist

When Lindqvist, in collaboration with Elia Heikel, drafted plans for the Neo-Renaissance Merkurius Building, he was only twenty-one years old and already displaying considerable artistic ability and professional maturity. The daring structural solutions in the house gained considerable attention. Instead of the usual load-bearing walls in the two first stories there was a mezzanine floor with squared openings, which was duplicated below, on the floor for shops, with cast-iron pillars. This gave a more airy ambience to the ground floor, thus avoiding the ponderousness that burdens, for example, the Grönqvist Building.

29

The Wrede Arcade 1888
Pohjoisesplanadi 35

Karl August Wrede

The Wrede Building differs from the other Neo-Renaissance structures along the Esplanade. In addition to a wing facing the street it contains two high transverse masses, and the façades facing the passageway have been dealt with in the same way as the façades facing the street, with two stories of shops. Wrede used the same solution in the Central Building on the Aleksanterinkatu side of the block. The result was the first continental-style shopping arcade in Finland: the Wrede Passageway. It differs from its Belgian or Italian prototypes in its small scale, and also because the planned glazed roof has yet to be constructed.

Today the Wrede Arcade has been degraded, serving as a parking area and loading zone. A competition was held in 1987 to revitalize the shopping arcade and surrounding buildings. The winning entry restores the Wrede Arcade to its rightful status, and directs pedestrian traffic through the block in a manner similar to the one P.E. Blomstedt employed in 1935 in his plan for the blocks around Aleksanterinkatu.

29

31

30

Svenska Teatern – the Swedish Theatre 1866
Pohjoisesplanadi 2

N. L. Benois

Originally a wooden theatre (1827) by C.L. Engel stood on the site. In 1860 a stone-built theatre by G.Th. Chiewitz was completed, but it was destroyed by fire two and a half years later. A public planning competition was held; but the contract, instead of going to the winner, went to N. L. Benois, member of the Academy of Arts in St. Petersburg. His theatre, completed in 1866, bears a striking resemblance to Chiewitz's, as it was constructed in part within walls that survived the fire. The greatest changes were made in the end facing the Esplanade Park.

Eliel Saarinen planned the extension toward the end of the 1910s and also, together with Hilding Ekelund in the 1920s and 1930s. The Swedish theatre was given its present appearance in 1936, from plans by Eero Saarinen and Jarl Eklund. Both wings and the end with the restaurant were rebuilt; while the central aisle in the auditorium was replaced with two side aisles, and the main entrance on Mannerheimintie, with two side entrances. The most visible change was the smooth exterior, which replaced rich ornamentation. A winter garden -type annex, planned by Olof Hansson, was added to the restaurant in 1978.

31

The Esplanade Chapel 1867
The Esplanade

Axel Hampus Dalström

The restaurant on the Esplanade had its modest origins in a refreshment booth opened in 1839 by confectioner J.D. Jerngren. During the following decades a number of plans were put forward to open a summer restaurant on the site but it was not until 1867 that sketches commissioned from Hampus Dalström were carried to completion. The floor plan of the Chapel was a cross. The middle section was articulated by tall Corinthian arcades, with two lower wings ending in bowed verandas. The restaurant seated 120.

In 1881 Konstantin Kiseleff drafted a plan for wooden annex pavilions. Ten years later the Chapel was enlarged to plans by Bruno F. Granholm. The wooden pavilions were replaced with cast iron and glass, the former main hall was enlarged, and the new annexes were joined with two terraces, producing the basic form of the Chapel as it is today. Its total seating capacity, including the outdoor tables, was 1000.

In 1887 an orchestra shell by B. Brynolf Blomqvist was built on the north side of the Esplanade Park. It was replaced at the end of the 1930s by a steel and glass bandstand by Valter Jung, and two smaller audience pavilions, which were dismantled in the 1960s.

Extensive renovations, by Aino and Pekka Laurila, intended to restore the Chapel to its 1891 appearance, were carried out in 1976.

32

33

32

The Ministy of Labour 1913
Eteläesplanadi 4

Armas Lindgren

The location of the building at the beginning of the Esplanade and the Market Place Square makes it an important element of the townscape. In 1913 it was the tallest building in Helsinki. The structures and fittings were modern: intermediate floors were concrete and it had central heating.

The state bought the house in 1911 while it was under construction. Nikolai Meder planned the necessary alterations. The National Board of Public Roads and Waterways had its offices in the building until 1982. The apartments in the top floors, among them the official residence of the Prime Minister, were later on converted to offices. The building was renovated for the Ministry of Labour in 1984, with the first story containing shops. The renovations were planned by Pirkko and Arvi Ilonen.

33

The Government Banqueting Hall 1824
Eteläesplanadi 6

Carl Ludvig Engel

Originally the house was the residence of the Chief Inspector of the Finnish Armed Forces. It was used as an interim university building while the university was being built. Thereafter it was used as the residence of the Russian Governor General and as various government offices. It has been called »the Smolna» after its famous namesake in Leningrad, having served as headquarters for the Red forces during the Finnish Civil War.

The-two story house is in the corner of the Esplanade and Fabianinkatu. The first story is rusticated and the main story is smooth. There is a two-phase broad central projection which continues as an attic over the cornice on the main façade facing the Esplanade. There is an Ionic colonnade above the balcony on the outer surface of the projection.

The building underwent extensive renovation while serving as the Governor General's residence. In 1851 a two-story annex by Ernst Bernhard Lohrmann was built in the courtyard. In 1866–68 extensive repairs and alterations planned by Carl Albert Edelfelt were undertaken. In the 1960s the Council of State took over the building mainly for use as a banqueting hall. Sirkka Tarumaa planned the renovation work carried out in 1964–66. The outer entrance hall and vestibule, with its paestum-type doric columns and cross vaults, have best retained the character of Engel's interior plans.

34

The Interior of the Savoy Restaurant 1937
Eteläesplanadi 14

Aino and Alvar Aalto

The interior of this restaurant was the Aaltos' first public commission in Helsinki. The restaurant is on the top floor of the Ahlström Building, and has a roof terrace. The restaurant seats 100, with space for an additional 150 on the terrace in the summer. Originally the terrace was divided by greenery into Japanese, southern European and Scandinavian sections. In the restaurant Aalto's furniture and lamps are complemented by elements and materials, such as birch, Oregon pine and mahogany, which contribute to the original expression and atmosphere. The so-called Savoy vase is in fact an entry in a glass planning competition arranged by the Karhula-Iittala glass works.

The Ahlström Building, by Walter and Bertel Jung, contains another space of cultural, historic and architectural value that has retained its original form: a 700-seat cinema. Today the Savoy Theatre is administered by the Municipal Centre for Cultural Affairs.

35

36

35

The Former
Wasa-Aktie-Banken 1899
Eteläesplanadi 12
Grahn, Hedman & Wasastjerna,
John Settergren

The Wasa Banken and the Argos Building at the end of Pohjoisesplanadi were among the last buildings to be constructed along the Esplanade in the 19th century. They marked a fresh stylistic phase characterized by a new historism and new materials. The Grahn-Hedman-Wasastjerna firm used diverse stylistic features to a late date, but was at the same time a pioneer of unadorned façades. The bank building indicates a desire to lower the reliefs and group the windows. As a result of these groupings the fairly large integrated wall surfaces dominate the façade, and its material, reddish sandstone from Ora in northern Sweden, is prominently displayed.

The motifs of the details in the façade come from medieval Venetian palace architecture and English Tudor-Gothic themes. A model for the Wasa Banken may be found in the Hallwyll Palace in Stockholm (1894), by I.G. Clason.

The first story, with its large windows, was originally given over to a magnificent bank hall, and the upper stories contained exclusive apartments.

The bank hall that dates from the turn of the century was renovated in the end of the 1960s, and the original structures and surfaces were hidden. Renovations by Egil Nordin were carried out in the 1970s and the bank hall regained its original appearance.

36

The Former Finnish
Mortgage Association 1908
Eteläesplanadi 16

Lars Sonck

This building heralded a new era in Finnish architecture. It broke away from the free form of the turn of the century and adopted a more classical approach. It rejects the asymmetric solutions in Sonck's earlier work – the Eira Hospital and the Telephone Company Building – for a symmetric classical façade with a colonnade. The return of the colonnade, order and symmetry can be seen in Sonck's later works and Finnish architecture in general. There is also a change in materials, the former rustic rubble-wall has been replaced by polished light gray Uusikaupunki granite. The general impression was spoiled by extra stories built in 1956 and 1967. Originally the building housed several banks. Subsequently it has been used by the Social Insurance Institute, the National Board of Education and, from 1977, the Ministry of Transport and Communications. Renovations, by Aili and Niilo Pulkka, were completed in 1977.

37

The Lassila & Tikanoja
Building 1935
Eteläesplanadi 18

Johan Sigfrid Sirén

The employer, a wholesale textile firm, held an invitational competition between four architects in 1934. It proved an interesting battle between two traditionalist and two functionalist entries. Siren's entry won first prize; and despite its symmetric and slightly monumental atmosphere, it is in many respects one of the first modern office buildings in Helsinki. The concrete pillars of the structure stand far apart, providing a versatile interior division, which is also served by a dense window axis division that corresponds to the beams of the intermediate floors. The façade material at street level story is polished black granite, and the top stories have stucco plastering.

39

40

38

41

The Bensow Building 1940
Eteläesplanadi 22

Uno Ullberg

The building is located in a block where two sites fronting Erottaja are out of line with the Esplanade. The Girsén Building (1891) by Theodor Höijer is in line with Bulevardi, whereas the Bensow Building is in line with the Espalanade. A small square in front of the building continues within as a courtyard with shops. There is a small restaurant in the second story on one side of the square. The top floors contain offices. The long sides of the deep site contain side corridor offices joined by two broader parts with central corridors. The eight-story building fronting the street and the four-story inner wings have steatite façades.

The offices of the Finnish Association of Architects are located in the Bensow Building.

The building in the corner of the Esplanade and Korkeavuorenkatu is by Keijo Petäjä (1975).

39

The Kirjapalatsi Book Palace 1969
Keskuskatu 1

Alvar Aalto, Elissa Aalto

An invitational competition for the building in the corner of Pohjois-esplanadi and Keskuskatu was held in 1961, and the completed building is based on the winning entry. Eliel Saarinen planned the Kinopalatsi Commercial Building for the same site at the end of the 1910s, but only the part fronting Keskuskatu was constructed, and the old corner building was left to stand until 1965. It contained one of the first cinema theatres in Finland. (Walter Jung, Emil Fabritius; 1916).

The main space in the Kirjapalatsi Book Palace is the three-story-high central hall lit with three big roof prisms. The floor and gallery railings in the central hall are of Carrara marble. The offices are in the top floors fronting the street. The façade material is copper.

40

The Former Kinopalatsi Commercial Building 1921
Keskuskatu 1 b

Eliel Saarinen

Originally the Kinopalatsi Commercial Building had been planned on the Keskuskatu and Pohjoisesplanadi sides of the site, but only the Keskuskatu side, adjacent to the movie theatre in the corner, was realized. At the same time the first phase of the Stockmann Department Store, a bazaar, was being built on the other side of Hakasalmenkatu – today Keskuskatu – a street planned by Saarinen. This commercial building was the last of Saarinen's Finnish period, and it formed a focal point for the later, harmonious, commercial buildings along Keskuskatu.

The façade is divided into three parts. The first story is granite. The middle part is brick, with three-story high arched window fields which have soft, curved edges. As the windows are set deep the surfaces between them appear as round pillars.

The Käsityöläis-Osake-Pankki Bank, having commissioned the building, was situated on the ground floor. The current occupant is a branch office of the Union Bank of Finland.

42

42

41

Rautatalo Building 1954
Keskuskatu 3

Alvar Aalto

In 1951 the central organizations of the hardware trade held an invitational competition for a commercial building in Keskuskatu, between what is known as the Litonius Building and the Union Bank of Finland Building by Eliel Saarinen. The completed building, based on the winning entry, is very discreet in its relation with the 1920s architecture of its nearest neighbors, and it is in harmony with the general image of Keskuskatu. The architectonic and functional central space of the building is the Marble Hall on the second floor. This three- story-high roof-lit space is framed with travertine-railed galleries that act as galleries for the office floors. Ever since the building was first constructed, there existed at the edge of the marble-floored central hall, beneath the gallery, a cafeteria with fountains, clinker slab, greenery, furniture, and other details, which had over the course of years become an inseparable element of the Marble Hall. The destruction of this milieu in the mid-1980s was considered a cultural scandal.

The Artek shop and showrooms are on street level and in a floor below, in a space that is in part naturally lit. The Keskuskatu façade of the Rautatalo Building is copper, with the end façade towards the Litonius Building in red brick.

42

The Stockmann Department Store 1930
Aleksanterinkatu 52

Sigurd Frosterus

The department store is based on the entry that won second prize in a public planning competition in 1916. During the first phase of construction four stories were built in the mid-1920s. The building reached its final height – eight stories above ground level – in 1930.

Even today the Stockmann Department Store stands beside its continental models as a full-fledged example of the genre. Its handsome features and spatial clarity are to a great extent based on the roof-lit non-rectangular central space, which follows the shape of the block. The brick façades are characterized by a simple vertical accentuation based on the structure of the building.

A public competition for an extension of the department store toward the Esplanade was held in 1983–84. The winning entry, by Kristian Gullichsen, Erkki Kairamo and Timo Vormala, retained the street-side façades of the Argos Building (Grahn, Hedman & Wasastjerna / John Settergren, 1897). The extension, based on the winning entry, was completed in 1989.

43

The Hermes Building 1897
Aleksanterinkatu 19, Keskuskatu 4

K.G. Grahn, E. Hedman,
K. Wasastjerna

The Hermes Building is the only extant 19th-century building on Keskuskatu. The oldest part of the street (between the Rautatientori Railway Square and Aleksanterinkatu) underwent radical changes in the 1930s, and more recently in the 1960s.

Originally the structure consisted of a principal mass and an annex connected to one of the main staircases. The annex was demolished in 1988. Originally the building contained business space and apartments, but the apartments have been converted to offices.

45

46

44

The Former
Liittopankki Bank 1929
Aleksanterinkatu 17

Pauli E. Blomstedt

Liittopankki was one of the five bank buildings constructed in the centre of Helsinki after planning competitions at the end of the 1920s. It is characteristic of periods of transition that the classical elements in the competition entries never saw completion in the finished buildings. The Liittopankki is based on the winning entry of a competition held in 1926. The arches of the street-level windows and the doorframes were still typical classicism, but the pronounced verticality of the top floors is a departure from it. One can find allusions to Louis Sullivan's Prudential Building skyscraper in Buffalo, New York. The two-story high ceiling-lit bank hall is placed in the inner corner of the two wings fronting Aleksanterinkatu and Keskuskatu.

45

The Lunqvist Building 1900
Aleksanterinkatu 13

Selim A. Lindqvist

The Lunqvist Building was the first exclusively commercial building in Finland. To a greater extent than the earlier Merkurius Building by the same planner, it corresponds to the late 19th-century buildings of the Chicago School. The façades and the superstructure are freestanding, large windows provide ample lighting to offices, which are easily altered due to the placing of the transverse bearing walls next to the two staircases, and the intermediate floors are supported elsewhere by slender cast-iron col-

umns and girders. The airiness and structural clarity of the Lundqvist Building, with its sumptuous roof silhouette, provides an impressive antithesis to the nearly contemporaneous castle-like solidity of the Pohjola Building on the opposite corner of the street. The building was among the last he planned together with the master builder Elia Heikel. Their collaboration produced architecture based on new materials: iron and concrete, combined with progressive structural solutions.

Heavy-handed renovation in 1981 retained the outer aspect of the building but destroyed its soul, as its progressive cast-iron fabric was replaced with a new superstructure. The building was made into a department store, and its outer expression changed when new windows were added in the attic.

46

The Pohjola
Insurance Company 1901
Aleksanterinkatu 44

Herman Gesellius,
Armas Lindgren,
Eliel Saarinen

Pohjola, the first fire insurance company in Finland, arranged a public competition in 1899 for the planning of its new office facilities. It was stipulated that the building be constructed of fire-resistant materials and the façades of native stone. The building is based on layout plans by Ines and Agathon Törnvall, whose entry won second prize in the competition. The final plans were developed by Gesellius, Lindgren and Saarinen.

In a manner typical of the period, the lowest stories contained shops and offices, and the upper stories apartments. The Pohjola Building was the first true National

47

48

Romantic building by the architectural trio, and became a prototype in its use of materials as well. The texture of the façade shifts gradually from rough to smooth from the street level upwards. In addition to the granite, Nunnanlahti steatite was used, especially in the ornamentation, executed for the most part by Hilda Flodin. The works of H.H. Richardson and in particular Louis Sullivan's Auditorium Building in Chicago are among obvious foreign influences.

Some of the interiors in the Pohjola Building are original. The staircase with its fine details is very impressive. The building is owned by the Kansallis-Osake-Pankki Bank.

47

The Former Main Office of the Union Bank of Finland 1898
Aleksanterinkatu 36 B

Gustaf Nyström

The UBF headquarters is the first building in which domestic granite was used as the sole material in the façade. This stemmed from a desire at the end of last century to employ genuine materials and the products of the domestic stonecutting industry. However, Nyström's palatial bank, dominated as it is by a colossal order, still utilizes the granite in a highly traditional manner. The spirit of National Romanticism then current introduced a new phase in the use of stone. The façade was severely marred when display windows were added to the ground floor.

The beautifully renovated bank hall is in the second story. The tall central part of the three-aisle hall is covered by a curved glazed roof. Today the old bank hall is used as an assembly room for the board of directors and as a meeting room and for social functions.

48

The Stock Exchange 1911
Fabianinkatu 14

Lars Sonck

Sonck's next major business building in Helsinki after the Mortgage Association Building was the Stock Exchange. The buildings are constructed on similar sites, and the composition and materials of their façades have much in common. The Stock Exchange Building contains the Stock Exchange, other office space, a restaurant and business facilities. The sky-light system of the Mortgage Association Building finds its counterpart in the covered courtyard of the Stock Exchange. The Stock Exchange courtyard can be characterized as a covered outdoor space; it is a semi-public forerunner of today's glass-covered public spaces. The interiors open towards the courtyard through a vaulted passageway, balconies, and a canyon-like passageway above. The restaurant is beyond the courtyard, and the Stock Exchange is over the restaurant. The general form of the façade and the relations of the windows draw parallels with early 20th-century works by Frank Lloyd Wright, particularly the Larkin building (1904).

51

53

49

The Former Atlas-Pankki Bank 1929
Mikonkatu 9

Jussi and Toivo Paatela

The Atlas-pankki Building was based on a purchased entry in a competition held in 1927. The horizontal nature of the competition entry was changed to a more vertical expression in the completed building, in consideration of its neighbor on Keskuskatu, the Lackman Building (Wäinö Palmqvist, Einar Sjöström, 1913). The red-brick façade of the Atlas-pankki Building has classical ornamentation, by Gunnar Finne, between the windows and on the wall surfaces of the notched corner segment. In 1936–76 the Rea Cinema Theatre operated in the building. The cinema entrance was in the corner, commonly known as the Rea Corner. The vertical motif of the Hallituskatu façade was highlighted when the adjacent Heimola Building (Onni Tarjanne, 1910) was replaced by a new Heimola Building by Toivo Korhonen. Its brick façade pillars continue the theme of the Atlas-pankki Building.

50

The Helsingin Suomalainen Säästöpankki Bank 1932
Kluuvikatu 8

Pauli E. Blomstedt

A competition for the bank was arranged in 1928. The façade of winning and completed entry, resembles the Liittopankki Building with its slightly monumental and vertical features. The top floor, however, is horizontal. The filleting emphasizes the vertical band windows and doors, otherwise the façades are completely unadorned.

The bank hall is a long roof-lit space. Its entrance is on the Kluuvikatu side. The building houses the Hotel Helsinki and its restaurants, with access on the Hallituskatu side.

51

The Porthania 1957
Hallituskatu 13

Aarne Ervi

A public competition for the Helsinki University Porthania Building was held in 1949. The building is based on the winning entry in the continuation competition. Plans for the University book storage rooms were included in the program.

The entrance forecourt fronts Hallituskatu. The student cafeteria is in a low pavilion in front of the building. The large lecture halls are in the entrance floor. The building also contains University departments, recreational space and book storage rooms. There is an underground passage from the University Library to the book storage rooms. The building was to a large extent constructed using prefabricated elements.

52

The Elonvara Office Building 1930
Kaisaniemenkatu 13

Yrjö Lindegren

The Pohja Life Insurance Company and the Elonvara Pension Insurance Company arranged a joint competition for their offices on wedge shaped corner sites on the opposite sides of the street. This double competition was part of a series of architectural competitions for commercial buildings in the end of the 1920s, in which functionalism gradually replaced classicism. The winning entry in the Elonvara competition, submitted by Yrjö Lindegren, still contained features of German new objectivity and the Hamburg tradition, in the vertical composition and use of brick in the exterior form. The building, completed in 1930, is particularly handsome and erect on its narrow northern side, where an extension of the main structure continues over the roof. The brick pillars are connected by horizontal molding protruding from the façade. The thickest part of the wedge-shaped building has a light shaft which provides natural light

54

55

to the staircases and some of the offices. The two bottom floors are shops and the top floors contain offices. There used to be a hotel in the building.

53

The Pohja Life Insurance Company Building 1930
Kaisaniemenkatu 6

Oiva Kallio

The Pohja Building has been called the first functionalist building in Helsinki. The band windows, a functionalist feature, make their first appearance in Helsinki's townscape, lending credence to this claim. It cannot be called a purebred functionalism, but in many respects the building is, however, a contrast to the Elonvara Building, a product of the same double competition. Similar sites produced similar solutions. Both buildings have light shafts in their thickest sections. The protruding part in the narrow side of the Elonvara Building finds its counterpart in the long façade of the Pohja Building. It continues over the roof as a light canopy. Protruding eaves and the delicately ornamentated trims which frame the windows and entrances in the lower stories are remnants of classicism, as is the ornamental niche which connects with the adjoining building on the Kaisaniemenkatu side.

54

The Palm House of the Botanical Gardens 1889
Unioninkatu 44

Gustaf Nyström

The Palm House was built to replace an old greenhouse (by Falderman, Engel and Arppe, 1832) which was proving inadequate and becoming dilapidated. The new greenhouse had an iron frame, principally of wrought iron, but with cast iron in the staircases and balconies. The central part of the Palm House is higher than the wings, the glazed roof is curved and culminates in a lantern. The general appearance and details of Nyström's greenhouse resemble several contemporary palm houses in Europe and their common prototype, the Kew Gardens Palm House in London, built in 1848.

The smaller greenhouse and the building of the Botany Department (1903) are also by Nyström. The University Botany Department and Botanical Gardens are to be transferred from Kaisaniemi to the Kumpula campus. There are plans to make Kaisaniemi a Natural Science Park and the present Botany Department building a Central Natural Science Museum, with geological, zoological and botanical museums. The Palm House remains in Kaisaniemi, and there are no plans to erect one in Kumpula.

55

The Finnish National Theatre 1902
Rautatientori

Onni Tarjanne

The National Theatre, originally the Finnish Theatre, is among the first public buildings in Helsinki in which the revival-style features have been displaced by National Romanticism.

In 1898 a public competition for the façade fronting Rautatientori Square was held and Jarl Eklund's entry won first prize. However, Tarjanne's entry was chosen because his stone architecture was deemed more advanced. The main façade (which has been influenced by Richardson) is of Uusikaupunki granite and Pielisjärvi steatite. The roof is red tile and copper.

The intermediate floors are reinforced concrete and the upper floor is supported by a steel structure.

The seating capacity of the theatre is about 1100. The National Theatre is a good example of a turn of the century interior. The visibility, lighting and acoustics of the theatre are good. In the 1930'ies an annex by Tarjanne was built on the Kaisaniemi side. It contains the stage set workshop, wardrobes and carpenters' workshops, etc.

Renovations in 1962 were planned by Kaija and Heikki Sirén, who also planned the small theatre on the Kaisaniemi side, with a seating capacity of 311. A third theatre, called Willensauna, seats 150.

57

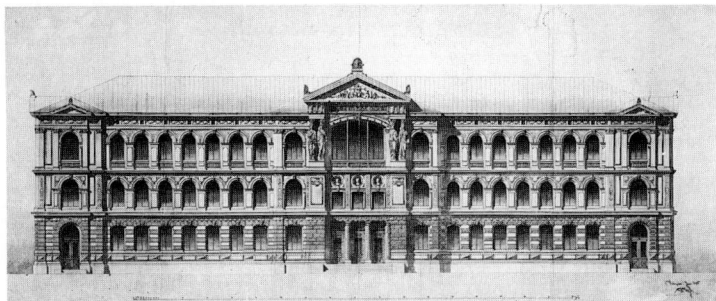

56

56

The Athenaeum 1887
Kaivokatu 2

Carl Theodor Höijer

»The Home of Art,» Finland's first art museum, saw the beginning of its collection in 1851, when Alexander II donated eighteen works of art as the germ of a future museum. Originally a grassroots initiative, the »Athenaeum» plan for an art museum and art school became a government project in the early 1880s. The building was completed in 1887, but only after a planning phase fraught with complexities and controversy. As with the Bank of Finland and the House of the Estates, an international competition for the Athenaeum building was held in 1883. Höijer received the commission after a further competition the following year.

The main façade of the Athenaeum has three projections, the central one highlighting the museum, and the side projections accentuating the former school. The four caryatids on the central projection symbolize painting, sculpture, architecture and graphic art. Busts depicting Raphael, Phidias and Bramante crown the main entrance.

The main entrance, entrance hall, massive staircase and exhibition galleries form a functional and architectonic whole. The Athenaeum was expanded in 1900–1901. Both wings were extended and the central hall was rebuilt.

Current repairs and an extension to be completed in the early 1990s will improve the building as an exhibition space. As the Academy School and the University of Industrial Arts have moved elsewhere the space for the permanent exhibition will be doubled. Even more is to be gained by enclosing one of the courtyards and extending the central wing towards the shopping arcade. The renovations were planned by Ola Laiho, Mikko Pulkkinen and Ilpo Raunio.

57

The Railway Station 1914
Kaivokatu, Rautatientori

Eliel Saarinen

The National Museum and the Helsinki Railway Station were among the largest government construction projects undertaken in the beginning of the century. Both buildings caused disagreement among architects. A station building had been commissioned from the German architect C.O. Gleim, who had won the planning competitions for the railway stations in Stockholm and Gothenburg. The Department of Railways attempted to conceal the project from the public, but protests by architects and a debate about the planning of the Railway Square, which had been kindled by a planning competition organized in 1902 by the Arkkitehiklubi Architects' Club, resulted in a public planning competition for the railway station.

58

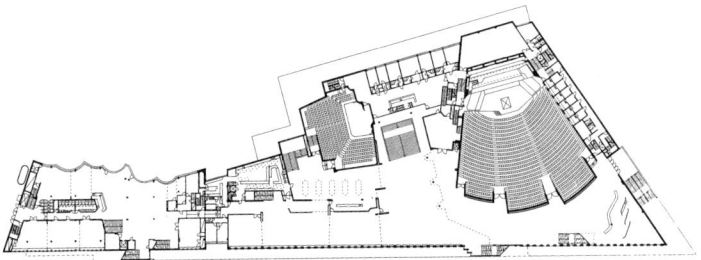

The entries were to follow a pre-set layout by Sebastian Gripenberg and Magnus Schjerfbeck. The competition was resolved in 1904 and Saarinen's entry took first prize. He had also submitted another entry to the competition together with Gesellius and Lindgren, but it was disqualified as too much like Saarinen's winning entry. This and several other entries indicated that the National Romanticism evident in the competition for the National Museum had gained wider acceptance. Many of the entries have features from castles and churches, and might well have been submitted to a continuation competition for the National Museum. Entries that were more in line with a terminus for railway traffic did not have a chance. The epoch-changing entry by Frosterus was met with ridicule.

Criticism of the competition and furious debate for a more rational architecture prompted Saarinen to make changes in his plans. A trip abroad strengthened his resolve. He moved from national influences towards the Viennese in both the whole and its details. Final plans were ready in 1909.

When the railway station was completed in 1914 it received international acclaim as a modern station building. The high vaulted station halls are an example of early 20th-century architecture at its finest.

The three-story plastered auxiliary building between the station and the Post Office was a part of Saarinen's general plan for the railway station area (1912).

58

Finlandia Hall 1971, 1975
Mannerheimintie 13

Alvar Aalto,
Elissa Aalto

The Finlandia Hall is the sole building in Alvar Aalto's plan for Helsinki's centre (1961–1972) to have seen completion. A part of the Töölönlahti shorefront plan, the concert building was constructed in 1967–71, and the conference wing four years later.

In addition to the entrance fronting Hesperianpuisto Park, there is another entrance from the lower parking level. The main rooms are in the auditorium floor, and the administrative facilities are in the gallery floor. The concert hall seats 1750, and the chamber music hall 350. The restaurant and its private rooms seat 300. The halls and lobbies can be combined in different permutations. The conference wing complements the concert wing. Two conference halls can be combined into one large space for 900 people. The composition and formal themes of the concert hall are a culmination of an idea Aalto developed over a considerable period.

The Finlandia Hall shows two sides, different in scale and character, the one toward Töölönlahti Bay and the planned terraced squares, and the other toward Hesperia Park and Mannerheimintie. The façades are clad in Carrara marble and, in part, black granite.

60

59

Villa Hakasalmi (The City Museum) 1844
Karamzininkatu 2

Ernst Bernhard Lohrmann

The Villa Hakasalmi was built in 1843–44 as a summer residence for the Procurator of the Senate, Privy Councillor Carl Johan Walleen, and is a copy of a Casino L'italienne-type dwelling derived from Italian Renaissance architecture. It was unusually grandiose for Helsinki and Finland, and has more in common with the local manor tradition than with town houses. The villa was situated outside the town limits, on the Hakasalmi shore, on a plot leased from the municipality. The lessee was required to develop the area into an English-style park, the origin of the present day Hesperia Park.

Upon C.J. Walleen's death in 1867, his stepdaughter Aurora Karamzin took over the villa for the duration of the lease and lived there until her death in 1902.

The town had bought the villa in 1896, and the City Museum has administered it since 1912. In the mid-1950s the villa was thoroughly renovated and a new exhibition plan was executed. The first extension plan dates from the same period.

A new extensive annex to the City Museum will initiate a massive development program for the Kamppi–Töölönlahti area. The completion of the annex will allow the museum to concentrate all its activities in various locations under one roof.

60

The National Museum 1910
Museokatu 1, Mannerheimintie 34

Herman Gesellius,
Armas Lindgren,
Eliel Saarinen

The National Museum is the best known monumental building of the National Romantic era, and the most prominent example of National-style stone architecture among public buildings.

Originally the museum was to have been a Neo-Renaissance palace, according to plans by the Department of Public Buildings. Armas Lindgren and a group of other prominent architects staged a protest, and their newspaper articles and the pamphlet »Vårt Museum» (Our Museum) resulted in a public competition. The pamphlet described new European museums employing the agglomeration prin-

59

61

61

ciple, according to which the various departments are distinct parts of the building, or otherwise distinguishable units. The winning entry was submitted by the GLS-trio. To a great extent it was in line with the principles outlined in the »Vårt Museum» pamphlet. On the other hand, the plan was a breakthrough for National Romanticism, and it was an architectonic statement of policy in a building with a preservative function.

The National Museum consists of a pavilion theme around two courtyards. The departments of archeology, history and ethnography are placed in halls which circle the courtyards. Medieval churches and castles are the dominant theme in the exterior form of the building. The tower of Martin Nyrop's City Hall in Copenhagen may have influenced the high tower.

The museum was completed in 1910, and the collections were opened to the public in 1916. A storage facility by Armas Lindgren was completed in the mid-1910s and the garden wall toward the end of the decade.

In 1987 a competition by invitation for the expansion of the museum was held in order to provide space for rotating exhibitions, lecture rooms and the conservation department. Aarno Ruusuvuori won the competition with an entry that places most of the new space under the courtyard.

61

The Parliament Building 1931
Mannerheimintie 30

J.S. Sirén

Originally the building for the new unicameral parliament was intended as an extension of the House of the Estates, and Gustaf Nyström drafted a plan for it in 1906. Two years later a competition for a Parliament Building on Tähtitorninmäki Hill was arranged, and Eliel Saarinen won first prize. Hilding Ekelund was awarded first prize in a placement competition held in 1923, and once the site was determined a public competition was held in 1924. J.S. Sirén drafted the final plans based on the winning entry, submitted by Kaarlo Borg, J.S. Sirén and Urho Åberg.

The Parliament Building, constructed in 1927–31, is the only example of monumental classicism in Finland. It was completed at a time when functionalism had already begun its triumphal procession in this country. The granite castle does not grow from within; on the contrary, it seems as if its contents were hewn from the stone mass. The severe exterior contains an extremely well and ambitiously planned and executed building, with its monumental series of spaces, details and furnishings. The most important interiors are the Chamber of Parliament, the Hall of State and the cafeteria.

Renovations planned by Ola Laiho, Pekka Pitkänen and Ilpo Raunio were completed in 1976–84, and they also planned the annex, constructed in 1972–78 on the basis of an entry awarded first prize in a public planning competition.

62

62

The Taidehalli Art Gallery 1928
Nervanderinkatu 3

Jarl Eklund,
Hilding Ekelund

A planning competition for the Taidehalli Art Gallery was held in 1917, and the entry by Jarl Eklund received first prize. However, this plan was not completed. Hilding Ekelund entered the picture in 1924, when the Taiteilijaseura Artists' Society commissioned him to draft preliminary plans for an interim exhibition building in the corner of Yrjönkatu and Ratakatu. This project also fell through. As a result of an competition by invitation held in 1927 for the present site it was decided to build Hilding Ekelund's façades around Jarl Eklund's layout, which resembled Ekelunds sketch for an interim exhibition building.

The division into a side-lit sculpture gallery and roof-lit painting halls is visible in the outer appearance of the Taidehalli as two divergent parts. The entrance exedra opens to a foyer hall, and a staircase leads to the lofty sculpture gallery. The straightforward and unaffected circuit continues to the bridged stairwell under a conical skylight, through the two painting halls lit with a clerestory to the small side-lit halls and back to the top of the staircase.

When the Taidehalli was built it was a notable Finnish exhibition hall and a synthesis of Scandinavian planning and realization. As a characteristic representative of 1920s classicism it is one of the principal works of the period.

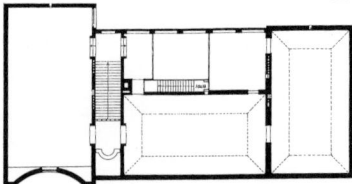

62

63

The Hankkija Building 1913
Salomoninkatu 1

Jarl Eklund

The Hankkija Building, which was originally called the Nikolajeff Building, is on the site of the former wooden Arkadia Theatre by C.L. Engel.

The Hankkija Building is one phase in the development of office buildings that was started by Selim A. Lindqvist and Elia Heikel. The structural rationalism, which is so manifest in the façade, makes the Hankkija Building a pure-bred example of an office building, and it served as a model for future development. This is clearly visible in the architectural competitions – and completed office buildings of the 1910s and 1920s.

64

Lasipalatsi »The Glass Palace» 1936
Mannerheimintie 22

Niilo Kokko, Viljo Revell,
Heimo Riihimäki

The Glass Palace is one of the most pedigreed examples of functionalism, on a impressive site where the former Turku Barracks once stood. Built as an interim shopping arcade, the Glass Palace displays the supple structural contours and large glass surfaces typical of the era, the Bio Rex cinema theatre in particular exemplifies the architecture of the night. The 800-seat theatre and its lobbies and foyers rank, both functionally and artistically, among the best utilitarian architecture of the era.

The present Bus Station is the only extant part of the Turku Barracks, which were destroyed in the storming of Helsinki in the Finnish Civil War in 1918. It forms a spatially and proportionally harmonious whole with the Glass Palace. It is attributed to C.L. Engel, but is probably the work of Colonel Burmeister, of the Russian Engineering Corps.

64

65

66

65

The Sokos Department Store 1939–52
Mannerheimintie 9

Erkki Huttunen

The Sokos Department Store is an important building in the townscape. On one side it fronts the Asema-aukio Station Square and its rounded corner is the starting point of the tall row of buildings on Mannerheimintie. The department store harmonizes well with the lower neighboring buildings, because the three top floors are gradually stepped back. The two bottom stories in the façade consist of large glass surfaces. In the higher floors the façade is polished granite. The building has, in addition to the department store, a hotel with a restaurant on the top floor, and a smaller street-level restaurant.

66

The Kaleva Insurance Company Building 1913
Mannerheimintie 7

Armas Lindgren

The Kaleva Building, currently the Helsingin Suomalainen Säästöpankki Bank, is the culmination of Lindgren's monumental office buildings in Helsinki. Here, unlike the Suomi Insurance Company Building, Lindgren planned both the exterior form and the interiors, down to the last detail. It is a seamless continuation of the New Students' House. The sedate and dignified façade accentuates the horizontal, with the ornamental balcony above the large display windows repeating the theme of the crenelated eaves and providing the sloping-sited structure with balance.

The sculptures at the main entrance and some of the interior reliefs are by Gunnar Finne.

The interesting thing from a constructional point of view is that for the first time in Finland concrete piles were used in the foundation. The structures were planned by Jalmar Castrén, who introduced steel-reinforced concrete into Finland and was an avid developer of the medium.

When the Seurahuone leased a part of the building while it was under construction, several important changes had to be made in order to incorporate the hotel and restaurant.

68

69

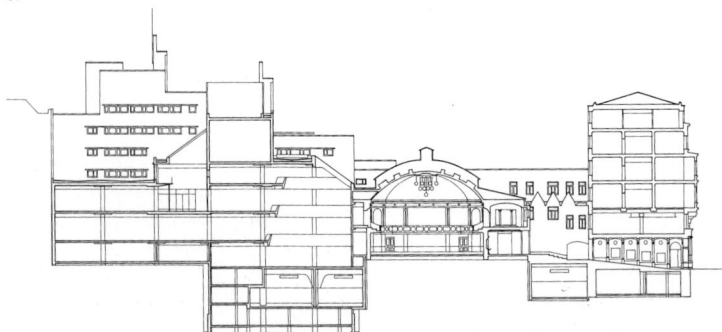

67

67

The Forum
Shopping Centre 1982–85
Mannerheimintie 20

Kari Hyvärinen, Kaarlo Leppänen,
Jaakko Suihkonen, Ilona Lehtinen

Mannerheimintie 16–18
Jan Söderlund

A public architectural competition
for the planning of the Forum
block was held in 1977. A continuation competition was held the following year, and the winning entry
served as a basis for the planning
of the new shopping centre. In
addition to a large new building
stretching from Mannerheimintie
to Yrjönkatu, alterations and an
expansion were carried out at the
Amos Anderson Art Museum.

An invitational competition was
held for Mannerheimintie 16 and
the block behind it, and Jan Söderlund submitted the winning entry.
In addition to new buildings, this
project contained structures and
interiors that were preserved, primarily the Capitol Cinema Theatre
(W.G. Palmqvist, Hilding Ekelund;
1926).

68

The New Students' House 1911
Mannerheimintie 5

Armas Lindgren,
Wivi Lönn

A competition by invitation between four architects for the New
Student's House was held in 1907.
The actual planners were selected
after a continuation competition.
Lindgren and Lönn placed the auditorium and regional students' associations closer to the Old Students' House, and the shops, offices, dining room and hotel in a
separate wing along Mannerheimintie. The two parts of the building are joined by a cupolaed tower. Today it is a landmark along
Mannerheimintie, together with the
towers of the Railway Station and
the National Museum.

The sculptures on the façade are
by Johannes Haapasalo. Lindgren
planned an extra story, completed
in 1925. The interiors have undergone considerable changes: today
the auditorium is a cinema theatre.

69

The Old Student House 1870
Mannerheimintie 3

Hampus Dalström

The construction of the Old Student House was an important ma-
nifestation of the national awaken-
ing during the second half of the
19th century, although the building
represents the international Neo-
Renaissance style typical of the period. A pioneering example of this

67

70

71

style, it was planned by Hampus Dahlström, assisted by Theodor Höijer, who supervised construction. As was befitting a public building, it stood apart from the low wooden houses on the rest of the block. It has an important series of Neo-Renaissance interiors: the auditorium, vestibule and staircases, and the barrel-vaulted music chamber above the main entrance. In 1898 the auditorium was expanded and a stage was added, according to plans by Yrjö Sadeniemi.

At the beginning of the century changes were made to the interiors, especially after the New Student House was completed in 1910 on an adjacent site. A terrace was built on the Aleksanterinkatu side in the 1920s, and behind it a side wing that connected the building to the Tallberg Mercantile Palace.

The Old Student House was severely damaged by fire in 1978. Subsequent repairs, planned by Vilhelm Helander and Juha Leiviskä, enhanced its utility and fire security, and the interiors were harmonized with the spirit of the original.

70

The Yrjönkatu Swimming Hall, interiors 1928
Yrjönkatu 21 b

Väinö Vähäkallio

From 1900 onwards there had been discussion for a swimming hall in Helsinki. In 1906 Selim A. Lindqvist drafted plans for a swimming hall in the Kaivopuisto Park, near the Ullanlinna Spa. For various reasons this project fell through, and the first swimming hall in Finland was inaugurated in the centre of Helsinki in 1928.

The spa-type Yrjönkatu Swimming Hall has two pools. The main pool is 25 x 10 meters. The dressing rooms are on the long sides of the hall. The balcony surrounding the pool contains the saunas, washing areas and dressing cubicles. Auxiliary space on the four sides are joined to the central pool area with high open-

ings, which end in an arch on the gallery floor. The 1920s classicism of the interiors is articulated in various details and the floor pattern. The Yrjönkatu Swimming Hall offered its patrons other services besides swimming and sauna baths. The building contained, for example, an institute for physical therapy, a hairdressing saloon and a gymnasium in the top floor. Later on the institute for physical therapy was replaced by athletic activities and the restaurant was converted to offices.

71

The Former Suomi Insurance Company 1911
Lönnrotinkatu 5

Armas Lindgren

The functional layout and most of the interiors of the Suomi Mutual Insurance Company Building were planned by Onni Tarjanne. Armas Lingren planned the façade. The only interiors assigned to him were the boardroom and the office of the Director General.

The façade towards the Old Church Park is sculpturesque, a »Renaissance palace» with a united eaves fillet, whereas the façades towards Yrjönkatu and Lönnrotinpuistikko are more modest, having the same alternating variation of windows characteristic of Lindgren's other buildings in Helsinki. Sculptures by Emil Halonen adorn the main entrance and the side projections.

In 1928 the Suomi Company arranged a public competition for an annex on the other side of Yrjönkatu. None of the submitted entries were completed. Oiva Kallio later planned a residential building on the site. It has been converted to offices.

An annex behind the original building was completed in 1938. It displays due respect for the original building through its choice of materials and their texture. The annex was planned by Risto-Veikko Luukkonen and Aarne Hytönen.

72

72

The Old Church 1826
Lönnrotinkatu 6

Carl Ludvig Engel

The Old Church – originally the New Church – was built to replace the Ulrika Eleonora Church (1727) razed to make room for the Senate Square. Built in what was then a suburb, it was meant as a temporary place of worship until the then Nicholas Church – now the Lutheran Cathedral – was completed. Viewed from the outside it resembles a cruciform church, an impression amplified by the ridge turret, a square »tempietto« with a dome roof. In fact it is a three-aisled hall church with brick columns supporting a wooden barrel vault above the nave. The interior of the church is unadorned and intimate, and its outer form is unassuming. Except for the columns of the ridge turret simple Tuscan columns and pillars and beams are the only elements of architectonic articulation. Once Nicholas Church was completed on the Senate Square the Old Church became known by its present name. The gate of the former cemetery and commercial councilor Johan Sederholm's mortuary chapel near the church are also by Engel.

73

The Taos Apartment Building 1912
Bulevardi 3

Sigurd Frosterus

The building, which faces the Old Church Park, has more in common with international Art Nouveau than the national Jugendstil. Its classical, refined expression refers to Henry van de Velde; Frosterus worked for him at the turn of the century. The park-side façade is symmetric. The protruding central part is framed by bays and topped by a curving gable motif. The two lowest stories are united by a natural stone surface, except for the bays.

The walls fronting the courtyard are a complete opposite to the refined elegance of the street façade, with free-flowing sculptural elements that are characteristic of National Romanticism. The Mortgage Association moved to the building in 1937.

74

The Academy of Fine Arts 1884
Yrjönkatu 18

Sebastian Gripenberg

The building was originally constructed as a girls' school and finishing school. Classrooms in the three-story school overlook the Old Church Park, the Yrjönkatu wing contains an auditorium and gymnasium. When built the school exemplified the latest in technical solutions and the organization of space, with practicality, hygiene, light and air as the key concepts. The building was occupied by the girls' school until 1981 and was then renovated for the Academy of Fine Arts in 1982– 1984. The former classrooms were converted for the most part into studios, the auditorium, into a classroom for drawing, and the gymnasium into a space for sculpture. A new tower with a staircase, elevator and sanitary facilities was constructed behind the house. The renovation was planned by Matti Nurmela, Kari Raimoranta and Jyrki Tasa.

74

75

75

The Former Keskuskirjapaino 1913
Bulevardi 2-4

Lars Sonck

The Helsingin Keskuskirjapaino ja Kirjansitomo Oy printers and book-binders constructed their building in the corner of Erottajankatu and Bulevardi in 1913. The printing presses were in an annex fronting the yard. Keskuskirjapaino sold the building to Helsingin Rakennusainekauppa Oy in 1917, taking a lease to it until 1924.

Long known as the Rake building, it forms a whole together with the former German Girls' School by F.A. Sjöström (1883). The printers' building has been joined with the old school by means of the façade material and a united molding. The façades are of Helsingborg brick fired to a purplish hue. The 3–4 cm-broad dyed seams ensure a cohesive surface. The gable on the Erottaja side has a colonnade bordered by a united wall surface resembling that of the Mortgage Association Building. The character of the building was altered in 1932 when an extra story was added (Väinö Vähäkallio).

After the offices and department store of the Rake Oy moved elsewhere a part of the building was taken over by the Postipankki Bank for bank and office use, and a part for an extension of the well-established Klaus Kurki Hotel.

76

The Otava Publishing Company 1906
Uudenmaankatu 8–12

Karl Lindahl, Valter Thomé

The building was completed in three phases. The middle part, from 1906, had been planned with a plastered brick façade. The re-cently- founded Suomen Kiviteollisuus Oy, a stone cutting company owned in part by some prominent architects, managed to convince the publishing company to use granite instead.

The printing rooms were completed in 1908 at Uudenmaankatu 12. The façade of the first story and stair hall are granite, the rest is plastered. The warehouse was completed in 1924, and in general it has the same type of façade. The façade composition, determined by the lay of the site, is exemplary. On this somewhat narrow street this important principle of composition has been completely forgotten in the 1960s office building in the next block, although it too is placed on three adjacent lots.

Some of the interiors and the office furnishings by Louis Sparre are still intact.

77

The Department of Forestry and the Customs Department
The Former Kaleva Building 1891
Erottajankatu 2

Carl Theodor Höijer

Originally the building was constructed as rental apartments and office space for the Kaleva Life Insurance Company. The offices of the insurance company were on the ground floor between the main entrance on Erottajankatu and the corner of Uudenmaankatu. The Säästöpankki Savings Bank had offices on the other side of the main entrance. Most of the five-story building was occupied by apartments. Kaleva sold the house to the state in 1914. The façade is articulated with reliefs and richly ornamented, a characteristic feature of Höijer's residential structures. Here, as in other examples of Höijer's work during this period, there are indications of influence from German commercial architecture of the 1870s and 80s.

78

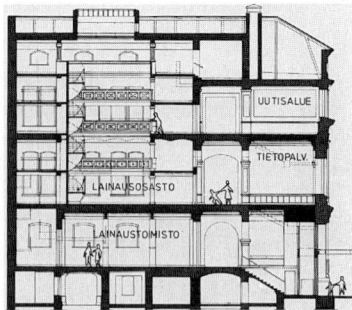

79

78

The Rikhardinkatu Library 1881
Rikhardinkatu 3

Carl Theodor Höijer

The building was originally built for the Helsingin Kansankirjasto ja Lukusali (Helsinki Popular Library and Reading Room), and it housed the Helsinki Main Library until 1986. As a municipal library it was a pioneering building in the Nordic countries, and served as a prototype for other libraries in our country. Originally the building had two stories, and the lending library and reading rooms were separate units. The lending library is in a separate wing towards the centre of the site, with illumination from two sides. The cast-iron pillars and wrought-iron joists that divided the space and supported the intermediate floor were characteristic of Höijer's work in the 1880s. The space above the lending library, reserved for a students' library in the original plans, it was initially in outside use. The reading room was originally two stories high, with a gallery supported by cast-iron pillars around a central space, but this was closed with an intermediate floor in the 1920s. The Neo-Renaissance-cum-Gothic mien and functional clarity of the building underwent an unhappy change when a third story, planned by Runar Eklund, was built in 1923.

With the Main Library now situated in Itä-Pasila, the building was renovated and restored in 1986–88 by Olof Hansson. The main staircase by Höijer was restored, the 1920s staircase was removed, providing space for an information area, and the former adults' lending department in the second and third stories was converted to form a five-story book hall. The building is now the Rikhardinkatu Branch Library.

79

The Helsinki Telephone Company Building 1905
Korkeavuorenkatu 35

Lars Sonck

When it was planned the Telephone Company Building had no precedent in Finland. The exterior appearance of the building, which contains offices, technical spaces and apartments, is at odds with its contents. The solid, fortress-like structure does little to suggest modern technical communication. The Telephone Company Building has details and material solutions in common with Sonck's Tampere Cathedral. The Uusikaupunki granite façade utilizes the same squared rubble technique. The windows in the top floor have subsequently been enlarged, and the tile roof has been replaced with copper sheeting.

78

80

81

80

Nylands Nation Students Union Building 1901
Kasarmikatu 40

Karl Hård af Segerstad

The students union building is on the north-west corner of Kasarmitori Barracks Square. The high gable motif and side towers of its façade form the end of Pohjoinen Makasiinikatu. The soapstone façade of the building is one of the earliest natural stone façades to utilize the Scottish squared rubble technique.

81

The Doctors' House, Residential Building 1901
Fabianinkatu 17

Herman Gesellius,
Armas Lindgren,
Eliel Saarinen

The Doctors' House on Kasarmitori Square is one of the first apartment buildings to break the bonds of the old layout composition. The plans of the apartments are more freely conceived and varied than during the previous century. The living spaces extend freely through the building from the street side to the courtyard, especially in the corners. The diversity of the living spaces from floor to floor is also evident in the façades, in their sculptural quality and free composition.

The smooth, unadorned and reliefless façade is enlivened with bays, towers, gable motifs and a loggia balcony, and arched windows at the street level. The sculptural quality is heightened on the corner, where an amusing frog supports a small tower, poking fun at the telamones on the corner of Höijers National Board of Customs Building. As is characteristic of National Romanticism and Jugendstil,

the roof is a visible element of the structure. Here, as in many other Jugendstil buildings, the original roof tiles have been replaced with sheet metal.

Originally the building contained apartments and reception rooms for doctors. Today it is mainly offices. The staircases display a change from the pomp of the previous century toward a more intimate character.

82

The Supreme Administrative Court 1901
Fabianinkatu 15

Waldemar Aspelin

Originally the main office of the Helsingfors Sparbanken Savings Bank, the building is situated at the Kasarmitori Square, flanked by two prominent Jugentstil apartment buildings: the »Doctors' House» and the »Torilinna». The palatial bank, which is almost contemporary with the residential buildings, contains remnants of the Neo-Renaissance, albeit with distinct allusions to the Jugendstil. The façade is of Ruskeala marble. The building was long known as the Radio House as the Finnish Broadcasting Company occupied it from the 1930s. In the 1950s the FBC expanded to an annex, planned by Jussi Paatela, on the Unioninkatu side.

The two buildings were renovated for the Supreme Administrative Court in 1982–1984 to a plan by Timo Jokinen. A building in the courtyard was razed to make way for a tower that contains a staircase and an elevator shaft. The courtroom of the Supreme Administrative Court is in the former bank hall in the second story. All the other conference and reception rooms are also in the Fabianinkatu building, whereas the Unioninkatu wing contains offices.

83

84

83

The Guard's Barracks 1822
Kasarmitori

Carl Ludvig Engel

Once the Helsinki battalion had been created the Guard's barracks were built on the central square for the part of town lying South of the Esplanade. The site was originally reserved for a theatre. The main building facing the square is the officer's barracks, built in 1819–22. Unlike the Naval barracks, which predate the Guard's barracks by a few years, there are no columns or pilasters on the façade. Instead, it is embellished with abundant reliefs and stucco ornaments which, especially in the side projection and portal of the central projection, bear military motifs.

The enlisted men's wing on the Fabianinkatu side was completed in 1825. The group of monumental buildings expanded around the central court. The Kasarminkatu wing by E.B. Lohrmann was completed in 1864. The southernmost building of the Guard's barracks is the Guard's manège (by A.H. Dalström), from 1877. Its massive oaken cross-structured roof slab spanned 30 meters.

The barracks suffered extensive damage in the bombardment of 1944. The officers' barracks were renovated in the 1950s, with considerable changes to the upper part of the building. The wings facing Fabianinkatu have been replaced by new buildings, by Viljo Revell and Heikki Castrén, based on the winning entry of a public planning competition in 1956.

Damaged by a fire, the manège lost its fine interior when it was divided into several stories to serve as the police garage.

84

The Leijona Apartment Building 1921
Korkeavuorenkatu 20
Einar Sjöström

This residential and commercial building was commissioned by the pharmacist Y.W. Jalander, founder of the Leijona Pharmacy, which still operates in the corner of Korkeavuorenkatu and Pieni Roobertinkatu. The red-brick building with a pitched roof is a good example of the first phase of traditional Nordic classicism. It was inspired by Danish architecture of the 1910's, which strove for ascetic simplicity, regularity and clarity. These points are particularly visible in the higher, Ratakatu part of the building.

85

86

85

The Museum of Applied Arts 1895
Korkeavuorenkatu 23

Gustaf Nyström

The Museum of Applied Arts was originally a school, but the three-story building by Gustaf Nyström has a such a distinct floorplan that its conversion to a museum offered no major difficulties. After renovations planned by Olli Borg were completed the museum was opened to the public in 1979. The permanent exhibition is on the first floor and in parts of the basement. The lecture rooms and other public facilities of the museum are to be located in an annex, the Center for Changing Exhibitions, due to be completed in 1992.

86

The Museum of Finnish Architecture 1899
Kasarmikatu 24

Magnus Schjerfbeck

The present museum was originally built for various scientific societies in 1899. According to the plans the three-story building was to have been as wide as the site, but initially only the central part was constructed, with the wings to be added later on in the 1920s. When the House of the Estates was made available to the scientific societies in 1931 the extension plans were abandoned. The cube-shaped building was used by the Helsinki University Gymnastics Institute until 1974. The Museum of Architecture took over the premises in 1980, and the alterations and renovation work were planned by Marjatta and Martti Jaatinen and Igor Herler. The exhibition halls, archive, research rooms, administration and library are grouped around an impressive staircase.

The Museum of Architecture and the Museum of Applied Arts are located in the same block. A planning competition for a Centre for Changing Exhibitions between the two museums was held in 1987, and the building, to be completed in 1992, will be based on the winning entry by Tuomo Siitonen.

85, 86

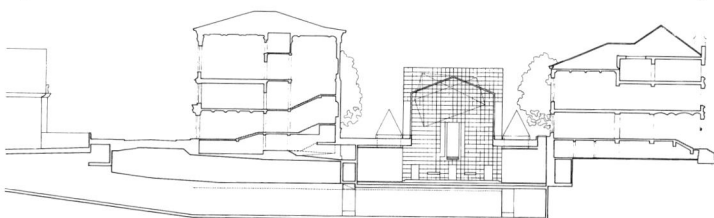

87

91

87

St. John's Church 1891
Korkeavuorenkatu 12

A.E. Melander

A great increase in the population of Helsinki toward the end of the 19th century necessitated a third Lutheran church for the southern part of the town. Finnish and foreign architects alike were invited to participate in a planning competition for the church. The Swedish architect A.E. Melander submitted the winning entry, albeit after the deadline for the competition. The church was completed in 1891 and at first it was called the New Church. Today it is known as St. John's, and with a seating capacity of 2600 it is the largest church in Helsinki.

88

The Sundman House 1818
Eteläranta 16

Carl Ludvig Engel

Like the Kiseleff House, the Sundman House is another example of a private residence Engel planned for affluent merchants prior drafting his plan for Helsinki's Empire style centre. The house, commissioned by Gustav Wilhelm Sundman, is the only extant 19th-century two-storied Empire style house in the block. The first story is rusticated and in the main floor a triaxial central projection with semicircular fields over the windows. There is a rich stucco frieze in the attic with a gable motif over it. The first story contained shops and storage space, and the second story was an impressive bourgeois residence.

The Sundman House was long known as the Victor Ek House, after the shipping agents' office there. A seven-story office building, planned by Jonas Cedercreutz and Helge Railo was built on the Unioninkatu side of the lot in 1962.

A shopping arcade bisecting the block from Eteläranta 16 to Unioninkatu was built in 1989. At the same time further construction was carried out on the lot, and the Sundman House was renovated to plans by Matti Vuorio.

89

The Market Hall 1889
Eteläranta

Gustaf Nyström

Alternative sites for Helsinki's second covered market were the Kauppatori Market Square, the Rautatientori Railway Square and the Kasarmitori Barracks Square, for which plans for a covered market had already been drafted. The hall finally built on the main Market Square in 1889 resembles the covered markets, exhibition halls and greenhouses built in Europe towards the end of the 19th century. The light façade and an integrated interior, with iron or steel superstructures, are characteristic features in these buildings.

Nyström's Market Hall has a tall transverse central part with two slightly lower wings somewhat basilica-like in cross-section. The elegant structures that run along the wings are Polonceau-style at its purest. Yellow and red bricks provide a simple ornamentation in the long façade. The more sumptuously accentuated gables relate the building to the Neo-Renaissance style of the period. The renovations carried out in 1988–89 were planned by Juhani Pallasmaa.

89

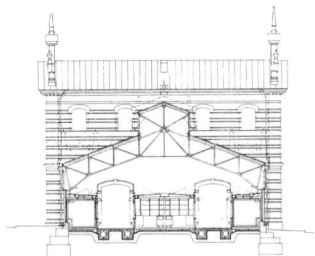

90 89

90

Teollisuuskeskus Industrial Centre 1952
Eteläranta 10

Viljo Revell, Keijo Petäjä

In 1949 some Industrial Employers' Organizations held a public competition for a large commercial building and hotel. Viljo Revell and Keijo Petäjä, together with Osmo Sipari and Eero Eerikäinen, won the competition, which aroused great interest at the time. The building, completed in Eteläranta in time for the Helsinki Olympic Games in 1952, was a final farewell to the Romantic trend of the 1940s.

The H-shaped building houses offices, a hotel, and restaurants, each in their own stories. The elevators and staircases are in the crossbar of the H. The two lowest stories cover the whole site, containing shops, cafeterias and restaurants. The façade fronting the sea is recessed in these stories, strongly articulated with double pillars. The six office floors have clearly drawn band windows. The hotel and restaurant floors in the nineth and tenth floors are, once again, set back. The façades are of polished concrete slabs which have in the course of time yellowed to resemble sandstone. Altered band windows by Keijo Petäjä in the 1970s did very little to diminish the effect of the façade. The Industrial Center, also known as the Palace Hotel, is a focal point in the Helsinki harbor area.

91

The Ekestubbe House 1887
Eteläranta 2

Sebastian Gripenberg

The four-story residential house was built for Lieutenant Colonel Ekestubbe. Situated atop a high hill, it forms the beginning of the three-block long Eteläranta shorefront façade.

It was the first stone building on the block and extends from Eteläranta to Bernhardinkatu and Unioninkatu. In this palatial residential structure Gripenberg utilized the two-story colossal system so popular in the 1880s, having already applied it to the Kirkkopuisto girls' school (now the Academy of Fine Arts). The fields between the façade's pilasters and the fillet were originally pink.

92

92

The Helsinki Observatory 1834
Kopernikuksentie

Carl Ludvig Engel

The Observatory was built on Täh-titorninvuori Hill at the southern end of Unioninkatu, the longest street in the city. Due to the elevated location, originally on bare rock, the building was visible from all sides, effectively dominating the townscape. Today the massive observatory and its three towers, hidden away among big trees, no longer achieve their full effect.

The approach to the building is through a forecourt enclosed by the annexes and walls. Narrow side wings contain the observatory halls that rise to form cylindrical observatory towers.

The refractor tower by Gustaf Nyström was built in 1889.

The buildings are still used by the Institute of Astronomy for teaching and research.

Gesellius, Lindgren, Saarinen: The Olofsborg Residential Building, 1902. (H2/15)

Selim A. Lindqvist: Villa Johanna, 1906. (H2/6)

anha Munkkiniemi
Gamla Munksnäs

73

72

71

74

Laajalahdentie

Munkkiniemen puistot

V. Saunalahdentie

Bre...

Pieni
Huopalahti
Lill
Hoplax-
viken

Paciuksenke

Uimaranta
Badstrand

MUNKKINIEMI
MUNKSNÄS

Meilahdentie

MEILAHTI
MEJLANS

Sauna-
lahti
Bastu-
viken

75

76

uusisaari
Granö

Granövägen

aarentie

Seurasaarent Fölis

Uimaranta
Badstrand

Seurasaari
Fölisön

H

Ulkoilupuisto
Friluftspark

ri

Kaskisaari
Svedjeholmen

Seurasaarenselkä
Fölisöfjärden

Mustasaari
Svartholmen

Ensö Katajaharju

Katajaharjunniemi
Enåsudden

Väs6terleden

Länsiväylä

Lauttasaarentie

Pohjoiskaari N:svängen

33

32

Drumsövägen

Isokaari

Storsvängen

34

Tallbergin puistotie

Lohiapajanla
Laxvarpsvik

LAUTTASAARI
DRUMSÖ

Uimaranta
Badstrand

Vattuniemenk

Vattuniemi
Hallonnäs

Hallon

© Kaupunkimittausosasto, Helsinki 1989
Julkaistu kaupungingeodeetin luvalla

Linnuston-
suojelualue
Fågelskyddsområde

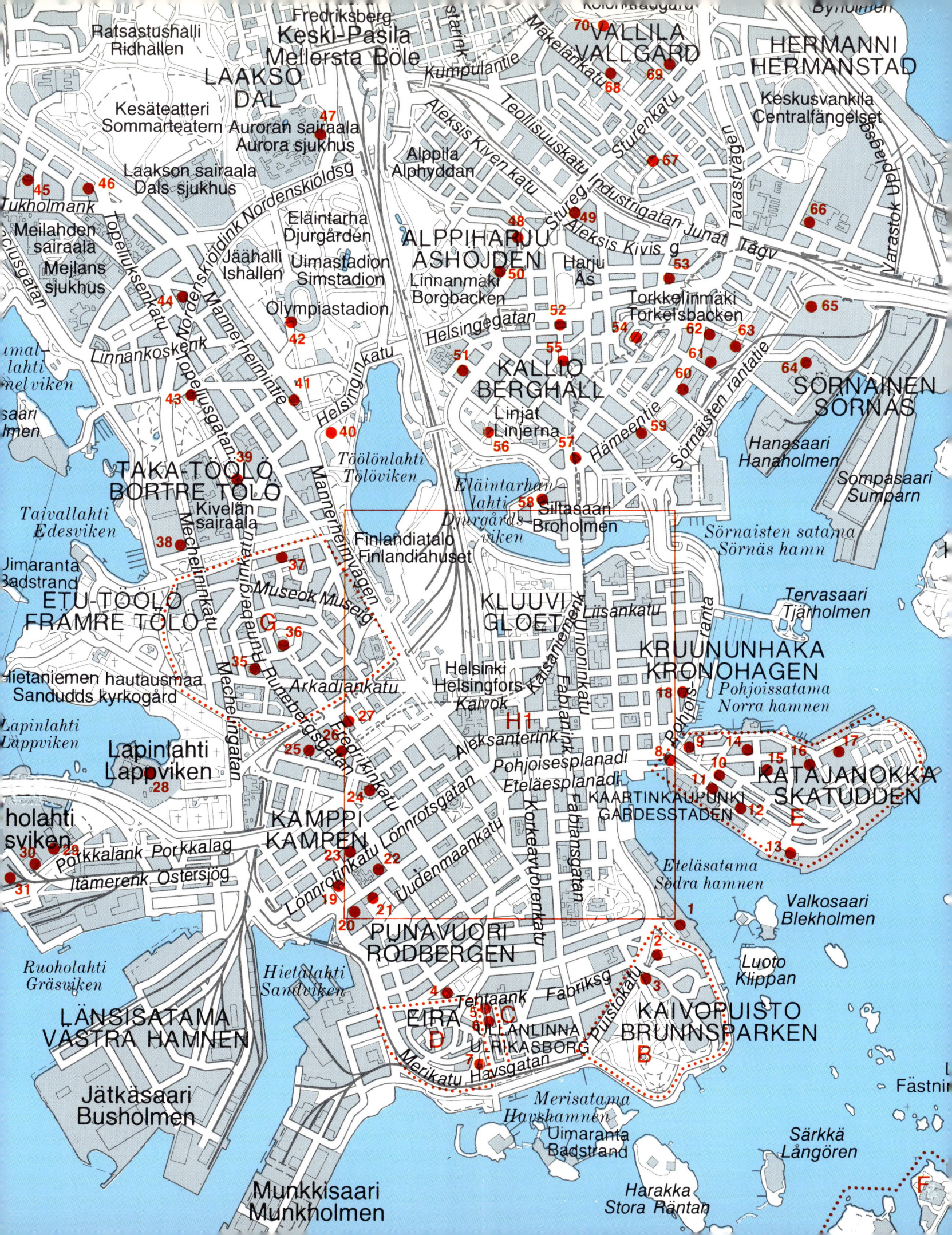

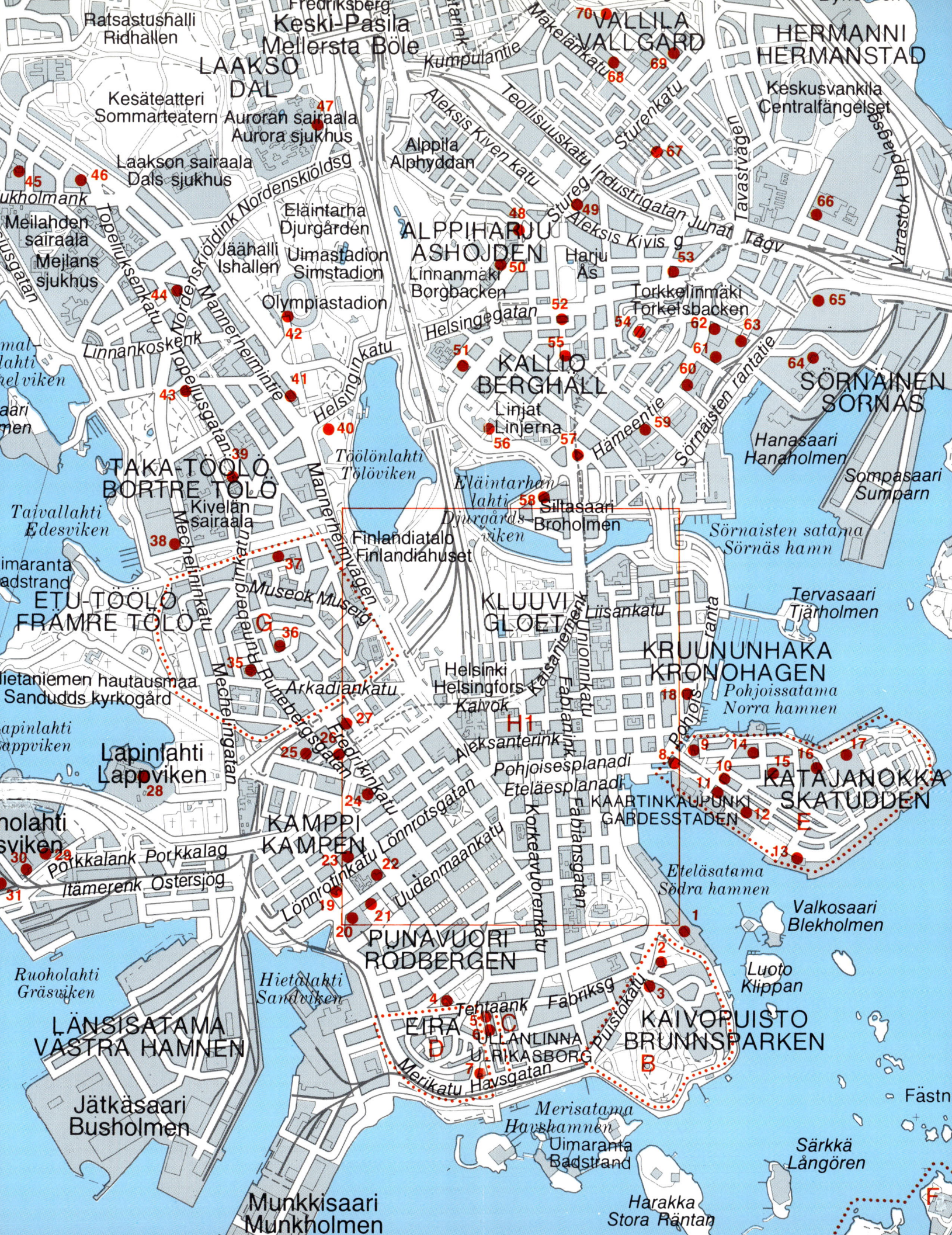

Fredriksberg
Keski-Pasila
Mellersta Böle
Ratsastushalli
Ridhallen
LAAKSO
DAL
VALLILA
VALLGÅRD
HERMANNI
HERMANSTAD
Kumpulantie
Mäkelänkatu
70
68
69
Keskusvankila
Centralfängelset
Kesäteatteri
Sommarteatern
Auroran sairaala
Aurora sjukhus
47
Alppila
Alphyddan
Aleksis Kiven katu
Teollisuuskatu Industrigatan Junat Tågv
Sturenkatu
Tavastvägen
Varastok Upp
67
Laakson sairaala
Dals sjukhus
Meilahden
sairaala
Mejlans
sjukhus
45
46
Tukholmank
Topeliuksenkatu
Nordenskiöldink Nordenskiöldsg
ALPPIHARJU
ÅSHÖJDEN
St Aleksis Kivis g
Aleksis Kivis g
48
49
Harju
Ås
53
66
Eläintarha
Djurgården
Jäähalli
Ishallen
Uimastadion
Simstadion
Linnanmäki
Borgbacken
50
Torkkelinmäki
Torkelsbacken
65
Olympiastadion
42
Nordenskiöldinkatu
Linnankoskenk
Topeliuksenkatu
Mannerheimintie
Helsingegatan
52
54
55
62
63
61
64
SÖRNÄINEN
SÖRNÄS
Linnankoskenk
Linnankatu
41
KALLIO
BERGHÄLL
60
Sörnäisten rantatie
43
51
Linjat
Linjerna
Hämeentie
59
Hanasaari
Hanaholmen
Sompasaari
Sumparn
40
56
57
Taivallahti
Edesviken
TAKA-TÖÖLÖ
BORTRE TÖLÖ
39
Kivelän
sairaala
Mechelininkatu
Töölönlahti
Tölöviken
Eläintarhan
lahti
Djurgårds
viken
58
Siltasaari
Broholmen
Sörnäisten satana
Sörnäs hamn
Jimaranta
Badstrand
38
37
ETU-TÖÖLÖ
FRÄMRE TÖLÖ
Museok Museig
Mannerheimvägen
Finlandiatalo
Finlandiahuset
Tervasaari
Tjärholmen
Hietaniemen hautausmaa
Sandudds kyrkogård
Runebergsgatan
Arkadiankatu
G
36
KLUUVI
GLOET
Liisankatu
KRUUNUNHAKA
KRONOHAGEN
Pohjoisranta
Pohjoissatama
Norra hamnen
Lapinlahti
Lappviken
Mechelingatan
35
Helsinki
Helsingfors
Kalvok
Katariinank
Unioninkatu
Fabianink
18
Katajanokka
Skatudden
9
14
16
17
Lapinlahti
Lappviken
27
H1
Aleksanterink
Pohjoisesplanadi
Eteläesplanadi
8
10
11
15
E
28
26
25
24
Fredrikinkatu
KAMPPI
KAMPEN
Lönnrotsgatan
Uudenmaankatu
Korkeavuorenkatu
Fabriksgatan
KAARTINKAUPUNKI
GARDESSTADEN
12
13
Eteläsatama
Södra hamnen
Valkosaari
Blekholmen
holahti
sviken
30
29
31
Porkkalank Porkkalag
Itämerenk Östersjög
23
22
LÖNNROTINKATU
Lönnrotinkatu Lönnrotsgatan
19
21
20
PUNAVUORI
RÖDBERGEN
1
2
Luoto
Klippan
Ruoholahti
Gräsviken
LÄNSISATAMA
VÄSTRA HAMNEN
Hietalahti
Sandviken
4
Tehtaank
Fabriksg
Puistokatu
3
KAIVOPUISTO
BRUNNSPARKEN
EIRA
D
5
C
ULLANLINNA
U. RIKASBORG
B
Jätkäsaari
Busholmen
Merikatu Havsgatan
Merisatama
Havshamnen
Uimaranta
Badstrand
Särkkä
Långören
Fästni
Munkkisaari
Munkholmen
Harakka
Stora Räntan
F

H2

Alvar Aalto: The House of Culture, 1958. (H2/50)

Itäinen Puistotie 7

Puistokatu 4

B Kaivopuisto

Helsinki's resort life in the 1830s was centered in Kaivopuisto Park, on the southernmost tip of the Helsinki Peninsula. The place was much favored by of both Helsinki society, and Russian officers and nobility. A resort firm constructed in 1838 the Ullanlinna Bathing Institute at the seaside, on the site of the present Café Ursula. The bathing institute building was destroyed by bombardment in 1944.

Along with the spa, the Kaivohuone Restaurant was completed along the Iso Puistotie esplanade that ran through the park. The original plans for both buildings were by C.L. Engel. Kaivohuone has been altered and expanded since the 1860s, first according to plans by C.A. Edelfelt, and in 1876 to plans by Th. Decker, for an industrial exhibition. Alterations, an expansion, and a music pavilion by Th. Höijer were completed in 1897.

The firm built villas on the rocky hill to the east of the park for customers of the spa and health waters institution. During the heyday of the resort, in 1830-50, a villa quarter grew in the area, with roads that freely followed the terrain. The oldest extant building from this period is the Kleineh Villa in Itäinen Puistotie 7. The villa (1839) shows shades of Engelian Classicism and is attributed to Jean Wik, a member of the firm's board. He also built a villa for himself in the area. The Villa Kalliolinna was built for F.J. Rabbe, manager of the resort firm, at Kalliolinnantie 12, with a perfect view of the sea. The villa, by E.B. Lohrmann, was among the first buildings to depart from the Classicism of the Empire period. After alterations and an expansion, the form of the villa resembled a feudal castle. Even as late as at the turn of the century Kalliolinna played an important part in the maritime landscape of southern Helsinki.

The Cygnaeus Gallery (F. Mieriz, 1870), the Mannerheim Museum (A. Boman, 1874; its exterior form has been changed), and a villa by Th. Decker from 1883, all of them in Kalliolinnantie, date from the close of the 19th century. Today there are several foreign embassy buildings in the area. The British Ambassador's residence, by Jarl Eklund, was completed in 1916 in Itäinen Puistotie 15, on the site of Rauhanniemi, or the Villa Jusupoff from the 1840s. The splendid Villa Baumgartner on the adjacent site was built by Lars Sonck in 1913 and razed in 1972, to be replaced in 1989 by a new British Embassy building by Stephen Quinlan.

The Salus Hospital (Kerttu Rytkönen, 1929) at Kalliolinnantie 4 is an individual interpretation of 1920s Classicism. Today it houses the Wihuri Research Centre.

Salus Hospital

Klippan

The Ursa Observatory stands on the summit of the park, bordered by old fortifications. It was completed in 1926, according to plans by Martti Välikangas.

Some villas were also built on the western side of Kaivopuisto Park. Dating from the 1870s and 1880s, two remain on Puistokatu. Puistokatu 4 houses the exhibition planning office of the Museum of Finnish Architecture.

The two restaurants on the islands lying off Kaivopuisto were built at the turn of the century. The Luoto (Klippan) Restaurant (1900) was planned by Selim A. Lindqvist, working at the Grahn–Hedman–Wasastjerna architectural company. The NJK Yacht Club Restaurant in Valkosaari (1900) was designed by Gustaf Estlander.

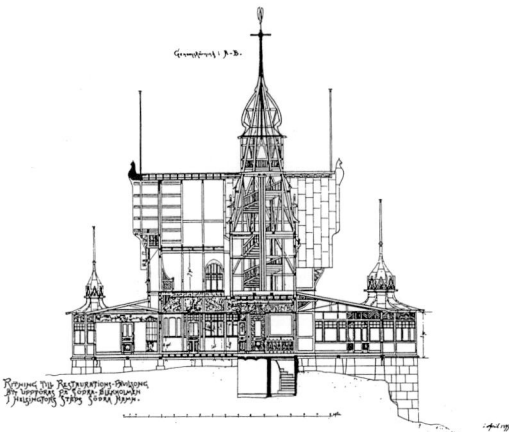

Klippan

1

The Meriasema Harbor Buildings 1952
Olympiaranta 1–3

Aarne Hytönen,
Risto-Veikko Luukkonen

An invitational competition for the Meriasema Harbor Buildings was held in 1949. The passenger pavilion is based on the winning entry and was completed in 1952, and the nearby Customs Warehouse two years later. The buildings mainly serve maritime passenger ferry traffic.

Because there is a six-meter difference in elevation between the wharf and the entrance level of the building, pedestrian traffic to and from ferries can be routed via bridges over the harbor installations. The main floor contains a waiting hall and customs offices. The top floor also has a restaurant. The wharf-side façades are dark brick. The top parts are concrete slabs covered with clinker.

The Customs Warehouse was converted to the Helsinki City Harbour House in 1986–88 according to plans by Juha Larkas.

2

3

2

Residential Building 1961
Myllytie 2

Aarne Ervi

The building is located on a valuable site in Kaivopuisto Park with a view over the sea. The building has three residential stories and has been composed to fit in the scale of the surrounding buildings and the varying elevation in the site. The two-staircase house has twelve sizable apartments, which share an entrance hall and sauna. The apartments have large balconies or terraces. The large roof terrace provides a communal leisure area and panorama view.

The façade materials repeat the marble surfaces of the adjacent Villa Keirkner by Eliel Saarinen. In the myllytie building the marble is in the form of slabs on top of the concrete elements.

3

Villa Keirkner 1916
Itäinen Puistotie 1

Eliel Saarinen

The industrialist and art collector August N:son Keirkner commissioned a large private villa in Kaivopuisto Park to house his art collection. It is also known as the »Marble Palace» because of its façade material. Saarinen had planned the interiors of Keirkner's previous apartment in the Tallberg Building in Katajanokka (Gesellius-Lindgren-Saarinen, 1898), they were transferred in part to the new residence. The exterior of the villa is cool and classical, but some of the interiors are interesting, with rich ornamental details: the hall and gallery are almost Baroque. The sculptors Emil Wikström and Gunnar Finne took part in the work.

In 1952 the state bought the house, and in 1984 it became the Court for Labour Disputes.

Huvilakatu 10–12

C Huvilakatu

Huvilakatu joins the four blocks in the southwestern part of Ullanlinna between Tehtaankatu and Merikatu. The quarter is Jugendstil in spirit, and these blocks form a most uniform whole. Also the inner parts of the blocks are functional and cohesively park-like along the alleys (Huvilakuja and Pietarinkuja) that cut through them. The buildings are, with one exception, from 1904-10. Most of them have three stories; near Tehtaankatu the number of stories increases to five.

The buildings in Huvilakatu are planned on small sites, with a garden at the back. The ground-floor façade fronting the street often differs from the other stories. Gable motifs, towers, bays and a spirited roof profile characterize the street, where the houses are also of different colors. The rhythm of the bays and other plastic motifs in the façades is at its most powerful along the stretch between Pietarinkatu and Merikatu, and does not let up until the Merikatu corner buildings: Huvilakatu 1 (Onni Tarjanne, 1906) and Huvilakatu 2 (Gesellius, Lindgren, Saarinen, 1904).

4

5

4

The Mikael Agricola Church 1935
Tehtaankatu 23

Lars Sonck

A planning competition for the Agricola Church (originally the Tehtaanpuisto Church) was held in 1930. The arrangers were put off by the modernism of the winning entries, and two years later they arranged a new public competition with a program that emphasized traditional forms of church architecture. They also invited several representatives of the older generation to participate, among them Lars Sonck. The winning entry by Sonck is a gable-towered basilica, with an interior dominated by cross vaults. The winning entry was criticized, and the completed church is more restrained and straightforward than the competition entry. The church complex also contains congregational facilities and apartments. The massive tower of the red-brick church narrows toward the top and terminates in a long spire.

5

The Eira Hospital 1905
Laivurinkatu 29

Lars Sonck

The Eira Hospital is a small private hospital originally built for a group of doctors. The character of the layout, the rich spatial composition, the number of balconies and other details all suggest a cozy private residence instead of an institutional structure. The residence-like exterior shares features with the concurrent Telephone Company Building, but here the wall surface is a light shade of plaster. The hospital blends in with the adjacent villa area, which Sonck collaborated in planning and which eventually took its name from the hospital. The annex on Tehtaankatu (1910) is also by Sonck.

6

Villa Johanna 1906
Laivurinkatu 25

Selim A. Lindqvist

Villa Johanna is among the most important Jugendstil buildings in Finland. It was named after the wife of Uno Staudinger, businessman and patron of the arts. The house was built next door to the Eira Hospital in 1906. Six years later an annex facing the alley was added. Villa Johanna was in private use until the late 1970s. For a while it was owned by TEOSTO (the Finnish Composers International Copyright Bureau).

Since renovations and repairs completed in 1988, the house has contained meeting rooms and entertainment facilities of the Postipankki Bank. The cellars and attic were converted during the renovation, which was planned by Juha Leiviskä.

Tehtaankatu 21

6

Merikatu

D Eira

Eira is a harmonious Jugendstil quarter from the first decade of the century. It is bordered by Laivurinkatu, Tehtaankatu and Merikatu. The ideological background for the new quarter was in the garden-city ideals of the turn of the century and the urban theories developed by Camillo Sitte, which were based on the organic growth of medieval towns, with their continuous and altering series of buildings and spaces, and the repeated detail motifs.

Lars Sonck proposed in 1898 that the area, which had been reserved for industry, be built up as a garden quarter. Because his proposal was unsuccessful, and because the area was in 1905 still without a plan, Sonck drafted a new proposal together with Bertel Jung and Armas Lindgren. According to the proposal, a company was to be founded to construct a villa quarter in the area. A preliminary plan by Sonck was attached to the proposal. It contained semidetached houses and single-family dwellings grouped in clusters along blind streets. The final plan, drafted by the authorities and approved in 1908, resembles Sonck's draft plan.

Most of the buildings in the area were completed before the First World War, in 1910-14. Instead of one or two-family villas, most of the buildings are low-rise apartment buildings that resemble villas only in externals. The semi-detached mode is fairly common in Eira. An often liberal reading of the plan and building order led to a rich and many-faceted quarter and a uniform archi-

Armfeltintie 4

7

tectural milieu, which, with few exceptions, has remained unchanged. An inseparable element of this whole are the period parks, which are characteristic of Eira and gracefully link the quarter to the rest of the town. The geometric structure of the plan is formed by the oval Engel Plaza and a central avenue leading from the plaza to the sea.

The late Jugendstil of the early buildings is replaced at times by monumental and mannerist classicism in the later ones. Armfeltintie 6 (Werner von Essen, 1911), Armfeltintie 8 (Jarl Eklund, 1916) and Armfeltintie 10 (Walter Jung, 1921) form a series which clearly depicts the history of construction in Eira: the first building is from the lively, predominantly Jugendstil early period, the middle one is from the final Classical phase, and the third signifies the end of construction in Eira and 1920s Classicism. The building opposite Armfeltintie 6 is the Villa Riviera at Armfeltintie 1 (Selim A. Lindqvist, 1910), which houses the Central Union for Child Welfare. The building on the other side of the avenue, at Armfeltintie 4, is by Lars Sonck (1913).

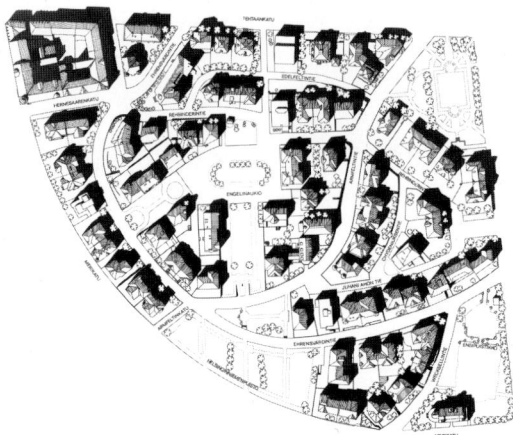

7

Villa Ensi 1911
Merikatu 23

Selim A. Lindqvist

Villa Ensi was named after the daughter of businessman par exellance Uno Staudinger, who commissioned this Jugendstil villa in Eira, as a maternity hospital in memory of his first-born daughter, Ensi. The villa is in the corner of Merikatu and Wecksellintie, with its long side towards Ensi Park. The layout resembles a ship. The simple mass, low profile, and espe-cially the façade facing the sea, resemble contemporary work by Josef Hoffman in Vienna and Brussels. The curved glass canopy over the main entrance complements the symmetry of the façade.

In the early 1930's the hospital was converted to nine apartments. The interiors were altered brutally. A renovation by Jan Söderlund is to be completed in 1991.

E   Katajanokka

Katajanokka is an islet adjacent downtown Helsinki, separated from the mainland by a canal. Of the current buildings in this quarter the Merikasarmi Naval Barracks buildings and the old part of the prison date from the first half of the 19th century, and the Mint, Uspenski Cathedral and some residential buildings date from the second half.

A town plan for Katajanokka was drafted in the early 1890s, and a railway line was built to the island. Construction according to the plan commenced at the turn of the century. The old residential area, the harbor warehouses and the new residential area in the eastern part of Katajanokka form distinct wholes.

The old residential area

The five residential blocks southeast of Satamakatu, with their citadel-like general form, prominent on the shorefront silhouette along the North Harbor, are a distinct entity in the townscape. The Jugendstil quarters in Katajanokka were constructed during the first decade of this century, the vast majority of them in 1903–06. The construction of a whole quarter in such a short time created, even on an international scale, a unique and uniform National Romantic townscape.

Luotsikatu and the parallel Kauppiaankatu, and the intersecting Katajanokankatu form the street network in a concise group of blocks shaped like a polygon on its outer perimeter. The angles of the corners of the blocks are acute in some places and obtuse in others. The corners are often accentuated with towers. The first buildings in this residential area were the Tallberg Building at Satamakatu 7 (the Gesellius-Lindgren-Saarinen company, 1898) and the AEOLUS Residential Building at Satamakatu 5 (Selim A. Lindqvist, 1903).

The last building on the northern side fronting the sea is the free- standing Wellamo Residential Building (Lindqvist, 1903).

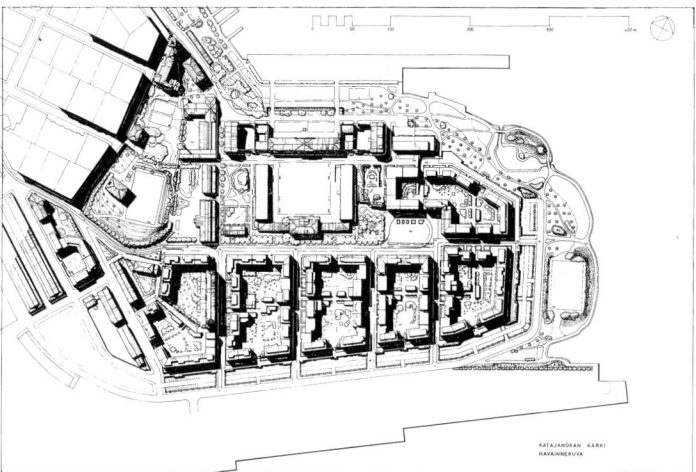

KATAJANOKAN KÄRKI
HAVAINNEKUVA

The Warehouses

The red-brick harbor warehouses and industrial buildings form a massive front that borders the east side of the Eteläsatama Harbor area. The oldest buildings are from the turn of the century, and the latest addition, The Kesko Building, was constructed in 1940.

Having become redundant, the warehouses have been put to new uses: The warehouse K 13 at Kanavakatu 12 (Elia Heikel, Selim A. Lindqvist) was converted to facilities for the Finnish Film Foundation (Juhani Katainen, 1985). The warehouses K 14 and K 15 at Laukkasaarenkatu 4 (Elia Heikel, 1898) were converted to a commercial, service and activities centre, »Wanha Satama,» by erecting a glazed roof over the street between the buildings (Timo Kauppinen, 1988). The SOK Warehouse Building, Kruunuvuoren-katu 4-18 (Selim A. Lindqvist, 1907), was converted to extra space for the Kesko Corporate Headquarters (Tapani Leppälä, 1988). The old part of the OTK Warehouse, Kanavakatu 9-17 (Elia Heikel, 1898), has been converted to office and business space (Matti Vuorio, 1989). The new part of the OTK Warehouse, Kanavakatu 3-7 (Georg Jägerroos, 1929), has been converted to office and business space. (Matti Vuorio, 1989) The Satamamakasiini Harbor Warehouse (Lars Sonck, 1913-28) is to be converted to a large hotel (Kristian Gullichsen, Erkki Kairamo, Timo Vormala, 1991) The warehouses on the northern waterfront in Katajanokka, Kanava-ranta 3 (Theodor Croll, Paul Björk, Waldemar Aspelin, 1867–1903), have been converted to office and business space and a restaurant (Juhani Katainen, 1987).

The new residential area

The eastern tip of Katajanokka was originally dominated by a garrison, docks and warehouses. When these activities moved elsewhere a considerable space was freed for the construction of a new residential area in the immediate vicinity ot the downtown area.

The residential blocks were constructed in 1977-86 around the renovated Merikasarmi Naval Barracks, which were enhanced with some new buildings. The frame of the outdoor public spaces in the residential area consists of a pedestrians and streetcar route which terminates at a square. The local services of the area have been placed in the ground floors of the buildings fronting the square. The main artery for motor traffic was placed in the background between the harbor and the residential area. The residential blocks follow the pattern of the Helsinki waterfront and present a unified front to the sea.

The local was demanding and the somewhat restrictive plan and its directions for the immediate vicinity, together with the careful selection of planners, was intended to ensure a uniform townscape. The cohesive and high-standard general view shows occasional indications of forced overplanning both in the streetscape and the view from the sea.

There are 1300 apartments in the area. Two-thirds of them are government-financed rental and owner-occupied apartments, and one-third was financed privately. The plan of the residential area was drafted by Vilhelm Helander, Pekka Pakkala and Mikael Sundman. It is based on their winning entry in a public ideas competition held in 1971–72.

9

10

8

**Headquarters of
Enso-Gutzeit** 1962
Kanavaranta 1

Alvar Aalto

The administration building of a large paper and pulp company terminates the Pohjoisesplanadi row of Neo-Renaissance and Empire- style buildings. It was formerly the site of the red-brick Norrmén Building by Theodor Höijer, which, as the gateway to Katajanokka and a central building in the harbor, formed a solid pair with Uspenski Cathedral. Aalto's building, on the other hand, is a part of a larger whole, the spatial and historic context of Neo-classicism. The architectural motifs in the building are classical: a uniform marble-clad façade and horizontal low roof. The building seeks harmony with the structures around the Market Square. At the same time, being free-standing and part of a different set of coordinates, it forms the main motif of the composition, which is further emphasized by its reflection in the water. The recessed top floor of the building contains a staff cafeteria and roof terrace.

9

The Uspenski Cathedral 1868
Kanavakatu 1

Aleksander Gornostajev

The Church of the Holy Trinity, the first Orthodox temple in Helsinki, soon proved too small for the growing congregation. With the new Lutheran Nicholas Church dominating the townscape, a new and impressive Orthodox church was called for. It was built on an outcropping in the Katajanokka quarter, on a site that had been intended for an imperial palace. Dedicated to »Uspenskij Sobor», or the repose of the Virgin Mary, the new church was consecrated in 1868. With its pavilion roof and gilt onion domes, it continues a long tradition of Byzantine and Russian architecture. The Russian motifs are complemented with western Romanesque elements. It is still the largest Orthodox church in Western Europe. In 1913 what was known as the Peace Chapel was constructed in a prominent location in front of the cathedral, to commemorate the conquest of Finland and the Peace Treaty of Hamina. It aroused mixed feelings, and had to be demolished in 1919 when vandals defaced its steatite façade.

10

The Kesko Head Office 1940
Satamakatu 3

Toivo Paatela

The approach to Katajanokka is dominated, after the Uspenski Cathedral, by the Kesko office building. This handsome example of brick functionalism stands as a gateway to the Katajanokka harbor area. The chimney and advertisement space in the corner, beside the staircase, accentuates the main entrance and balances the horizontal elements of the building. It fronts three streets and fills the whole block. Originally it housed three functions, each located along different streets. The warehouse on Kanavakatu has clearly defined band windows, the façade of the office building on Satamakatu has separate vertical windows. Originally the building on Kruunuvuorenkatu contained production facilities – for example a coffee-roasting plant. The dark brick façades of the Kesko office building blend in with its neighbors, Nyström's Customs House and Sonck's warehouse.

12

11

11

11

The Customs House and Bonded Warehouse 1901
Kanavakatu 6

Gustaf Nyström

The new Customs House and bonded warehouse from 1898–1901 is from Nyström's transition period between the Neo-Renaissance and the Jugendstil, when he was searching for a new architectonic expression. The composition resembles to some extent the Kauppahalli Market Hall in Eteläranta, with its transverse tall central element and two extending wings terminating in round corner towers. The brickwork of the façade is unusually ingenious. The main portal is of steatite. The impressive customs hall in the second story of the north wing has retained its original form, with visible structural elements and a glazed roof.

12

The Harbor Magazine, Katajanokka 1913–1928
Kanavakatu 8

Lars Sonck

The Harbor Magazine is the largest of Sonck's buildings. The brick-clad, monumental building is more than 140 meters long. Its material is in keeping with the older architecture in Katajanokka, with Nyström's Customs Warehouse in particular. The reinforced concrete structure of the building was planned by Selim A. Lindqvist in 1911. Although the use of the building was ordinary in function its place in the cityscape was crucial, and so a competition for its façade was held. However, the work was not awarded to the winners (Blomstedt, Taucher, Cajanus); it went instead to Sonck, winner of the continuation competition. The mainly five-story building is accentuated by two tower-like side-projections. The vertical windows in the three top stories become broader in the second story. The street level has arched windows.

13

14

13

The Katajanokka Passenger Terminal 1938
Katajanokanlaituri

Gunnar Taucher

The curved, red-brick building on the Katajanokka wharf was built as a customs warehouse (K8). It contains warehouses, offices and a cafeteria in three stories above ground level and a cellar. The intermediate floors are supported by mushroom pillars that narrow from floor to floor. There is a terrace fronting the sea. Large curved brick surfaces, door openings with curved edges and the terracing contribute to the pronounced plastic character of the building.

In 1975–77 the warehouse was converted to a passenger terminal according to plans by Kari Unelius. Pedestrian traffic between the terminal and ships is directed from the second story of the building through two connecting bridges, a passenger bridge parallel with the dock, and mobile gangplanks.

14

The EOL Apartment Building 1903
Luotsikatu 5

Herman Gesellius,
Armas Lindgren, Eliel Saarinen

The EOL Apartment Building resembles the other residential buildings on corner sites by the same firm: the Olofsberg Building and the Doctors' House. In the EOL the layout is slightly more rigid, lacking the advanced corner solutions of the Doctors' House. The façade has elements similar to those of the other two buildings, but the general impression is heavier and more fortress-like. The entrance hall from Katajanokankatu is particularly impressive.

15

The Olofsborg Residential Building 1902
Kauppiaankatu 7

Herman Gesellius,
Armas Lindgren,
Eliel Saarinen

Both the layout and the façade composition of the Olofsborg Building resemble the Doctors' House (1901) on Kasarmitori Square. Both buildings contain large living spaces which extend through the house, with the corner apartments in particular very open. The numerous bays enhance the views from the apartments. There are only three apartments per floor, the layout varying from one to another. Fireplaces and alcoves create a distinctive and cozy atmosphere in the apartments.

The façade resembles those of the country houses the trio planned during the period. A large, round, tapering tower dominates the tile roof on the Kauppiaankatu side. A rough natural stone plinth course joins the arched shop windows and portal frames. The façade is plastered. The impressive staircases are a characteristic feature of Jugendstil.

17

16

Katajanokka Primary School 1985
Laivastokuja 6

Vilhelm Helander

The school buildings, west of the Merikasarmi Naval Barracks, are old renovated red-brick buildings with altered interiors. The manège and workshop are part of the general barracks plan drafted under the direction of E.B. Lohrmann in 1844. The school's gymnasium and dining room are in the old manège, and the administrative facilities and special classrooms in the old workshop. The classrooms are in a turn-of-the-century machine workshop between the two buildings – one of the earliest iron-reinforced concrete interiors in Finland. Its tall, roof-lit central part offered a good starting point for the creation of a dynamic and functional school milieu.

A former wood and metal workshop from the beginning of the century is situated to the south of the school and contains a children's day-care centre, and further back an old bakery has been converted to club facilities. The renovations of these buildings were planned by Vilhelm Helander and Merja Nieminen.

17

Merikasarmi – Naval Barracks 1820
Laivastokatu 22

Carl Ludvig Engel

The main wing of the Merikasarmi Naval Barracks and the Old Town Hall were among the first monumental buildings Engel planned in Helsinki. The seamen's building, the first to be erected along the artillery court dating from the 1770s, forms the central part of a composition over 200 meters in length. Transverse officers' wings abut it with massive portaled walls. The western officers' wing was built in 1833– 36; its temple-like gable is modelled on the lateral projection of the Admiralty in St.Petersburg. The composition remained incomplete until the eastern officers' wing was built in 1987. A hospital by A.F. Granstedt was built in 1838 on the Artillery Court, opposite the seamen's building.

Originally the barracks were constructed for the Imperial Russian Navy. In the 1960s and 1970s they were used by the Valmet shipyard, and in 1984–89 the buildings were renovated according to a plan by Erik Kråkström to house the Ministry of Foreign Affairs.

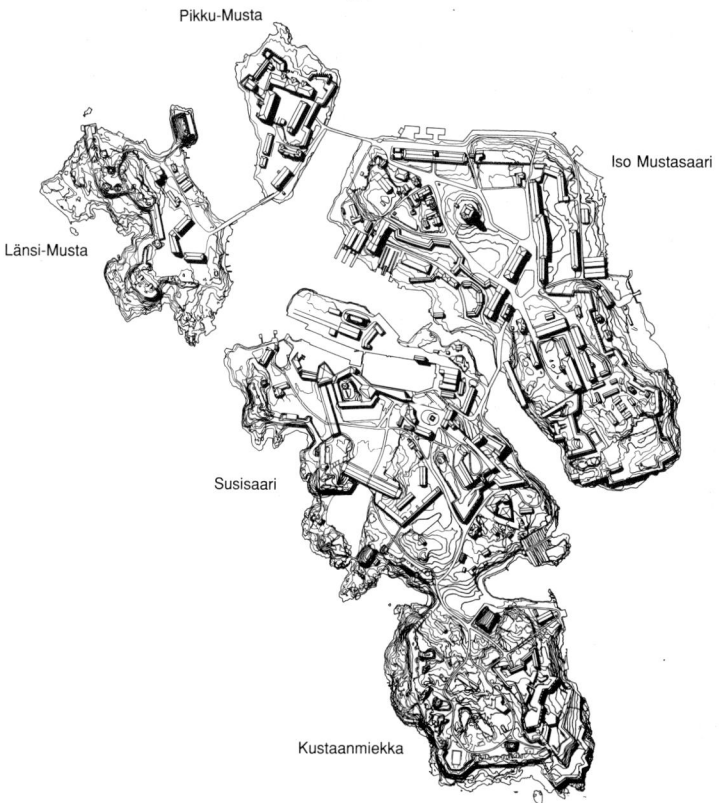

Pikku-Musta

Iso Mustasaari

Länsi-Musta

Susisaari

Kustaanmiekka

F   Suomenlinna 1748–88

The fortification of the islands in front of Helsinki began in 1748 under the leadership of Augustin Ehrensvärd. The fort was to be the main base for the defence of the eastern parts of the Swedish realm. It was called Sveaborg in Swedish, and the Finnish name became Viapori. For six decades the fortress was Sweden's shield against Russia, until it capitulated in the Finnish War of 1808. Viapori then served as a Russian fort until Finland's independence in 1918. The island fortress was given its present name in 1918, and was a Finnish garrison until 1973, when it came under civilian administration. The main construction period in Viapori was 1748–1788, and although Ehrensvärd died in 1772, his plans were carried out and complemented in the final phase by Nils Mannerskantz.

Between 1790–1808 few buildings were constructed. After capitulation new fortifications were devised, but these plans were soon out of date. New construction work produced the church, some barracks, hospitals and kitchens. When a joint English and French force bombarded the islands in 1855, Viapori proved totally outdated as a fortress. A new maritime defence line built on Helsinki's outer archipelago minimized once and for all Viapori's significance and it became an administrative and logistics center.

Iso Mustasaari Island

Iso Mustasaari Island is primarily a residential area, with few fortifications. Of the planned Army Fleet buildings to be placed axially around the courtyard, only the eastern wing, »Noah's Ark», was built. In the 1850s a Russian Orthodox church was constructed on the square, and eventually converted into a Lutheran church. The Crown Fort Ehrensvärd was built in 1774–1784 to house the headquarters, workshops and magazines of the Finnish Squadron of the Island Fleet.

Susisaari Island and Kustaanmiekka

The main fortress is on Susisaari Island and consists of two concentric bastion rings and to the south a separate fortress called Kustaanmiekka (»King Gustav's Sword»). The central fortress is an oblong group of buildings enclosing three courtyards. The most noteworthy is the Linnanpiha courtyard, the only courtyard plan by Ehrensvärd to be realized. It suffered extensive damage in the 1855 bombardment. The old Commandant's house contains the Ehrensvärd Museum.

There is a dry dock north of the Linnanpiha court. The Palmstierna courtyard is ringed by the bastions »Virtue», »Honour» and »Good Conscience». »Good Conscience» houses a summer theatre. Kustaanmiekka fortress was built in 1748–56 on the southernmost of the islands. The Kings Gate, facing Kustaanmiekka Strait, was built in 1753–54 as the main entrance to the fortress. An old barracks in the fortress houses the Armfelt Museum.

Pikku Mustasaari Island

The fortress (which is closed to the public) on the island consists of four bastions and a tenaille. The bastions ring a square which has buildings on three sides. The building on the north side, from the 1820s and attributed to C.L. Engel, was originally a hospital. The buildings are used by the Naval Academy.

Särkkä

Construction of the fortress began in 1749. It covers the whole of the island. The fortress is dominated by two tall caponieres joined by a two-sided curtain.

Later Development in Suomenlinna

When Viapori came under Finnish rule in 1918 no overall plans for the fortress were made for almost fifty years, despite the fact that Kustaanmiekka and Susisaari were decreed historical landmarks in 1919. The most important individual project was the transforming of Suomenlinna Church from Orthodox to Lutheran. Einar Sjöström won the planning competition and alterations based on his entry were completed in 1928. In 1922 Oiva Kallio designed a yacht centre and restaurant for the Merenkävijät Yacht Club. In 1947 Aulis Blomstedt initiated plans for the revitalization of the Kustaanmiekka fortress, including the Walhalla Restaurant within the caponieres »Delvig» and »Boije» and an extension adjoining them. The restaurant was opened in 1950 and renovated 1984.

Comprehensive planning for Suomenlinna began in the 1960s and extensive reparations in 1971. In 1970–71 the City of Helsinki organized a general planning competition for Suomenlinna. Since 1976 renovation has been the responsibility of Suomenlinna administrative body, which is appointed by the Council of State; and a plan for the use of Suomenlinna was approved in 1974 to provide guidelines. Its main goal is the preservation of Suomenlinna as a historical monument and its development as a living residential area and work environment.

The plan served as a basis for several renovations, among them the conversion of a Russian barracks to house the Nordic Art Centre (Pekka Helin & Tuomo Siitonen, 1985) and the conversion of the Palmstierna barracks to house artists' studios (Severi Blomstedt, 1981); both projects on Susisaari.

19

20

18

The Standertskjöld Building 1885
Pohjoisranta 4
Carl Theodor Höijer

The apartment house on the corner of Pohjoisranta and Kirkkokatu, built for Lieutenant General C.A. Standertskjöld, and now functioning as an office building, is the most impressive in a three-block row of domestic buildings. Its structural depth is considerable and the plan is labyrinthine. The main staircase, which has cast-iron pillars and consoles, resembles the side staircases of the Athenaeum. An entrance hall with a coffered barrel-vaulted ceiling leads from the street to the staircase. The angled corner of the building has a tower similar to that of the Grönqvist Building. The façade is mainly red brick. An unsightly extra story was added in the 1950s.

Lars Sonck and Onni Tarjanne continued the corner-tower theme in a house completed in 1900 at Pohjoisranta 10.

19

The Hietalahti Market Hall 1904
Hietalahdentori

Selim A. Lindqvist

The Hietalahti Market Hall resembles, except in façade material, a later work by Lindqvist, the Kaarti Market Hall, demolished in 1958. The building consists of a main hall with slightly lower apsides at both ends. The entrance wings face the market place. The geometry of the building is simple and coherent. Brick buttresses protruding from the façade reinforce the outer walls, whereas the semicircular exterior walls of the apsides are themselves structurally reinforcing. The red brick façade has plaster fields in conjunction with the windows. The Hietalahti Market Hall serves its original purpose, and its interior is largely intact. There is a café in one of the apsides.

20

The Brewery Boiler-room Building 1970
Bulevardi 42

Woldemar Baeckman

The Boiler-room Building is in the Hietalahdentori Square side of the Sinebrychoff industrial area. Vast glass surfaces front the square. Because the Boiler-room operates round the clock, its façade enlivens the square also even in the dark. The rest of the building is red brick, which harmonizes with the other buildings in the industrial area, particularly the old brewery building by C. Th. Höijer.

The six-story building consists of the actual Boiler-room, hops and sugar warehouses, the company computer center, and the staff dining room in the top floor. The malt silos tower above the building.

21

The Sinebrychoff House 1842
Bulevardi 40

Jean Wik

The Finnish Academy of Art museum for classical foreign art has been located in the former residence of industrialist Nikolai Sinebrychoff since 1980. Originally the house was Empire style, but Theodor Höijer added neo-renaissance features to the façade. There is an English-style park from 1835 behind the house and brewery, with a brick watchtower on its highest point.

In 1959 a public planning competition was arranged to convert the site into a business zone. The plans would have called for the razing of the Sinebrychoff House. The state bought the house in 1975, and at the same time the city acquired the adjacent park.

The museum has a permanent collection and a small space for temporary exhibitions, with a total

---

21

23

22

23

exhibition area measuring about 1500 square meters. The renovation was planned by Sirkka Tarumaa.

The wooden dwelling behind the Sinebrychoff House was moved to the present site from Suomenlinna in 1823, serving as the Sinebrychoff residence until 1842. It was converted to office space in 1988–89.

22

The National Opera 1879
Albertinkatu 34 B

Benard, Koschperoff

In 1879 the Neo-Renaissance Alexander's Theatre was built along the Boulevard to meet the cultural needs of Helsinki's Russian community. It was planned by Lieutenant Colonel Benard, and Colonel Koschperoff of the Engineering Corps was in charge of construction. The interiors were designed by the Russian architect Ieronim Osuhovski, and his successor, the Finnish architect Jac. Ahrenberg.

The Alexander's Theatre is a rectangular structure comprising a stage, a 500-seat U-shaped house, and a lobby with corner staircases. The chambers behind the handsome boxes were reserved for the private use of the holders. The Imperial box had its own entrance from the Boulevard, with a massive portico that dwarfs the modest canopy over the main entrance

on Albertinkatu. In 1918 the building was acquired by the Finnish Opera, now the National Opera.

23

The Poli (the Former Polytechnic Students Union Building) 1903
Lönnrotinkatu 29

Walter Thomé,
Karl Lindahl

In 1901 a competition was held for the building of the Polytechnic Union, with Walter Thomé's entry winning first prize in the continuation of the competition. The Students Union financed the project with lotteries and subscriptions and Sampo, a construction company founded for the purpose. The building was completed in 1903, and contained meeting rooms, an auditorium, a restaurant, and shops. The façade was originally planned to be plastered, but it was changed to natural stone. The interior contains columns of natural stone supporting plastered vaults. In the auditorium dark timber beams are combined with plaster, and massive wooden pillars support the gallery.

In 1928 a competition for the Teekkarila, the building next door, was arranged for students of architecture. By Kaj Englund, it was completed in 1931, and contained shops, apartments, and a barrel-vaulted hall with tennis courts.

24

25

24

The Luther Church 1931
Fredrikinkatu 42

Hilding Ekelund

When the building of the Finnish Lutheran Evangelical Society in the corner of Fredrikinkatu was renovated, the old prayer hall, designed by K.A. Wrede in the 1890s, was enlarged into the Luther Church. The Society's offices and apartments were constructed over the prayer hall, with Wrede's Neo-Gothic red-brick façade as the back wall of the entrance to Ekelunds Residential Building.

The main part of the Luther Church extends into the courtyard, whence the church hall receives natural lighting. The lenghty church hall has galleries in the back and along both long sides. Pillars in line with the front of the side galleries support a barrel-vaulted roof.

25

The Kamppi Triangle 1986–
Runeberginkatu, Eteläinen rautatiekatu, Malminkatu
Eric Adlercreutz (Runeberginkatu 2–4 a, Malminkatu 3)
Raimo Teränne (Runeberginkatu 4 b and 4 c)
Kirsti Sivén (Eteläinen rautatiekatu 16 a)
Pentti Riihelä (Eteläinen rautatiekatu 16 b)
Tapani Kajaste (Eteläinen rautatiekatu 14 b)

In 1983 the City of Helsinki held a public architectural competition for the planning of a block it owned and which was in nonessential use. The aim of the competition was to find an integrated approach to urban block development and to study forms of urban habitation and its supplementary services. The block was built according to the principles put forth in the winning entry, submitted by Eric Adlercreuz, with other prize-winners planning some of the residential buildings. The façades are differentiated in order to display the quarter's original site boundaries.

Some of the apartments are designed for the elderly and disabled. The Kamppi Service Building on Malminkatu contains multipurpose facilities, leisure workshops for the elderly, and gymnasiums. The Southern Helsinki Social Work District Office is also in the group of buildings.

A hotel and convention centre is being constructed on the square at the end of Salomonkatu.

27

31

26

The Kamppi Metro Station 1983
Fredrikinkatu 46–48

Eero Hyvämäki,
Jukka Karhunen,
Risto Parkkinen

The Kamppi Metro Station is based on the winning entry of a public competition held in 1971. For the time being it is the western terminus of the short metro line. The pavilion-type ticket hall is well lit with skylights and side windows. The façades and interiors of the ticket hall are granite, bronze and glass.

The Other Metro Stations
Railway Square Metro Station, 1976
Rolf Björkstam, Erkki Heino,
Eero Kostiainen

Hakaniemi Metro Station, 1976
Mirja Castrén, Juhani Jauhiainen,
Marja Nuuttila

Sörnäinen Metro Station, 1976
Jaakko Kontio, Seppo Kilpiä

Kulosaari Metro Station, 1976
Jaakko Ylinen, Jarmo Maunula

Herttoniemi Metro Station, 1977
Jaakko Ylinen, Jarmo Maunula

Siilitie Metro Station, 1982
Jaakko Ylinen, Jarmo Maunula

Itäkeskus Metro Station, 1982
Juhani Katainen

Kontula Metro Station, 1986
Toivo Korhonen

27

The Tennis Palace 1937
Fredrikinkatu 65

Helge Lundström

Originally known as the Automobile Palace, this barrel-vaulted building, squeezed between granite and aluminum edifices in Kamppi, lightens the massive row of buildings. Together with the Bus Station, which predates it by a hundred years, it is a member of an endangered species.

The top floor of the building contains the best indoor tennis courts in Helsinki, with their original, springy playing surfaces.

The long sides of the top floor contain dressing rooms, offices and clubrooms. The three lower floors have a similar plan. A wide central part is framed by a separate space, mostly shops and offices. The original automobile showrooms and garages have been replaced by other facilities.

28

Lapinlahti Hospital 1841
Lapinlahdentie

Carl Ludvig Engel

The Lapinlahti Hospital is the last and most unadorned of the four hospitals Engel planned in Helsinki. With the Old Clinic he had already done away with columns and pilasters. In the Lapinlahti Hospital there are no framed windows to brighten up the façade. The ascetic look is due in part to the location in Lapinniemi, a long way from town in those days.

The psychiatric hospital, in an agreeable, park-like setting, is a large two story-building shaped like the letter H. A front yard facing the city is enclosed with a fence and gate. Another, larger yard opens towards Lapinlahti Bay. A red brick building, called »Venice,» is also a part of the hospital.

29   30   31

29

The Salmisaari B-Power Station 1984
Porkkalankatu 11

Timo Penttilä,
Heikki Saarela,
Kai Lind

The B-Power Station is a continuation of the bold brick architecture of Salmisaari; earlier examples include the Alkoholiliike State Alcohol Monopoly Building from 1940 and the A-Power Station from the early 1950s. This group forms an important entity in the cityscape, viewed from both Itämerenkatu and Lapinlahti Bridge. Just like the old power station, the new building is also terraced toward the street. The brick-slab façades are divided with horisontal concrete stripes. The façade fronting the sea is clad with dark steel plating.

30

The Salmisaari Power Station »A» 1947–53
Porkkalankatu 11

Hilding Ekelund,
Hugo Harmia,
Vera Rosendahl

This steam turbine power station was planned in the Helsinki City Building Office under the direction of the City Architect, to secure electric power for the capital. Only a half of the original plans were completed. The red brick Power Station forms a vigorous and dynamic pair with the adjacent Alkoholiliike State Alcohol Monopoly Building (1940), continuing the architectural tradition it displays. The parts fronting Porkkalankatu gradually decrease in height toward the street. In the background the chimney stack, conveyors, staircases and staff pavilion form a contrast to the monumental form of the main building.

31

Oy Alko Ab – The State Alcohol Monopoly 1940
Salmisaarenranta 7,
Porkkalankatu 13

Väinö Vähäkallio

Pauli Blomstedt, who had planned restaurant interiors and those of the former administrative building for Alko, drafted a plan in 1935 for Alko's offices and warehouses in Salmisaari. However, this plan was not realized, and in 1936 Alko arranged a combined invitational and public competition for its industrial and warehouse complex. In the winning entry each function forms a characteristically distinct part of the extensive whole. The low parts of the building contain storage and transport facilities, the high part production units and laboratories. An adjoining portal building contains the factory offices. The company headquarters are in an annex facing the sea.

Alko's Itämerentalo Baltic House, by Einari Teräsvirta (completed in 1970), is on the other side of the street, next to the Lauttasaari bridge.

32

33

32

Apartment Building 1939
Lauttasaarentie 7

Aarne Ervi

The apartment building on Lautta-saarentie by Aarne Ervi is one of the best examples of a humane and sensitive interpretation of 1930s functionalism. The principal part of the building consists of four stories of apartments parallel with the street. The site is sloping and the height of the shops varies. The top floor contains communal space and a roof terrace, with a boldly protruding eaves that contrasts with the rest of the building. The tall central part of the façade fronting the street is enlivened by folds in the exterior walls and adjacent balconies. These deviations also lend variety to the views from the street- side apartments.

33

Ekonomitalo Residential Buildings 1952
Gyldenintie 17,
Taivaanvuohentie 12

Ahti and Esko Korhonen

The group of buildings consists of three terraced building units, two apartment houses and a building containing communal space. The two-story terraced houses contain a total of 26 apartments consisting of from four to five rooms and a kitchen. The apartment buildings contain 32 small and medium-size apartments. The terraced houses enclose a protected yard on a gentle slope. The placement of the residential units, a considered window pattern, the use of corner windows, and other simple architectural effects have resulted in an interesting and varied residential milieu. Both the terraced houses and apartment buildings have brick façades. Construction was financed by government loans.

34

Lauttasaari Church 1958
Myllykalliorinne 1

Keijo Petäjä

The church is based on a purchased entry in a public competition held in 1954. The building is located in park-like surroundings on the slopes of Myllykallio Hill, at the end of Tallbergin puistotie Avenue. The tall belfry occupies a dominant position on the Lauttasaari skyline. The composition begins with a military cemetery in the end of the avenue (Dag Englund, 1945), and continues with concrete slab covered levels bordered with native stone walls and a flight of steps to the church court bordered by the church on three sides. The whole consists of the church hall, several parish halls, a gymnasium, parish office, club rooms, apartments, and the facilities of the Swedish-speaking congregation. The church halls are closed in character, lit from the top part of the side walls. The interior walls are clad with sandblasted white concrete tiles, which are also the main façade material.

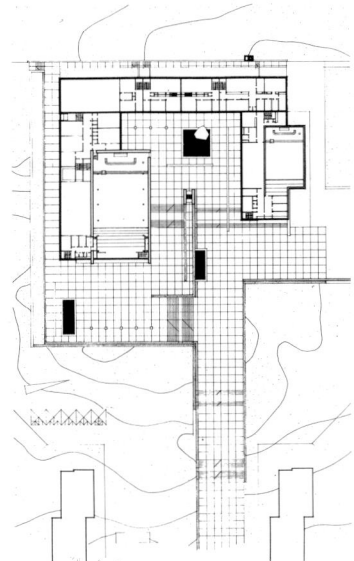

G   Etu-Töölö

The Etu-Töölö residential area in the immediate vicinity of the downtown area was constructed for the most part in the 1910s and 1920s. The planning and building in Töölö reflect the new trends in town planning and urban architecture.

Lars Sonck was familiar with the theories of Camillo Sitte, and he initiated a competition for the Töölö town plan, held in 1898. After a continuation competition the final plan, drafted by Gustaf Nyström and Lars Sonck, was approved in 1906. If one compares it with the competition entries, the approved plan is a compromise that relinquishes the surprises and small scale of the Sittean urban ideal. A proposal for a modification of the plan submitted by Bertel Jung further trimmed irregularities from the plan, in line with then-prevailing Classical trends.

Temppeliaukio Square, the highest elevation in the area and the terminus of radial streets, was given its final form in Jung's plan. After many stages a church was built there in the 1960s. The National Museum is another public building with an integral position in the early phases of the Töölö plan. The construction of the Parliament Building on a site reserved for the opera and a music institute restricted the planning of the immediate vicinity.

The first residential blocks in Töölö were built at the beginning of the 1910s, and the area filled out at the end of the following decade. The first-phase street vistas are united by continuous eaves lines, but it is still characterized by the rich details – the numerous bays and multiformed windows – of the later Jugendstil. The residential building at Museokatu 3, in the corner of Museokatu and Töölönkatu (Sigurd Frosterus, 1913), is an example of this phase. The two blocks at the end of the street, at Museokatu 27–37 and Museokatu 40-46, are examples of the uniform townscape of the second phase. United roof and eaves lines, regular simple windows, and other characteristics of 1920s Classicism are present in this strong urban vista. The residential blocks in Etu-Töölö have large courtyards or several adjoining courtyards. The buildings at the end of the 1920s were for the most part constructed by founder contractors, and the master builders played a significant role in the planning.

The westernmost residential blocks in Etu-Töölö, on the Hietaniemi side of Mechelininkatu, were constructed in the 1930s.

35

36

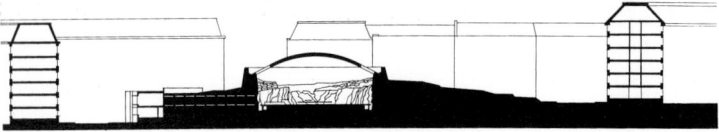

36

Remnants of Classicism meet the distinctive features of Functionalism, particulary in the details. Perhaps the most interesting building in the row of blocks is the Pergola Residential Building, at Väinämöisenkatu 29 (Sven Kuhlefelt, 1934). Its gateway ends in a courtyard with a pergola and fountain. What is known as Töölö Functionalism can largely be found in Taka-Töölö, the 1930s blocks north of Hesperiankatu. The residential apartment buildings at Pohjoinen Hesperiankatu 9-11 and 32, by Kaarlo Borg, are representative of residential buildings in which the façade composition is based on reflecting the inner function of the apartments. The livingroom bay and designed balconies, together with the staircase halls, are in the spirit of the period.

35

The School of Economics 1950
Runeberginkatu 14

Hugo Harmia,
Woldemar Baeckman

A public planning competition for the School of Economics was held in 1941, with the winning entry constructed in 1948–50. The building whole consists of parts dissimilar in nature and distinctly identified in the façade of the entrance side. The lecture halls and auditorium are at the centre of the building, beyond the main entrance and the uninterrupted plane enlivened with reliefs that crowns it. The theoretical and practical teaching areas are in different segments of the ringlike building, enclosing a courtyard, where the auditorium protrudes as a separate wing. The auditorium seats 772, and has extra-curricular uses. The large lecture hall seats 600. The façades of the building are light yellow clinker tile.

36

The Temppeliaukio Church 1969
Lutherinkatu 3

Timo and Tuomo Suomalainen

Public planning competitions for the church were held in 1933, 1936, and finally in 1960, when the entry by Timo and Tuomo Suomalainen was awarded first prize. The basic idea – a church quarried in the bedrock, with a tunnel from Fredrikinkatu – was already present in P.E. Blomstedt's entry in the first competition in 1933. Otherwise the present church is an independent and individual work.

The church, which only barely rises above the rock surface, is lit with a window that circles the central cupola between the dense radial beams that support the roof. The walls of the hall are bedrock and quarried stone. The powerful atmosphere of the church makes it one of the best known sights in Helsinki, and it is also a popular concert hall.

37

39

37

The Lallukka Artists' Residence 1933
Apollonkatu 13

Gösta Juslén

A public competition was held in 1931 for an artist's residence bequeathed by Juho and Maria Lallukka. The building was constructed according to the third- prize entry by Gösta Juslén. The H shaped building is situated between Eteläinen Hesperiankatu and the eleven-meters-higher Apollonkatu. The buildings fronting the street are connected by a cross-bar which divides the central part of the site into two courtyards. The building contains 49 artists' apartments, 21 of them studios for visual artists. There are two large studios on the Hesperiankatu street level. Each of the upper floors contains three studios with living quarters. The main entrance to the building is on Apollonkatu. A meeting room is located one floor down on the courtyard side.

The Hesperiankatu façade of the Lallukka Artists' Residence, beautifully proportioned and slightly classical in its interpretation of functionalism, stands out in a long row of residential buildings.

38

The Guards Batallion Barracks 1935
Mechelininkatu 32

Martta Martikainen

The building known as the Helsinki Motorized Company and later the Motorized Battalion is, together with the Tilkka Military Hospital, among the most important works of the Ministry of Defence Construction Office. Perhaps the spare and Spartan expression of functionalism and the character of the building type work in harmony, much like Engel's Empire style in his barracks and military hospitals.

The position of the Barracks building is emphasized by its location in natural park-like surroundings; standing at the street corner, it seems to be waiting for the block to fill out.

The buildings contains a tall building for enlisted men and one-story garages.

39

The Töölö Church 1930
Topeliuksenkatu 4

Hilding Ekelund

A planning competition for the Töölö Church and Congregation Building was arranged in 1927. Placed on the central axis of the Topelius Park, the winning entry by Ekelund was a symmetric, almost monumental composition with a Baroque-like stairs and an arched passage that circles the church. The completed building resembles the competition entry, but the 700-person church hall was not constructed. The entrance to the church is from the park side, in the middle of the tall tower which terminates in an open belfry. This story contains two wings with social facilities and confirmation classrooms. The church hall and baptismal and wedding chapels are in the next floor. The choir and organ space adjacent to the church hall is located in the second story of the tower.

The altar end of the church hall has a side-lit apse. The ring beam oft the casette roof protrudes in the churh hall and is supported by two freestanding round pillars. This gives the impression of a columned rotunda. The ceiling of the hall is divided by visible beams and the surfaces between them have a simple band ornamentation. The classicism of the 1920s is evident not only in the details but also in the use of colors in both the interiors and the exterior. The main color is pink, supplemented with light blue.

40

41

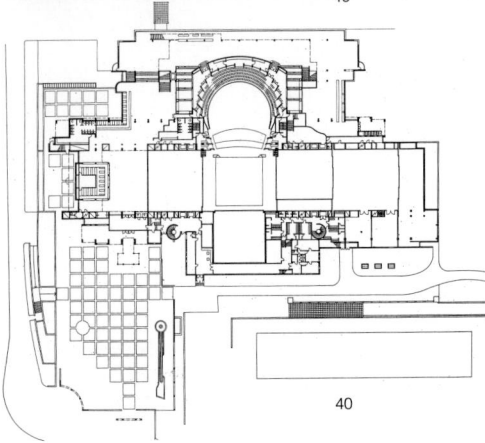

40

40

The Opera 1992
Mannerheimintie, Helsinginkatu

Eero Hyvämäki,
Jukka Karhunen,
Risto Parkkinen

Since the beginning of the 19th century four different sites were proposed for the Opera before its final location, on Töölönlahti Bay, was decided. A two-phase architectural competition for the Opera was held in 1975–77, and the building under construction, to be completed in 1992, is based on the winning entry.

The building contains two theatres, with the Opera hall seating 1350 and the modifiable studio theatre 450. In addition to the performance and public facilities it contains diverse rehearsal rooms, workshops, prop storage rooms, and a ballet school.

41

The Former Exhibition Hall 1935
Mannerheimintie 17

Aarne Hytönen,
Risto-Veikko Luukkonen

The Suomen Messut Finnish Exhibition Cooperative held a public competition for the planning of the Exhibition Hall. The completed building is based on plans by the winners of a continuation competition, Aarne Hytönen and Risto-Veikko Luukkonen. The first phase of construction was completed in February, 1935; and as the largest interior in Finland, it opened its doors to 7000 guests in celebration of the centenary of the Kalevala, the Finnish national epic. The Exhibition Hall was used not only for exhibitions but also for large festivals, athletic events, concerts, congresses, etc. The main hall is the size of four tennis courts. A gallery spans it on three sides, and there is a restaurant on the fourth side, above the former main entrance. According to the original plans the façade on the main entrance side was to be a multi-storied, windowless wall above the restaurant for the display of advertisements. This wall and an adjacent hotel wing were not constructed due to lack of funds, and the profile of the barrel-vaulted roof became the distinctive feature of the building.

The first expansion of the Exhibition Hall was completed in 1941. In the 1950s the smaller B-Hall, with a capacity of 2000, was constructed adjacent to the main hall. Likewise barrel-vaulted, it recalls the streetcar halls with their curved roofs on the other side of Mannerheimintie, themselves pioneering work in iron-reinforced concrete by Selim A. Lindqvist from the 1910s. Since the completion of new exhibition halls in Itä-Pasila in the 1970s, the Exhibition Hall has been primarily used as a sports facility.

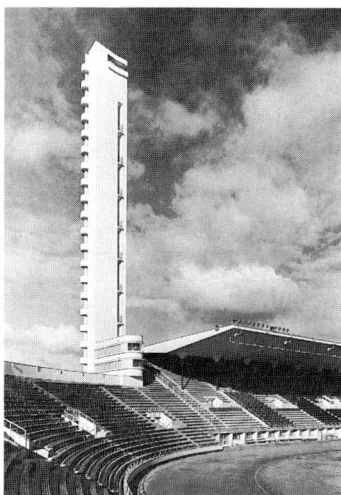

42

43

42

The Helsinki Olympic Stadium 1940
Paavo Nurmen tie

Yrjö Lindegren,
Toivo Jäntti

The Olympic Stadium is one of the most significant examples of Finnish functionalism. In 1930 the City of Helsinki held an ideas competition for the stadium and athletics park to determine, among other things, the location of the stadium. The actual public competition for the stadium was held by the Stadium Foundation and it closed in 1933.

Lindegren and Jäntti won the continuation competition and were awarded the work. The first phase of construction on Tivolinmäki Hill in Töölö was completed in 1938. The 12th Olympic Games were to be held in the new stadium in 1940. The Games had been awarded to Tokyo, but due to the Sino-Japanese War they were transferred to Helsinki. Because of the Games the capacity of the stands was doubled by constructing the east stands and erecting supplementary wooden bleachers, which were later replaced by steel-reinforced concrete stands for the Helsinki Games held in 1952. Wooden bleachers also had to be erected for these 15th Olympic Games in order to increase spectator capacity to the required 70 000. The stadium underwent a last, and least successful, metamorphosis, when the space under the supplementary stands was converted to office space. Although these extensions to the stadium destroyed

much of its original whiteness and linear clarity – the powerful tension between the horizontal and the vertical – it remains a notable symbolic building in Helsinki. The stadium has best retained its original character around the Sports Museum, the back of the main stands, and the tower. The fine details in the radio broadcasting rooms, the stairs of the tower and the entrance to the Sports Museum also illustrate the spirit of the original.

The nearby Swimming Stadium by Jorma Järvi was intended for the 1940 Games. The pools and the frame of the building were completed before the war, and construction was completed in time for the 1952 Olympic Games.

43

The Töölö Branch Library 1970
Topeliuksenkatu 6

Aarne Ervi

The library building is in the northern end of Topeliuksenpuisto Park. The part fronting the street is fairly closed, but a curved glass wall offers a broad view of the park. The most important public facilities have been placed in the side facing the park. The ground floor contains a newspaper reading-room, and a children's library with a park-side courtyard of its own. The next, tall story contains the reading rooms and lending library in the galleries. The music library, club rooms and public cafeteria are in the recessed top floor.

44

45

44

The Social Insurance Institution 1956
Nordenskjöldinkatu 12

Alvar Aalto

An ideas competition for the Social Insurance Institute Building was held in 1948, and Aino and Alvar Aalto won first prize. The program included government office space, commercial and private office space, and furthermore, a large Sibelius Concert Hall. The planned site was the block where the Inter-Continental and Hesperia Hotels are today. As the site was unavailable due to zoning policies, the SII Building was constructed on a smaller, triangular site originally reserved for the Opera. The site is set back from Mannerheimintie, and its long south-western flank fronts the sloping Kirjailijapuisto Park. The Lastenlinna Children's Hospital is at the far end of the park.

The building is grouped around a courtyard which forms a continuation of the park, is elevated from street-level and sheltered from the noise of the traffic. The work space borders it as a terraced building, with the staff cafeteria and library in pavilions. The tall office section continues on the other side as a multifaceted monumental structural mass.

The Social Insurance Institute Building contains several impressive interiors with fine details and materials. The staff library develops the idea of the form of the Vyborg Library. The tall central hall was planned as a customer services area. Its clerestory resembles delicate glass prisms. The central hall and its function have subsequently undergone unfortunate changes. In the 1970s it ceased to function as the customer services area of the SII District Office and it was converted to an open office space, retaining the walls of the former customer services area. In 1988 these walls were removed, and the lower part of the hall underwent considerable changes when it was converted to a Personnel Training Centre.

45

Meilahti School 1953
Jalavatie 6

Viljo Revell,
Osmo Sipari

The City of Helsinki held a public planning competition for this school in 1949. Completed according to the winning entry, it was one of the first examples of a new, less rigid method of planning schools.

It is located in the northern part of a crowded and irregular site, in part fronting Valpurintie. The row of classrooms fronts south and curves to enclose a sheltered playground. Most of the classrooms in the curved two-story building are placed along a windowed side corridor. In the first story there is a recessed rain shelter. The equivalent second-story space contains administrative offices. Special classrooms, a gymnasium, and cafeteria facilities are on the north side of the corridor.

The façades of the school are red brick. Glass bricks contrast with it in the gymnasium and staircase windows. The interiors also occasionally contain red brick worked fair.

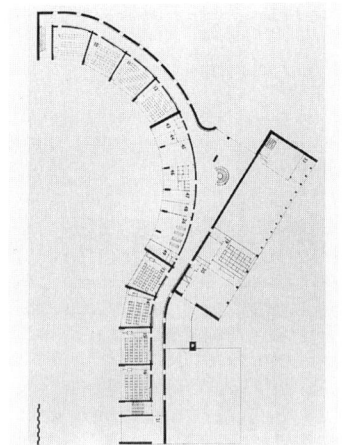

47

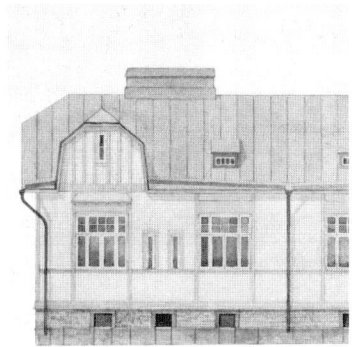

48

46

Tullinpuomi Residential Building 1943
Mannerheimintie 118

Olli Pöyry

This residential and commercial building is based on the entry awarded second prize in a competition held in 1939. The nine-story building, a landmark on Mannerheimintie, heads the northernmost row of street-side buildings.

The recessed top floor contains a restaurant and outdoor terrace. The street-level floor has shops, and the other floors are apartments. Over the years both the top floor and the street-level floor, which originally contained the lobby of a cinema theatre, have been altered; but it remains a handsome, albeit late representative of the 1930s.

47

Auroranlinna Residential Buildings 1989
Paulankatu 2

Juha Leiviskä

The group of residential buildings is located to the east of the Aurora Hospital area, and at the same time it provides a conclusion and a scale change for the heavy row of office buildings in Länsi-Pasila.

Viewed from the east, the partly staggered residential buildings form a varied, sculptural entity bound to the slope by its tall base. Vehicle traffic and parking has been arranged in conjunction with this foundation wall. The rocky park to the west remains as a secluded court, on to which most of the apartments face. The principal façade material is light yellowish brick.

The Aurora Hospital Chapel has been renovated as club facilities for the inhabitants.

48

Workers' Apartments 1910, 1913
Kirstinkuja 4

Albert Nyberg,
Onni Tarjanne

Four out of the six wooden houses were built by the city for municipal employees according to plans by Albert Nyberg. The two others were planned by Onni Tarjanne for Workers' Housing Association Kumpu. The houses are board-clad timber. There are handsome trees in the yard framed by the houses. This residential area is an early example of a combination of hygienic and architectonic principles to improve the dwelling standard of workers in a rapidly industrializing town. The dwellings and their organization were considered exemplary at the time they were built.

49

The SOK Production Facilities 1934–1938
Sturenkatu 17–19

Erkki Huttunen

This group of buildings is a good example of the distinctive features in the architecture of commercial and industrial buildings Erkki Huttunen created while working at the SOK construction department at the close of the 1920s. Among the external features of this »White Functionalism» are smooth white-plastered façades and long band windows with narrow steel frames. The windows often continue around corners.

The industrial complex in the corner of Sturenkatu and Aleksis Kiven katu were constructed in several phases. The first buildings constructed were the coffee-roasting plant and warehouses; the food processing plant and textile mill were constructed later.

The nearby HOK production facilities were designed by Erkki Huttunen and completed in 1938. A notable feature are the vertical exterior split screens of the bakery fronting Aleksis Kiven katu.

50

The House of Culture 1958
Sturenkatu 4

Alvar Aalto

The building consists of a five-story office block and a large curved concert and congress hall joined by a two-story section containing meeting rooms. The three parts of the building frame a courtyard through which the office wing and meeting rooms are entered. The different parts are joined on the Sturenkatu side by a canopy over the entrance to the hall. The concert hall, renown for its good acoustics, seats 1500. Its fan-shape is familiar from Aalto's other works. In the House of Culture the fan is asymmetric, with a vigorously curved back wall. The façade of the concert hall is of a brick specially designed for the House of Culture, which allows construction of wall surfaces with different curve radi. In the other parts of the building the façades are primarily copper.

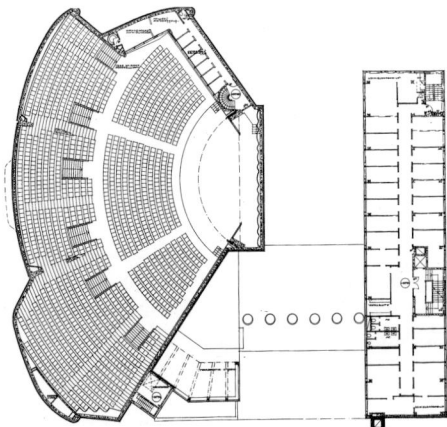

51

52

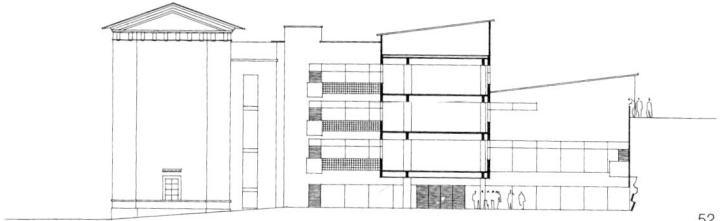

52

51

The House of Cities 1982
Toinen linja 14

Heikki Castrén, Mirja Castrén,
Juhani Jauhiainen, Marja Helenius

The Finnish Union of Municipalities Building is based on the winning entry in a public architectural competition held in 1977. Situated near the Diakonissalaitos Hospital, its façade material is a continuation of traditional red-brick architecture.

The clear composition is based on a H-shaped plan. The crossbar of the H contains common rooms and divides the site into a public entrance forecourt, and on the other side a more private, terraced courtyard fronting the park. A gradually narrowing roof-lit hall is the central, unifying interior. The offices in the sides of the H represent a typical double-corridor solution with separate rooms.

52

The Helsinki Worker's Institute 1927
Helsinginkatu 26

Gunnar Taucher

The Institute building is another example, along with the Mäkelänkatu residential buildings, of the superior architecture the Helsinki City Buildings Office produced under Gunnar Taucher. Both buildings are refined examples of the 1920s Asplundian-Italian classicism. It is probable that P.E. Blomstedt,as the building office's »façade architect» played a considerable part in both the Institute building and the Mäkelänkatu residential buildings.

At the time of its completion the simply proportioned, purplish four-story building rose proudly over the surrounding wooden dwellings. There is a two-story high portal in the middle of the building. The layout is a simple side- corridor system. Twin stairs protrude into the courtyard as a separate element. An extension to the Institute was started in the 1930s, with excavations in the vacant part of the site, but the war put an end to this plan. An annex by Aulis Blomstedt was completed in 1959. The new part is behind the old building, parallel with it, and connected to it with a joint between the twin stairs. The substantial difference in elevation between Helsinginkatu and Alppikatu, which borders the site to the south, has been utilized in the placing of the large auditorium. The cut in the rock face at the back of the site, with its colored concrete slabs, forms an effective frame for the courtyard and entrance to the building. The extension of the Institute is among the most successful examples of good coexistence between an old and a new building.

53

The Ebeneser Foundation 1908
Helsinginkatu 3-5

Wivi Lönn

The Ebeneser Nursery-school Teachers' College and the Hotel Helka are the only two buildings in Helsinki Wivi Lönn designed independently, despite her long career in Helsinki.

The four-story college contains lecture rooms and a day-care centre on the ground floor. The freestanding Jugendstil building, set back from the street, is a stark contrast to the tall apartment houses around it.

54

55

54

Torkkelinmäki Hill 1926-28
Torkkelinkatu, Torkkelinkuja

The re-zoning of Torkkelinmäki Hill was drafted by Birger Brunila, and the villa quarter type plan was ratified in 1914. The blocks that surround the square Torkkelinmäki Park contain three-story and four-story residential buildings completed in 1926–28. The outer edges of the blocks front two parks: Pengerpuisto Park and Franzéninpuistikko Park. High up on the hill the low and spaciously built group of buildings stands in striking contrast to its surroundings - the tall and densely built stone city of Kallio. From Helsinginkatu the area can be viewed from Harjutori Square, and from Kaarlenkatu, from the top of the steps that rise from Franzéninkatu.

An important feature in the Torkkelinmäki residential milieu is its distinct and articulated spatial structure, which is supported by uniform and balanced buildings. The sites were sold on the condition that the buildings conform with façade schemes set by the »Control Commission of Façade Plans». The residential buildings have a touch of 1920s classicism and are unpretentious. The steep, visible roofs are accentuated by handsome chimneys. Variation is provided by details and the varying pastel hues. Most of the buildings were designed by Jalmari Peltonen. Garden Advisor Elisabeth Koch designed the greenery.

The former Yhteiskunnallinen Korkeakoulu College, which today houses the Helsinki University Department of Social Science (Väinö Vähäkallio, 1930), and the Helsingin Teknillinen Oppilaitos Technical School (Yrjö Sadeniemi, 1929), are in the vicinity of Torkkelinmäki.

55

The Kallio Church 1912
Itäinen Papinkatu

Lars Sonck

Lars Sonck submitted the winning entry in both the public planning competition for the Kallio Church (1905–06) and the subsequent continuation competition between the prize winners. Although some changes were made to his plans during construction, the layout of the church is a Latin cross: the sanctuary, topped with an apse forms the upright of the cross, and the choir and side wings, the arms. The exterior form of the grey granite church is dominated by the tower, which rises from the intersection of the cross and forms the end point of the longest straight street axel: Unioninkatu and Siltasaarenkatu. The broad nave of the church is covered by a large barrel vault with arched openings from the galleries to the nave. During repairs in the 1950s the organ was moved from above the altar to the rear gallery, adding visibility to the semicircular choir. The renovation in 1987 was planned by Heikki Havas.

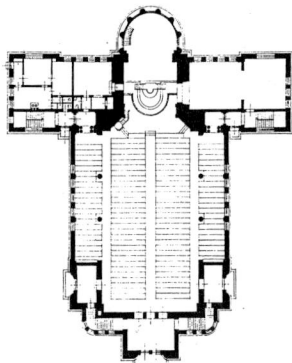

56

57

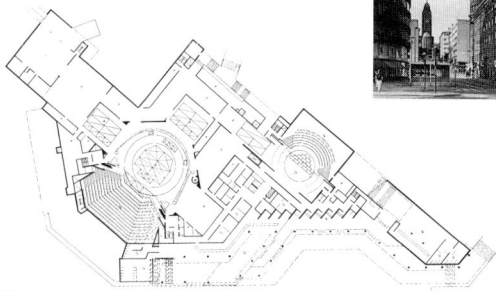

56

56

The Helsinki City Theatre 1967
Eläintarhantie 5

Timo Penttilä

The first prize in the competition for the City Theatre was awarded to Timo Penttilä and Kari Virta for their joint entry. The theatre is set in park-like surroundings on the northern edge of the site, partially embedded in a steep outcropping. The public space is grouped in the part fronting the park; and the cloakroom of the main theatre, the upper lobby staircase, the lower lobby and the cafeteria offer a view toward the park and Eläintarhan-lahti Bay through a large glass wall. The 920-seat theatre is traditional in its basic composition. The house is fairly broad and shallow. The small, adaptable studio theatre seats 220-300. Its lobby and cloak-room in the inner part of the building are intimate and closed in character.

The theatre building is fixed in the park landscape with granite walls, entrance canopy and a powerful horizontal principal mass. The scenery tower on top of the step-terraced building is a prominent element of the townscape. The façades are clad in white ceramic clinker tiles. An annex in Ensi linja was completed in 1989.

57

The Arena Building 1923
Hämeentie 2

Lars Sonck

The Arena Building consists of a triangular block, the red-brick façade encompassing three large corner towers (turrets) which give the building the appearance of a castle and are landmarks on the Unioninkatu-Siltasaarenkatu axis. The Hämeentie façade forms a pair with the brick Market Hall. Staircases and auxiliary spaces front the triangular courtyard, and the outer façade thus has rows of evenly spaced windows. The original small-paned windows have been replaced with large ones, breaking the closed appearance of the building.

The closest neighbors, the Posti-pankki Building (Antero Pernaja, Nils-Henrik Sandell; 1960) with its rounded corner, and the circular Ympyrätalo (Kaija and Heikki Sirén; 1969) were constructed with respect for the Arena Building.

The red-brick Hakaniemi Market Hall (1914) opposite on Hämeentie is by Karl Hård af Segerstad and Einar Flinkenberg.

59

58

58

The Helsinki Workers' Association 1908
Paasivuorenkatu 5

Karl Lindahl

The entry by Karl Lindhal and Max Frelander won first prize in the general competition for the Helsinki Workers' Association Building. Lindahl added a massive tower to the plan, and during construction the material of the façade was changed from plaster to granite, in order to utilize the abundant on-site supply.

The simple, castle-like form of the building indicates a departure from the ample forms of National Romanticism. The lack of national motifs in the ornamentation may also be an allusion to the international nature of the labor movement. The sumptuous and ornamental interiors are a counterpoint to the unadorned exterior. The most important interiors are the assembly hall, main staircase and the downstairs restaurant. The building is a relatively early example of the use of concrete and iron in the bearing structures.

During the Finnish Civil War in 1918 the house - an important symbol - was subjected to extensive artillery fire. The tower was altered during repairs.

An annex by Lindahl was built on the corner of Paasivuorenkatu and Saariniemenkatu in 1925. The most recent extension on the Paasivuori park side was completed in 1955 (Heikki Sysimetsä).

Karl Lindahl has also planned the residential building on the corner of Saariniemenkatu and Säästöpankinranta, opposite the Workers' Association.

59

The First Block in the Näkinpuisto Residential Area 1984
Hämeentie 7–9

Timo Vormala,
Jaakko Sutela

This block of residential buildings began the transformation of the Kone ja Silta (today Wärtsilä) industrial area into a residential development. An invitational competition for the block was held in 1980, and the residential buildings in the corner of Hämeentie and Haapaniemenkatu are based on the winning entry. The red-brick façades fronting the street link them with the old industrial and commercial buildings in Sörnäinen, particularly the neighboring building, the former separator factory (Armas Lindgren, Bertel Liljeqvist; 1916), which has been converted into office space.

On the side fronting the courtyard red brick has been used only in the lower part of the buildings. There are 161 apartments of various sizes and eight shops in the first block.

61

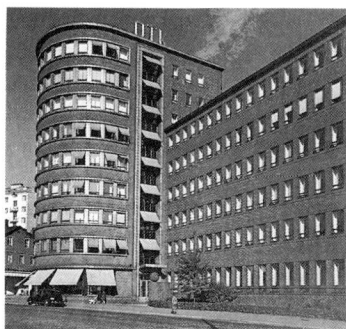
62

60

The Elanto Cooperative Head Office 1928
Kaikukatu 2

Väinö Vähäkallio

In 1919 the Elanto Cooperative organized a competition for the use of its industrial sites, and the entry by Väinö Vähäkallio was awarded second prize. His plan for a block containing the cooperative headquarters, industrial buildings and warehouses was only partially realized. The pitched-roofed administrative building, completed in 1928, fronts Kaikukatu, with the tall clock tower on Hämeentie. The red- brick surfaces are accentuated with numerous bays, and the archways of the gate passage are framed by a pillar and beam motif. The main entrance is in the lower part of the tower, in a granite-framed field of doors and windows. The ground floor used to contain shops with arched windows. The offices in the administration building are on both sides of a central corridor. The top floor contains an auditorium and foyer, the staff cafeteria and library. The most impressive interiors are in the tower, beginning with the round entrance and continuing with a barrel-vaulted passage to the entrance hall and main staircase. Birger Hahl was in charge of interior design.

In 1929 a low annex fronting Kaikukatu was added to the Co-operative Headquarters, and in 1942 it was raised as an extension to the main mass according to plans by Väinö Vähäkallio and Antero Pernaja.

61

The Eka Warehouses in Sörnäinen 1927
Lintulahdenkatu 4

Väinö Vähäkallio

The central warehouse of the OTK Cooperative Union consists of two perpendicular wings. The massive ten- story red-brick building is ac-centuated by the pillars between the vaulted openings in the loading arcade and the projecting stepped eaves. The delicate vertical disposition of the façade has an airy effect: it is related to the near-contemporary Elanto Head Office. The second floor contains office and exhibition space, the other floors are warehouses. The intermediate floors are supported by concrete mushroom pillars. It is one of the earliest frame structured warehouse buildings in Finland.

62

The Eka Head Office 1933
Hämeentie 19

Väinö Vähäkallio,
Georg Jägerroos,
Antero Pernaja

The head office of the OTK Co-operative Union and the Kansa Insurance company were completed in 1933 in the corner of Hämeentie and Käenkuja. The building is an abbreviated version of a planned larger whole. The most recognizable part of the office building is a nine- story building mass with a curved gable dominating the curve in Hämeentie. It serves as a landmark for Elanto's and OTK's mainly red-brick industrial, warehouse and office area, beginning with the Elanto Headquarters tower. In the OTK Building the Neo-Classicism of the Elanto Building has been replaced by a more rational and graceful touch. The curved tower resembles Central European models, particularly the famous department stores by Erich Mendelsohn.

The main entrance is in the juncture of the tower and the lower wing fronting Hämeentie. The framed recess as high as the tower seems to await a staircase, but this is on the opposite side of the tower. The spacious entrance hall and main staircase - and also the other interiors and details - show traces of classicism, accented by numerous works of art. The sculpture before the main entrance is by Gunnar Finne.

63

64

63

Partek Group Helsinki Office 1988
Sörnäisten rantatie 23

Kaarina Löfström,
Matti K. Mäkinen,
Mauri Tommila

The Partek Office Building is the first part of the development program of the Lintulahti industrial blocks, bordered by Hämeentie, Käenkuja, Sörnäisten rantatie and Kaikukatu.

The building is on Sörnäisten rantatie, on a triangular site, and it culminates in a rounded corner, counterbalancing the other corner-site buildings in the Lintulahti blocks: the Elanto and Eka Buildings. The plans had to take into account the conveyor from the cement plant to the harbor, an important feature in the Sörnäisten rantatie streetscape.

The scale of the building is harmonized with the old massive redbrick industrial and warehouse buildings in the area. The façade material, green glazed ceramic tile, links it to our own era and the renovated surroundings. The office solution is based on separate rooms. The office wings are based on a double-corridor solution, and have a private character, while the circular part joining the wings contains lobbies and adjacent auditoriums, meeting rooms and cafeterias, and thus represents a more public area intended for visitors. In the fairly low framed office wings a feeling of confinement has been avoided by means of the curved ceiling of the corridor, interior windows and indirect lighting.

64

Hanasaari Power Plant 1974, 1976
Parrukatu

Timo Penttilä

The power plant houses the more detatchable process facilities, such as offices, staircases, coal conveyors and maintanence facilities, by grouping them freely in spaces around the heavy machinery. Uniform materials and details draw the different parts of the power plant into an impressive whole in the cityscape.

The power plant was constructed in two phases, in 1971–74 and 1974–76.

65

The Former Suvilahti Power Plant 1908
Sörnäisten Rantatie 20

Selim A. Lindqvist

The City of Helsinki was one of Lindqvist's most important clients after 1900. He planned, for example, the Vallila and Töölö streetcar halls, the Kallio Fire Station, the Hietalahti and Kaarti market halls, and various buildings for the municipal Electricity and Gas Companies. When his productive collaboration with Elia Heikel came to an end at the turn of the century he started working with Jalmar Castrén, a pioneer of constructive engineering and an unprejudiced developer of steel and reinforced concrete.

The first phase of the Suvilahti coal-burning power plant was completed in 1908. It acquired its current form when the boiler room and turbine hall were expanded in 1913. The adjacent Gas Company buildings, with their monumental gas storage tanks, are also by Lindqvist. The barrel and cupola-roof-

65

66

ed buildings; together with the power station, form a cogent whole.

With parallels to the industrial architecture of Peter Behrens and the concrete architecture of Auguste Perret, the Suvilahti Power Station, including its interiors, is a most impressive example of industrial architecture. The turbine hall is particularly refined, with traces of the Vienna Postal Savings Bank by Otto Wagner. The three-aisle boiler room, with its double pillars and narrow, vertical band windows, is of comparable interest.

Power production in Suvilahti was terminated due to low efficiency, and new uses for the plant have been sought. For a while it was a meeting place for installation art and the theatre. It was then repaired and used as a warehouse and recreational facility. Renovations and repairs in 1985 were planned by Reino Huhtiniemi and Kimmo Söderholm.

66

The Helsinki Municipal Slaughterhouse 1933
Työpajankatu 2

Betrel Liljeqvist

The slaughterhouse is a part of the Helsinki wholesale foodstuffs trade centre located at the foot of the Agros Hill in Hermanni. The slaughterhouse occupies several buildings in the area; the administration building, machine centre with its refrigeration tower, the heating centre and a curved-walled gate building front Työpajankatu.

As a fine example of municipal architecture the slaughterhouse can be compared with the wholesale meat market in Copenhagen (Kødbyen, 1931). Liljeqvist replaced the white functionalism of the latter with a more humane brick rationalism with classical details. Although the Helsinki Slaughterhouse has undergone many changes due to ponderous expansions and changes in roof shapes, there remains much of the spirit and atmosphere of the original.

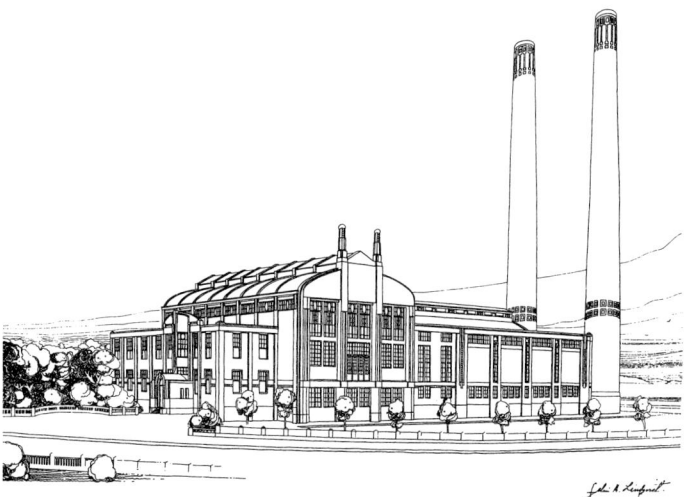

67

68

67

The Vallila Residential Area 1910–1927
Sturenkatu, Mäkelänkatu,
Päijänteentie, Roineentie

The origins of the Vallila residential area are an early example of municipal working-class residential policy at the turn of the century. The population had passed the 100 000 mark and was growing at an accelerating rate. A division plan for the area was initiated in 1908, with the streets narrow and the lots small. The garden-suburb principle emphasized the proximity of nature and the significance of gardens.

Construction in Vallila began in 1910. The first buildings were for the most part small rental houses without modern conveniences, planned by the master builders and contractors. In the early 1920s the fairly big residential cooperatives and companies in the area were founded. The standard of these buildings was much higher than of those built in the 1910s. Several prominent architects such as Armas Lindgren, Bertel Liljeqvist, Martti Välikangas, and Jussi and Toivo Paatela designed the buildings. The buildings were timber clad with board, and built according to type plans.

In the 1970s the Vallila residential area was under threat of urban renewal. Activity among the residents to save their residential area increased and in 1980 a conservation plan was ratified, recognising the significance of the area as a cohesive residential area which reflectes turn-of-the-century architectonic and social ideals. Vallila is among the test areas for the new law concerning renovations, which commenced in both the privately and municipally owned buildings in 1980.

68

Mäkelänkatu 37–43 Residential Building 1926
Mäkelänkatu 37–43

Gunnar Taucher

This municipal residential building was planned in the City Buildings Office under the supervision of Taucher, who was City Architect. The actual plans were drafted by P.E, Blomstedt. The building is almost 160 meters long and it consists of a four- story central part set back from the street and two three-story wings. The central part of the façade is accentuated by a massive portal motif; otherwise ornamentation is minimal. The smooth window jambs and the small Empire-style reliefs between them lighten the plastered wall surface. The monumental gable is accentuated by small arched windows near the top of the façade, and an ornamental door. The light wall surfaces and small windows made the building a pure-bred example of 1920s classicism, and it is an important illustration of residential architecture for workers. The building contains 87 apartments consisting of one room and a kitchen, and four shops. There are only two apartments per landing and as the frame of the building is fairly narrow they extend through the house

69

and are draft ventilated. They were also relatively thoroughly equipped. The building was renovated in the end of the 1970s.

The buildings on the adjacent site, Mäkelänkatu 45, are also by Taucher, and are a harmonious continuation of the row of buildings. Another example of harmonious townscape is on Mäkelänkatu 13–31, on both sides of the Sturenkatu corner. These residential buildings were constructed in accordance with the façade schemes drafted at the Planning Department of the City Buildings Office.

69

The Kone ja Silta oy Workers' Apartments, the Sammatti Block of Flats, 1918, 1927–29
Somerontie 14, Kangasalantie 9–14

Armas Lindgren,
Bertel Liljeqvist,
Elisabeth Koch

This residential block is an excellent example of how the architecture of socially motivated residential construction and cohesive townscape gave dignity to working class residential areas. The large park-like courtyard is enclosed by a narrow three-story building, which, for Finland, formed an unusually large courtyard block, but which was the most common form of construction in Central Europe. The most representative examples of this type of construction are the workers' apartment buildings or »Hofs» in Vienna. An earlier Scandinavian example are the so-called

»Governors Houses» in Gothenburg.

The initiative for building a workers' apartment house in block 555 in Vallila came from one of the biggest employers in the city: Kone ja Silta, nowadays called Wärtsilä.

The company built one quarter of the block in the end of the 1910s. The rest fell to the City of Helsinki, which completed the building in two phases, in 1927 and 1929, by a semi-municipal construction company. The standard of the building was raised by the courtyard, designed by Garden Advisor Elisabeth Koch together with Lindgren. Most of the apartments were one and two-room. The number of inhabitants in the block has varied from 700 in the late 1920s and early 1930s to the present-day 250.

Other examples of combined social and architectonic goals are the nearby:

Asunto oy Sture Apartment Building 1926

Sturenkatu 40,
Martti Välikangas

Asunto oy Eura Apartment Building 1920

Sturenkatu 37–41
Jussi and Toivo Paatela

Asunto oy Hauho Apartment Building 1925
Hauhontie 4–8

Akseli Toivonen and
Martti Välikangas

and the apartment building at Sturenkatu 43, by Lars Sonck and Matti Finell, 1928.

70

71

70

Vallilanrinne Student Housing (HOAS-50) 1987
Karstulantie 8

Pentti Piha

The lamellar houses on the steep northern slope form a bordering wall for some dreary 1960s point blocks. This solution has fused the random northern side of the residential area, visible all the way to Vallila Valley and Kumpula. At the upper part of the slope the buildings have mainly three stories, those below have five. On the high northern side a two-story projection from the frame of the building forms a base for the residential buildings. The lively roofs, balconies and a cheerful color scheme have enhanced the environment and given a positive mien to student dwellings.

71

The Social Insurance Institution Staff Residential Area 1954
Riihitie 12–14

Alvar Aalto

Three longish lamellar buildings in this four-building group are in line with the street; the fourth, out of alignment with the street, is pronouncedly accentuated and is thus a central element in the composition, drawing the group together around a small square. The four-story and five-story buildings have red-brick façades, and those fronting the park have balconies with white concrete railings which form powerful horizontal lines.

72

Villa Aalto 1936
Riihitie 20

Aino and Alvar Aalto

Originally built as a residence and office, the house is situated on a southwest slope among pine trees. The main materials, stuccoed brick and vertical boarding, are visible in the closed façade fronting the street. The living and dining rooms of the residence in the first floor and the roof terrace on the second floor face the garden and the adjacent sports field. The darkened wood curves from the street side to the garden as the exterior cladding of the bedrooms, and continues as the terrace railing. In the west side the façade of the partially two-story office is brick. Toward the yard and terrace the façade is painted board. The structure of the house is formed, in addition to the bearing walls, of round steel pillars filled with concrete.

The house in Munkkiniemi contains several features which set it apart from the functionalism of the period. As an example of Romantic Modernism it marks, between the Villa Tammekann in Tartu and Villa Mairea in Noormarkku, an important phase in the development of a series of private residences designed by Aalto.

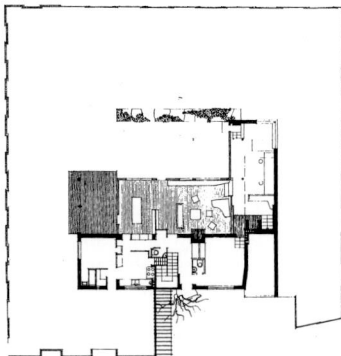

72

73

74

73

Studio Aalto 1955
Tiilimäki 20

Alvar Aalto

The studio building is strongly horizontal and closed toward the street. Over the garden wall one can catch a glimpse of the roof, which descends in line with the grade of the downhill street, and a wall, which curves slightly in line with the street. The secluded outward expression of the building changes in the inner courtyard, which follows the slope, forming a semi-enclosed amphitheatre-like outdoor space.The studio and office have their own vestibules and conference rooms and storage spaces. The façade materials are stuccoed brick and white board.

74

The Administrative Development Agency 1919
Hollantilaisentie 11

Eliel Saarinen

Saarinen drafted the Munkkiniemi-Haaga general plan in 1910-1915. The only parts that were completed are the Sigurd Stenius Park, some streets, a few terraced houses and the Munkkiniemi Boarding House. The boarding house was dimensioned for about 100 guests. It ran into financial difficulties after three years of operation and the government took over the company in 1922. The Cadet School operated in the house from 1923 to 1940 and from 1940 to 1973 it was the headquarters of the Air Force. After extensive renovations were completed in 1976 the building has been used by the State Training Centre and from 1988 by the Administrative Development Agency.

The most interesting interiors are the high entrance hall, the dining room and the tower lounge.

Saarinen's terraced two-story houses, located nearby at Hollantilaisentie 12–20, have mansard roofs. Soft bright colors that change from one unit to another and windows with small square panes are characteristic features in the harmonious and simple building mass.

75

76

75

Hirviniemenranta
Residential Buildings 1981
Hirvilahdenkuja 5

Timo Penttilä, Heikki Saarela

The buildings are located on park-like northerly headland and placed on the site in a manner that spared a great number of the valuable trees. Each residential unit has a small stretch of the shoreline and views toward Laajalahti Bay and Munkkiniemi. The group of buildings curves around a common forecourt with a handsome oak and a stand of tall pines. The buildings are unadorned and closed toward the yard to ensure privacy. Narrow vertical band windows are the only connection between the apartments and the forecourt. The façade fronting the sea is a complete contrast, open and exuberantly sculpted.

The group contains four large apartments (from six to twelve rooms and a kitchen), and three small apartments in the second story of the maintenance building. The structure is concrete poured on site. The bearing pillars on the side fronting the sea are outside the building frame. The closed façades and walls are clad in Carrara marble. The garden wall beside the main gate holds a sculpture depicting an elk, by Kari Juva.

76

Studio Ervi 1962
Kuusiniementie 5

Aarne Ervi

Aarne Ervi's former architectural firm is built in conjunction with his residence, which was constructed in 1950 on the Kuusisaarensalmi side of the site, near the shore. The workrooms have a view to the bay and the adjacent park. The office consists largely of one single space. It is connected with the ground floor of the residence, where the staff cafeteria, library and archives are located.

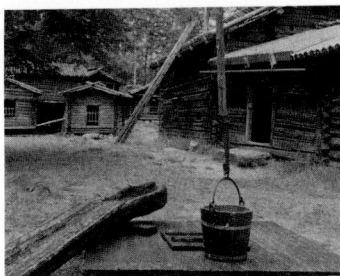

H The Seurasaari Open Air Museum
17th to 19th centuries Seurasaarentie 15

Modelled on the Skansen Museum of Stockholm, the Seurasaari Open Air Museum was founded in 1909 by the folklorist Axel O. Heikel, whose goal was to gather together typical buildings from the various Finnish provinces to depict living conditions and construction. At present the museum is administered by the National Board of Antiquities and Historical Monuments as a national outdoor museum.

Today the museum consists of almost one hundred buildings. The Niemelä Croft from Konginkangas, the enclosed courtyard Antti Farmstead from Säkylä and the Karelian Pertinotsa House from Suojärvi give the best picture of regional habitation. The oldest building in the museum is the wooden church from Karuna, which was built in 1686. The rest of the buildings are mainly from the 18th and 19th centuries.

The Urho Kekkonen Museum (Sigurd Frosterus, Gustaf Strengell; 1904) is located near the entrance, at Tamminiementie 2.

Ilmo Valjakka: Yhtyneet Kuvalehdet Building, 1987. (H3/6)

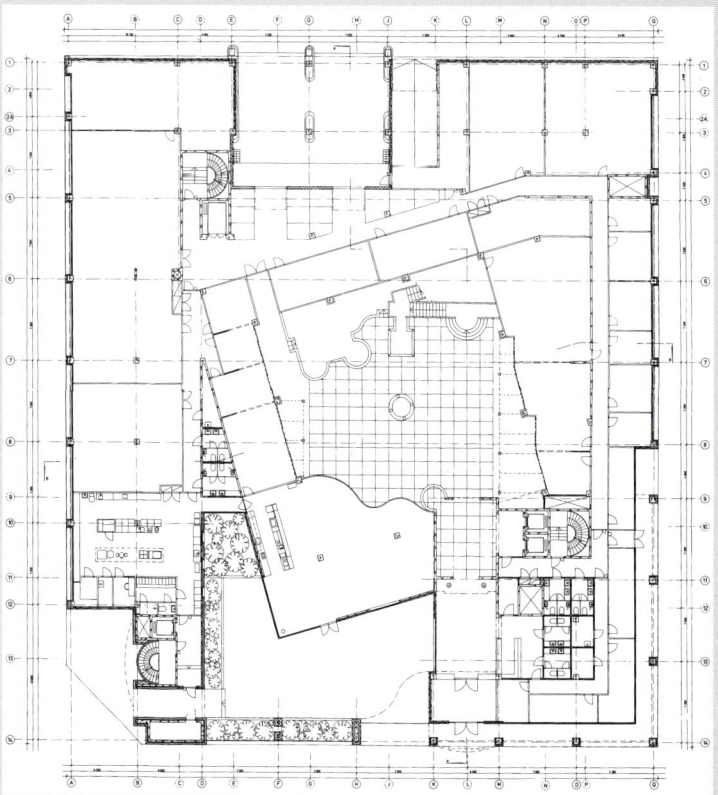

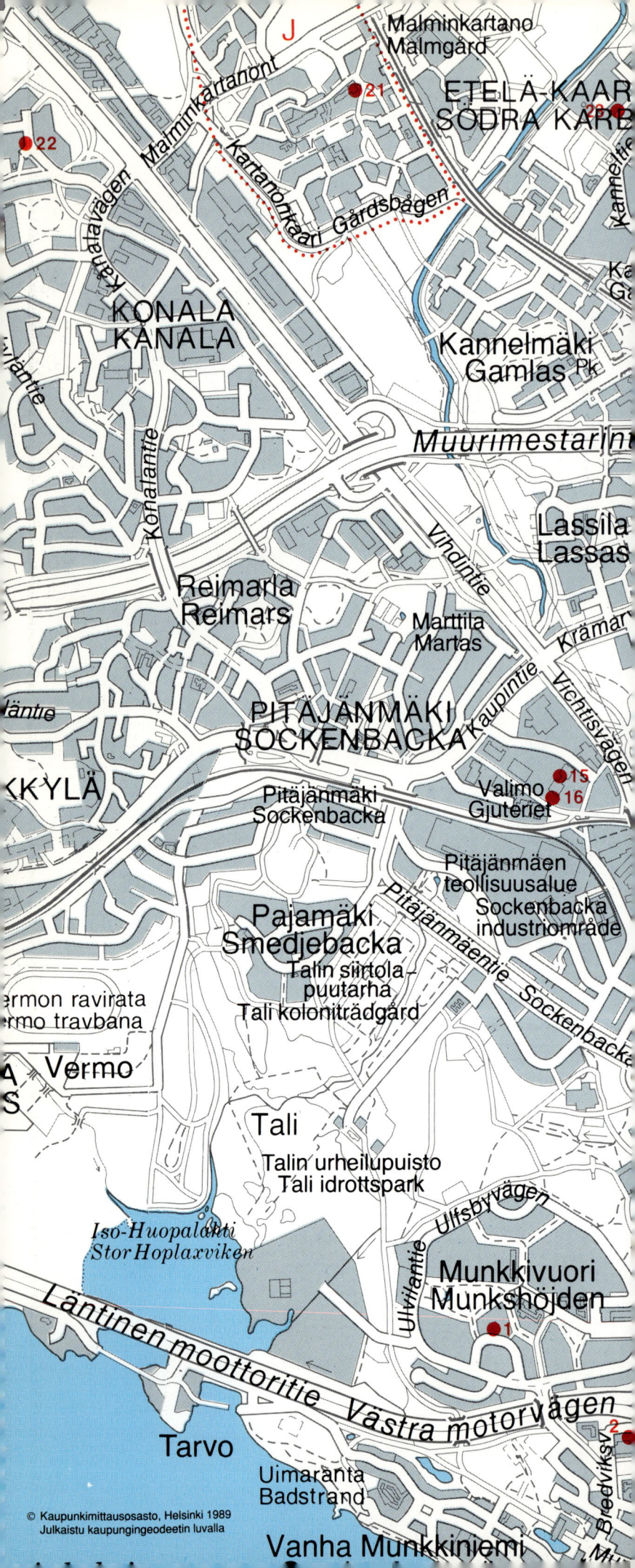

J

Malminkartano
Malmgård

● 21

ETELÄ-KAAR
SÖDRA KÅRE

● 28

● 22

Malminkartanont

Kanalavägen

Kartanonkaari Gårdsbågen

Kannelt

Ka
Gå

KONALA
KÅNALA

Kannelmäki
Gamlas *Pk*

Muurimestarin

Vindintie

Konalantie

äntie

Lassila
Lassas

Reimarla
Reimars

Marttila
Martas

Krämar

KKYLÄ

PITÄJÄNMÄKI
SOCKENBACKA

Kaupintie

Vichtisvägen

Valimo
Gjuteriet

● 15
● 16

Pitäjänmäki
Sockenbacka

Pitäjänmäen
teollisuusalue
Sockenbacka
industriområde

Pajamäki
Smedjebacka

Pitäjänmäentie Sockenbacka

Talin siirtola-
puutarha
Tali koloniträdgård

rmon ravirata
rmo travbana

Vermo

A
S

Tali

Talin urheilupuisto
Tali idrottspark

Iso-Huopalahti
Stor Hoplaxviken

Ulvilantie

Ulfsbyvägen

Munkkivuori
Munkshöjden

● 1

Läntinen moottoritie Västra motorvägen

Tarvo

Uimaranta
Badstrand

● 2

Breeviksv.

Vanha Munkkiniemi

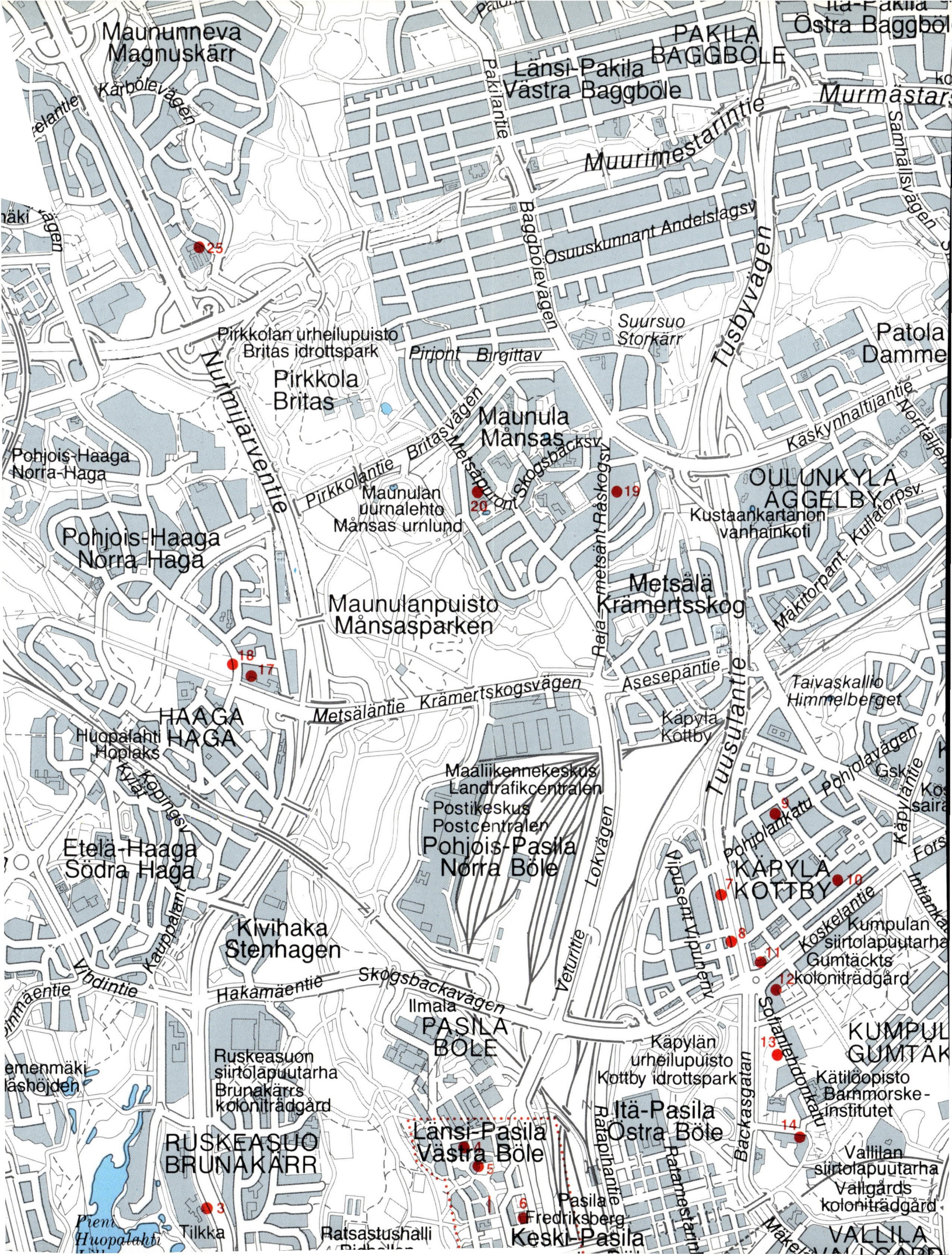

Maunumneva
Magnuskärr

PAKILA
BAGGBÖLE

Östra Baggbö

Länsi-Pakila
Västra Baggböle

Ita-Pakila

Murmästar

Muurimestarintie

Käböleväden

Osuuskunnant Andelslagsv

Tusbyvägen

Samhällsvägen

Samhällsvägen

●25

Pirkkolan urheilupuisto
Britas idrottspark

Pirjont Birgittav

Suursuo
Storkärr

Patola
Damme

Norrtäljer

Pirkkola
Britas

Maunula
Månsas

cksv

OULUNKYLA
ÅGGELBY

Kåskynhaltijantie

Pohjois-Haaga
Norra-Haga

Pirkkolantie Britasväden

Maunulan
urnalehto
Månsas urnlund

●20

●19

Kustaankartanon
vanhainkoti

Patola
Damme

Pohjois-Haaga
Norra Haga

Metsälä
Krämertsskog

Maktorpant. Kulfatorpsv

Maunulanpuisto
Månsasparken

Raja- metsänt-Råskogsv

Asesepäntie

Taivaskallio
Himmelberget

●18

●17

Käpyla
Kottby

Metsäläntie Krämertskogsvägen

HAAGA
HAGA

Huopalahti
Hoplaks

Köpingsv

Kytät

Maaliikennekeskus
Landtrafikcentralen

Postikeskus
Postcentralen

Pohjois-Pasila
Norra Böle

Lokvägen

Pohjolaväden

Gskle

Ko
sair

●9

KÄPYLA
KOTTBY

●7

●10

Etelä-Haaga
Södra Haga

Kauppalant

Kivihaka
Stenhagen

Veturitie

Viipusent-Viipurinv

●8

Koskelantie

Kumpulan
siirtolapuutarha
Gumtäcks
koloniträdgård

●11

●12

Vihdintie

nmäentie

Hakamäentie

Skogsbackavägen

Ilmala

PASILA
BÖLE

Käpylän
urheilupuisto
Kottby idrottspark

Sofianlehdonkatu

KUMPUL
GUMTAK

Backasgatan

●13

emenmäki
äshöjden

Ruskeasuon
siirtolapuutarha
Brunakärrs
koloniträdgård

Itä-Pasila
Östra Böle

●14

Kätilöopisto
Barnmorske-
institutet

RUSKEASUO
BRUNAKÄRR

Länsi-Pasila
Västra Böle

●4

Ratapihantie

Ratamestarin

Vallilan
siirtolapuutarha
Vallgårds
koloniträdgård

●5

Pieni
Huopalahti

●3

Tilkka

Ratsastushalli

●6

Pasila
Fredriksberg

Keski-Pasila

Mäk

VALLILA

H3

Kari Järvinen: Sofianlehdonkatu 10 Residential Block, 1988. (H3/14)

Martti Välikangas: The Käpylä Residential Area, 1920–25. (H3/9)

1

1

Residential Area 1958
Porintie 5

Hilding Ekelund

This group of residential buildings in Munkkivuori is located near the Ulvilanpuisto Park. It consists of six-story lamellar houses, straight and terraced rows of three-story and four-story lamellar houses, and gradually curving two-story terraced houses. The garages and residential buildings frame a sheltered and well-lit courtyard. The entrances of the apartment buildings and terraced houses are toward the yard. The courtyard forms an entity which derives its distinctive character from the grouping of the buildings, the composition of their scale, and the flora.

3

central space of the annex is framed on one flank by a staircase hall which joins the different phases of construction. The three other sides are framed by the separate rooms of the combi-offices.

2

The IBM Building 1979, 1987
Tietokuja 2

Osmo Lappo, Juhani Westerholm

The IBM Building is in Munkkiniemi, near where the Western Motorway enters the city. The multinational conglomerate places considerable emphasis on how its buildings portray its corporate image, and this one is a well planned addition to its series of buildings all over the world. Its dark and closed exterior expression includes features that unite it with its international family. The exterior form does little to express the organizational model of office work it represents. The staircase and elevator towers that protrude from both phases of the building suggest vast open-plan office spaces, but the glass prisms atop the annex, visible from the motorway, indicate another sort of solution.

The first phase was completed in 1979 and contains open office spaces, whereas the annex, from the end of the 1980s, has a combi-office solution. The tall glazed

---

3

The Central Military Hospital (Tilkka) 1936
Mannerheimintie 164

Olavi Sortta

The building was planned at the Ministry of Defence Construction Office under the supervision of Olavi Sortta. The nine-story main mass of the military hospital is highly visible in the open landscape. The curved main staircase at the gable forms a split cylinder, which is accentuated by ring-like balconies. The reserve staircase is also exterior to the structure and it continues as a curved piece above the eaves of the main mass. A perpendicular four-story wing is joined to the main mass with a joint. The first story contains a waiting room and outpatient clinic. The kitchen, laboratories and doctors' offices are in the second story. The seven top stories contain about 250 hospital beds.

In 1965 the wing was extended toward Mannerheimintie with a slightly curving annex which contains hospital rooms, an outpatient clinic, a laboratory and a military pharmacy.

4

I   Länsi-Pasila

The area consists of three main components: Itä-Pasila in the east, Länsi-Pasila in the west, and Keski-Pasila, which lies between them. Originally it was planned as an extension of the downtown area, with sufficient jobs to lighten the load of traffic to the centre of the city. In later plans the places of employment were to give way to apartments. Residential buildings are concentrated in Länsi-Pasila, whereas Itä-Pasila remains more pronouncedly a workplace area. Construction in Itä-Pasila began in 1972 and in Länsi-Pasila in 1979. The latter was, after Katajanokka, the largest residential construction project in the downtown area.

The urban milieu in Itä-Pasila has provoked considerable criticism of the two-level traffic system, dense construction and heavy concrete environment. This criticism, together with a change in the ideology of planning, resulted in a different scale and principles of town planning in Länsi-Pasila. There the two-level street network gave way to a traditional composition of ground-level streets. Parking is concentrated in four underground parking areas. The block structure is no longer based on a strict rectangular grid layout, and more attention has been paid to creating a diversified urban townscape. Ground level, small scale site division and partial preservation of the original terrain, are characteristic features of the planned urban milieu. The other residential areas that were constructed in Helsinki after Itä-Pasila, particularly Katajanokka and Malminkartano, are examples of a more humane urban structure in an apartment-building environment.

The location of Länsi-Pasila – between the railway yard and Central Park – was the starting point for the functional structure of the area. The main artery is located beside the railway yard, in front of a line of office buildings. This zone of office buildings reflects the grid layout of Itä-Pasila and shelters the residential area that lies behind it. The functional composition of the area is based on three large squares and the streets that join them. Most of the commercial services in the area are located along the squares and in arcades in the ground floors of the buildings. A central urban space forms the public urban milieu of the area and connects the residential buildings to the places of employment. A school and parish centre (Eric Adlercreuz and Mikko Heikkinen, 1983) is situated in Maistraatintori Square.

The Helsinki Main Library (Kaarlo Leppänen, 1986) is in Itä-Pasila, in Rautatieläisenkatu 8.

KESKUSTA - PASILA

5

4

5

Experimental Construction Area in Länsi-Pasila 1983
Radiokatu 8

Jan Söderlund

The Experimental Construction Area is a part of the Helsinki City development project for apartment building construction. A public competition for the block was held in 1979, and the buildings are based on an entry that shared first prize. A group of eight point blocks frames a courtyard. Narrow greenhouses join the buildings to create a string-of-pearls. Horizontal and vertical staggering enlivens the profile of the buildings. The principal façade material is pale fired brick.

Leanpuisto Apartment Buildings 1982
Leankatu 4

Gullichsen, Kairamo, Vormala/Reijo Jallinoja

The three single-staircase, three-to-four-story residential buildings have been placed on the norhern slope of Hertanmäki Hill in Länsi-Pasila and grouped on the north-ern edge of the site. Part of the site has been left in its park-like state, and contains the renovated wooden houses of Old Pasila, that date from the turn of the century. The buildings utilize a split-level solution. The plan is T-shaped, with two small apartments in the vertical element and two larger ones transversing from them. The top floor contains the largest split-level apartments with terraces. The façade material is a pale fired brick.

A day-care centre by Kari Järvi-nen and Timo Airas was built among the old wooden houses lo-cated on the site.

6

7

6

Yhtyneet Kuvalehdet Building 1987
Maistraatinportti 1

Ilmo Valjakka

The Magazine Publishing House is located centrally in a compact urban setting, in a row of Länsi-Pasila office buildings. While it blends in with its settings, it displays a rich and varied composition based on the use of surprising elements. The basic architectural idea of the structure consists of concentric buildings with coordinates varying by sixteen degrees. The inner, twisted building encloses a tall central space with a curving glazed roof. The square-like central space is the functional centre of the Publishing House. It joins different spaces to one another, and acts as the setting for a number of functions. The space for client contacts has been placed in the entrance floor around the square, which also contains most of the meeting, cafeteria and restaurant space in the building. The separate office rooms are in the top floors, opening either on to the central space or the periphery of the inner building. The wedge-like spaces resulting from the shift in axis are in part open-plan offices, and in part tall canyon-like lighting shafts, which are joined to the office corridors with square openings or balconies.

The collage-like interiors and the geometry of the interior and exterior surfaces of the Yhtyneet Kuvalehdet Building testify to the strong personal touch of the designer, but also to connections with current international architectural trends.

The Käärmetalo (Serpentine House) Apartment Building 1951
Mäkelänkatu 86

Yrjö Lindegren

The Serpentine House consists of three alternately curving apartment buildings with from four to seven lamellae, and a separate maintenance building. A native stone wall joins the elevated site with the street-level. The maintenance building is in line with the street, and in part protects the courtyard from disturbance from the street.

The curves in the apartment building provide varied street-side views, the natural state of the site has been preserved, and the apartments face advantageous directions. Despite the curves, the apartments are rectangular with staircases and auxiliary space located in the irregular parts. The structure of the building is visible in its exterior form, as the ends of intermediate bearing walls give rhythm to the façade surface.

The group of buildings contains 190 state-financed apartments. Originally the maintenance building contained a day-care center, a sauna, a laundry room and central heating unit. The use of the maintenance building has undergone some changes.

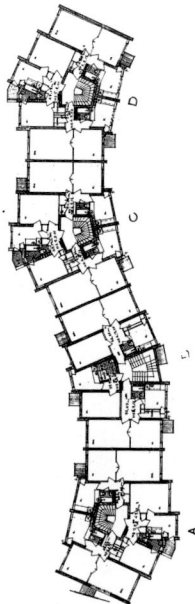

9

8

The Paragon Building 1973
Mäkelänkatu 84

Aarno Ruusuvuori

The four-story office building has a square plan, with approximately fifty meters on a side. The main staircases and elevator groups are placed outside the frame of the building. The open office spaces fit particularily well within this framework. The bearing pillars are grouped in 8-by-16-meter rectangles. The façade material is natural colored anodized aluminium.

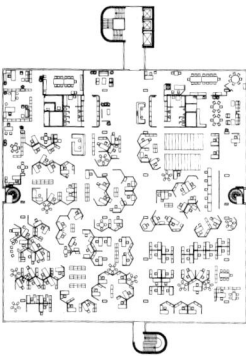

9

The Käpylä Residential Area 1920–25
Pohjolankatu

Martti Välikangas

The Käpylä residential area is a unique application of the garden city idea. It is the most noteworthy of the workers' housing developments from the 1920s, and the most extensive and versatile example of 1920s classicism.

The City had leased land to the Helsingin Kansanasunnot Company and two cooperatives: Käpy and Käpylä. Birger Brunila drafted the plan, based on the continuation plan Brunila and Otto-Iivari Meurman had submitted in 1918. It includes features of English garden suburbs and has also drawn some influences from old Finnish Empire-style plans, in which the yards were an essential part of the whole. All buildings were planned by Martti Välikangas. He was also in charge of grouping the buildings, as the plan lacked site and building boundaries. Originally there were only two types of buildings, both types containing four residential units. Each unit in the two-story building had direct access to the yard, which contained garden plots assigned to each unit. Elisabeth Koch, Helsinki City Garden Advisor, was assigned the design of the gardens. At the time of its completion the treeless residential area with its slightly boxlike buildings was considered alien. Today the full-grown trees and well-planned greenery contribute to the very pleasant atmosphere of the area.

In 1960 the City held a town plan competition in order to chart more effective building in the Käpylä area. Irreplaceable cultural values were at stake and an intensive debate followed. The alternative favoring renovations gained support only gradually, and not until1971 was a conservational town plan for the area ratified. From 1972 on the buildings have been renovated according to plans by Bengt Lundsten. The large rooms have provided ample space for introduction of the sanitary facilities the buildings lacked. The systematic construction techniques and prefabricated construction method employed in the original work have facilitated technical renovations.

Käpylä Church, built in 1930 on Metsolantie, is the dominant feature of the area, and the only Functionalist-style church in Helsinki. Martti Välikangas and Ilmari Sutinen tied for first prize in the planning competition for the church, and Sutinen was awarded the work.

10

11

10

11

The Olympic Village 1940
Untamontie 2–12

Hilding Ekelund,
Martti Välikangas

The first phase of the Olympic Village was constructed in 1939–1940 to house the male athletes of the 1940 Helsinki Olympic Games. The apartment types and the first-phase block plan were drafted collectively by Alvar Aalto, Hilding Ekelund, Kaj Englund, Georg Jägerroos and Martti Välikangas.

The Olympic Village is an example of a Finnish interpretation of the open block solution that had become common in Europe in the 1930s. The lamellar houses are fairly short and they are freely situated in deference to the hummocky terrain and its vegetation. The gentler and close-to-nature urban planning of the 1940s was anticipated in the point blocks adjoining the lamellar houses, which provide variety. The Olympic Village is a key example of Finnish architecture and in many respects the first modern urban residential area in Finland. In addition to developing urban building and revitalizing residential planning the Olympic Village was also the first example of regional construction aimed at the common weal.

The second phase of the Olympic Village was completed in 1948 according to plans by Hilding Ekelund.

The Kisakylä Village, by Pauli Salomaa, is situated opposite the Olympic Village (Koskelantie 7–27, Sofianlehdonkatu 7–9). It was completed in 1952 to house participants in the Olympic Games.

The Head Office of Amer Group Ltd 1987
Mäkelänkatu 91

Helmer Stenros

The building is located at the busy intersection of Mäkelänkatu and Koskelantie, and forms the other half of the gateway to Käpylä. It is also, when approached from the centre of town, at the end of a long straight stretch of Mäkelänkatu. Situated at the end of the Olympic Village, in both scale and materials it fits in with its neighbors.

The public milieau of the side fronting the street has been carefully planned. The arcades and the recessed part in the façade take the scale of the pedestrian into account as well. The park-like character of the open portion of the site is emphasized in its interior, where the semi-public surrounding space, with its water motifs and ornamentation that recalls the firm's logo, joins the interiors, the lobby of the auditorium and the staff cafeteria. The main entrance is through an arcade from Mäkelänkatu to a lofty central space. The office space in the second floor is grouped as combi-office cells around the central hall.

12

Office Building 1983
Koskelantie 5

Jan Söderlund

The building forms a traffic noise barrier between Mäkelänkatu and the Kisakylä Village. Together with the Amer Building on the other side of Pohjolankatu, it forms a gateway to Käpylä, and particularly the Olympic and Kisakylä Villages. The building contains for the most part ordinary office rooms. The staff cafeteria in the first floor fronts a lush courtyard toward the south. The basement contains leisure facilities.

14

15

13

Sofianlehdonkatu 10
Residential Block 1988
Sofianlehdonkatu 10

Kari Järvinen

The residential block is located on a high forested hill between Mäkelänkatu and Sofianlehdonkatu. Its southern side connects with the former Sofianlehto Home (Gunnar Taucher, 1929). On the other side of Sofianlehdonkatu there are buildings that belong to the Kisakylä (Olympic) Village.

The outward expression of the block is closed, the three-story buildings bordering a large communal court in the manner of a folded wall. The day-care centre divides the courtyard into two parts. Corner windows, balconies and their supporting structures enliven the side fronting the courtyard. The block contains 125 apartments.

14

Isoniitty Residential Area 1988
Isonniitynkatu

Reijo Jallinoja

A two-phase invitational competition for the planning of the area was held in 1983. The area is based on the winning entry, with slight modifications. The composition of the plan is in five sections, each grouped around a central parking area and entrance square.

The building type is based on narrow three-story structures articulated with balconies and external staircases. The free-form roof shapes and façades provide the area with variety within the context of a unifying entity.

15

Valio Head Office 1978
Meijeritie 6

Matti K. Mäkinen,
Kaarina Löfström

In the business and production facilities it has commissioned since the 1960s, the Valio Central Dairy Cooperative, in its striving for a good working enviroment and high architectural quality, has displayed a pioneering spirit comparable to that of the OTK and SOK cooperatives in the 1920s and -30s. The Valio headquarters may be considered a good example of how a commission can be a demonstration of faith in the architectural possibilities of creating an exemplary working milieu and an confidence-inspiring corporate image.

Two square pavilions with rounded corners have been constructed as a part of a projected larger whole . The inner parts of the four- story pavilions are spatially and structurally delineated open offices, with separate rooms at their margins. A connecting element between the two pavilions forms the main entrance hall on the first floor, and has lobbies and adjacent conference rooms in the other floors. Exterior staircase towers and ventilation channels have been integrated to the exterior wall in a manner charged with machine-like and fururistic power.

13

16

18

17

16

The Valio Computer Centre 1985
Meijeritie 6

Antti Katajamäki,
Osmo Syrjänen

The Computer Centre is the first phase of a centre for information management, information processing, research and product development. It is located near the Valio headquarters, of which, in overall form, it is the counterpart, approaching it in rhythmic scale and materials. The side fronting the Headquarters resembles a stepped pyramid. Behind it are open-plan and combi-office spaces, whereas the part near the massive rear façade contains single office rooms. The computer halls are within the deeply sunken frame of the bottom floor and lit by angled, pointed skylights.

17

The Haaga Vocational School 1967
Ilkantie 3 a

Timo and Tuomo Suomalainen

The school building contains automotive repair and metalworking departments and common rooms. The sloping site has been utilized in the placing of the workshops, which are all on ground level. The communal lecture rooms between the two departments are also on the same level as the recess yard.

The deep-structured building is lit with large windows and skylight turrets, giving exterior of the building an expression of generosity and vigor.

18

Multipurpose Building of the Associations of the Deaf 1987
Ilkantie 4

Jaakko Laapotti

The joint multipurpose building of the Finnish Association of the Deaf and the Finnish Federation of the Hard of Hearing contains offices and a cultural centre for the hearing-impaired, with a theatre, museum, video production unit for sign language material, and a video tape library. The building also houses the sixty-student Folk Academy of the Deaf and rehabilitation facilities for hearing-impaired children and young people.

The building is on a hillside and its different parts are grouped around a two-part courtyard in a castle-like enclosed fashion. The curving shape of the theatre-auditorium and the semicircular projection of the staff cafeteria lead to the main entrance on Ilkantie.

The special needs of the hard of hearing have been taken into account by choosing room shapes and lighting that facilitate the use of sign language.

19

20

19

Oulunkylä Apartment Buildings Sahanmäki Apartment Buildings 1951–56
Rajametsäntie 25–33

Hilding Ekelund

The residential area in Maunula contracted by The Helsinki City Residential Production Committee was built in two phases on a hillside which can be seen from afar. In the first phase 22 terraced houses were constructed on the lower slope. The next phase brought four angular point blocks, which form a powerful contrast with the horizontal lines of the roofs of the terraced houses. A curved rank of lamellar houses rises in the background. The area forms a compact whole, in which the buildings have been placed freely according to the contours of the terracing. The divergent buildings form interesting street compositions and there is a strong sense of space in the area. The façades are light plastered surfaces, with occasional red brick.

The terraced houses have been placed on the slope with a split-level solution. The apartments in the point blocks are situated spirally around a central staircase, with one apartment to a landing.

20

Maunulan Kansanasunnot Apartment Buildings 1949–53
Metsäpurontie 25–31

Viljo Revell,
Keijo Petäjä

The apartment buildings contracted by the Helsinki City Housing Production Committee were financed with government loans and constructed in three phases in the early 1950s. The group of buildings consists of apartment buildings, a day-care centre, and a sauna building on the little square on Metsäpurontie. Originally the sauna building contained a sauna, a commercial laundry and shops. There are 252 apartments, from 24 to 94 square meters in size, in the area. The apartment types and building structures varied from on construction phase to another, as did the materials and details. Red brick and plaster are unifying materials, together with the concrete balcony elements.

J   Malminkartano

Malminkartano is a suburb along the Martinlaakso railway line, with apartments for some 9500 inhabitants, and light industry, shops and offices. A two-phase idea and planning competition for Martinlaakso was held in 1972-73. The goal was to develop something other than a dormitory suburb, and this was done by combining jobs and a residential area. The places of employment have been placed visibly in the residential area along pedestrian streets. Separate one-story and two-story buildings for light industry blend in with the residential buildings.

In 1978 an invitational competition was held for the planning of the Malminkartano Experimental Construction Project, as part of the Helsinki City Residential Apartment Buildings Development Project. The best entries to the competition were realized in 1981-84, in the Kartanonkaari 18-24 block: Kartanonkaari Residential Building, by Eric Adlercreutz; Tollinpolku Residential Building, by Esko Kahri and Kai Lohman; Kartanonkaari Residential Building, by Raili and Reima Pietilä.

A residential area with terraced houses and low-rise apartment buildings by Ralph Erskine was constructed in 1985-87 next to the Malminkartano Railway Station.

The Kaarnatie 5 Residential Building by Pekka Helin and Tuomo Siitonen highlights the townscape in the northern part of Malminkartano. A street runs through an articulated gate-like opening in the building, and the corners of the building are also emphasized.

The nearby Pihkatie 1 by Sakari Laitinen has a low basic fabric, which culminates in one corner in an eight-story tower.

21

22

21

Puustelli Multipurpose Building 1985
Puustellintie 6

Kari Järvinen,
Timo Airas

The Puustelli Multipurpose Building is based on a long semi-public enclosed street, thus extending the urban structure from Puustellinaukio Square, toward which the more public parts of the building incline. The entrance from the square is between the library and the gymnasium. The other service facilities – the dining room, the special classrooms, the youth work facilities and the day-care centre for schoolchildren – open to the indoor street. The homeroom classes of the primary school and the administrative facilites are along a gallery passage in the second floor. The façades of the multipurpose building are red brick. The parallel roofs slant south, toward the school yard, accentuating the whole.

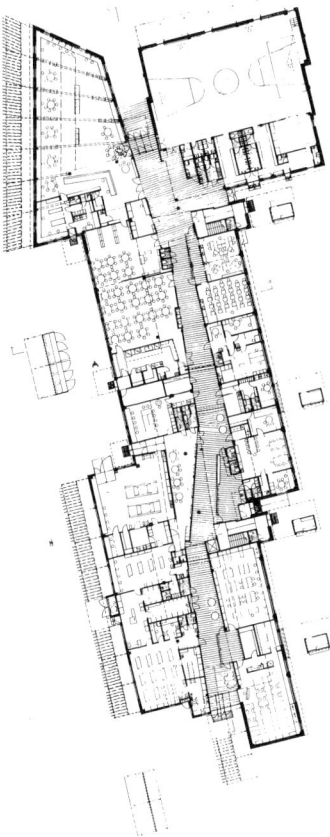

22

Vitsaskuja Housing Area 1980
Vitsaskuja 1

Timo Vormala,
Marja Lapinleimu

The Vitsaskuja houses are a part of a larger housing project in Konala, with some 200 residences and, among other things a children's day-care centre. The government-financed houses were constructed on the basis of the winning bid for the turn key-project competition.

The Vitsaskuja 1 development consists of one-story and two-story terraced houses of five residential units, totalling 65 apartments. The one-story part in the middle of each terraced building contains small apartments. The plan of the top floor has made it possible to vary the size of the larger units. The rhythmically undulating façades of the terraced houses are clad in horizontal white board, and the visible sloping of the roofs are dark corrugated steel.

24

25

23

Kannelmäki Residential Area 1975
Vanhaistentie 14

Esko Kahri

This residential area is based on the turn key-project competition the Helsinki City Bureau of Residential Production held in 1972. The area borders open fields and consists of two-story wooden frame terraced houses, a total of 191 residential units. The smallest units consist of one room and a kitchen, the largest units have five rooms, a kitchen, dining room, and sauna.

A group of units consists of three or four terraced houses of different lenghts. Each group has its own playground. Each unit's yard faces this common area.

The rooms fronting the yard can be altered, which makes the plan flexible. The utility areas on the entrance side are fixed. Except for the small units, each unit has its own storage space, yard and balcony. Those with from three to five rooms and a kitchen also have a sauna.

The Domino pillar-slab construction system has been employed. The exterior walls are prefabricated wooden elements, and the intermediate floors are made of steel and wood slabs.

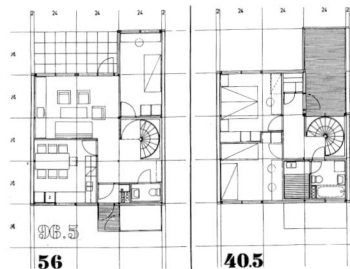

24

Kannelmäki Church 1968
Vanhaistentie 6

Marjatta and Martti Jaatinen

The church is based on the winning entry in an invitational competition held in 1967–68. The placing and exceptional form of the church hall emphasize its sacred character. The roof of the hall is formed of four hyperbolic paraboloid surfaces, which are bordered by windowed edge beams. The thirty-meter-high tent-like church is located on a high elevation and it dominates its surroundings. The parish meeting rooms and offices are in a low wing.

25

The Finnish-Russian School 1965
Kaarelankuja 2

Osmo Sipari

The school is a dynamic composition of functional units that form three schoolyards. The regular classrooms, the special classrooms, the dormitories and day-care centre are each in separate wings. They are combined by a transverse wing which contains the cafeteria, library, and administration facilities. A separate wing with an auditorium and gymnasium borders the other side of the entrance court. The buildings are terraced with a split-level solution conforming to the terrain.

Kristian Gullichsen: Malmi Church, 1980. (H4/5)

by

Kuninkaantammentie

Niskala
Nackböle

Tammisto
Rosendal

Laamannintie Lagmansvägen

Torpparinmäki
Torpparbacken

TUOMARINKYLÄ
DOMARBY

1

Lainkaarentie

Vanha Tuusulantie

Sexmansvägen

aloheinä
vedängen

Tuomarinkartano
Domargård

2

Sysimiehentie

Yhdyskunnantie

Pakilan
siirtolapuutarha

Ui
Ba

Uimaranta
Badstrand

Itä-Pakila
Östra Baggböle

Baggböle
koloniträdgård

PAKILA
BAGGBÖLE

si-Pakila
ra Baggböle

Murmästarsvägen

Muurimestarintie

Sittavoudintie

Samhällsvägen

Mikkolantie

Osuuskunnant Andelslagsv

sbyvägen

Suursuo
Storkärr

Patola
Dammen

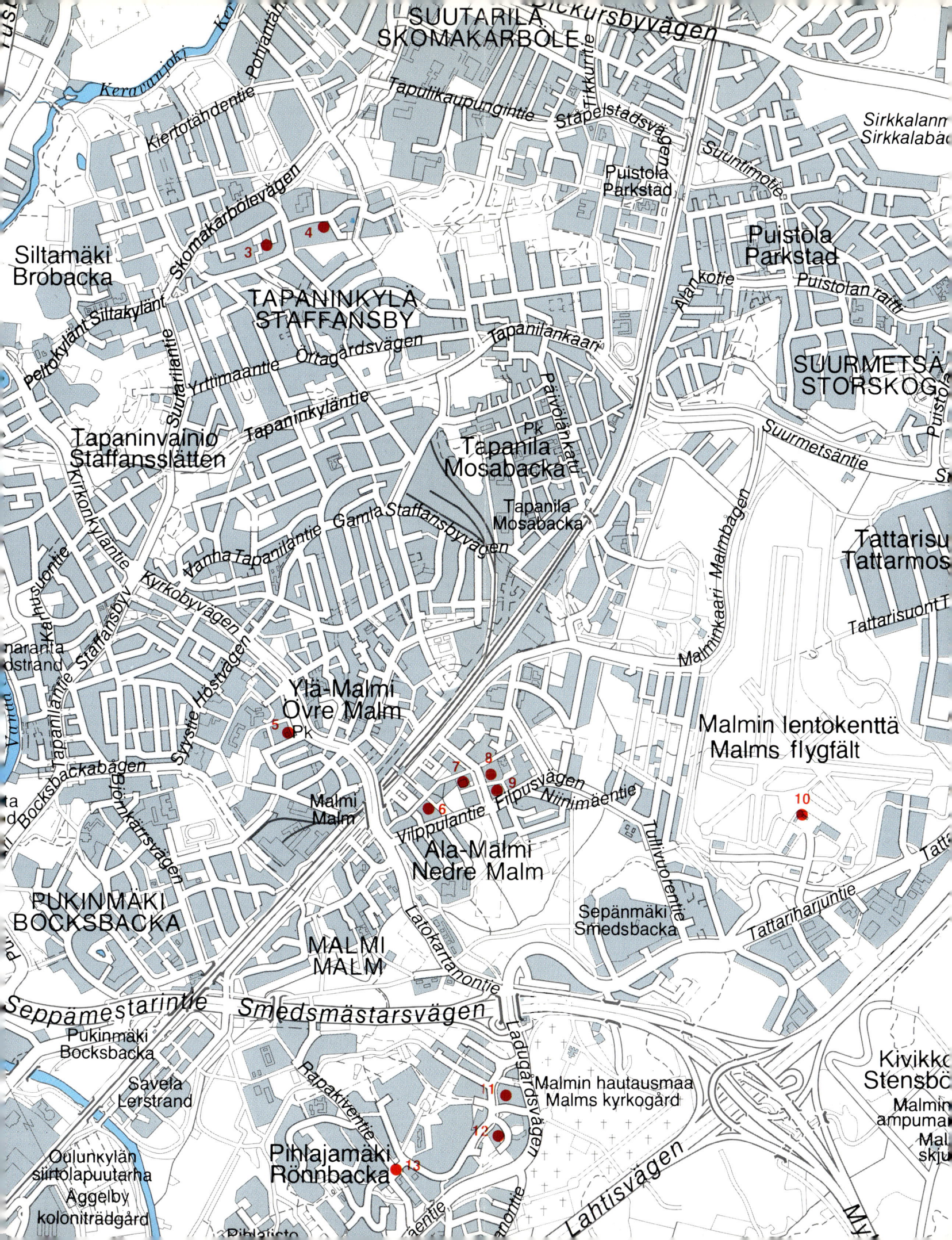

SUUTARILA
SKOMAKARBÖLE
Dickursbyvägen

Keravanjoki

Tapulikaupungintie
Stapelstadsvägen
Strikkurtie
Suuntimotie

Puistola
Parkstad

Sirkkalann
Sirkkalabä

Ponnantä

Kiertotähdentie

Puistola
Parkstad

Siltamäki
Brobacka

Skomakarbölevägen

3
4

Alankotie

Puistolan raitti

TAPANINKYLÄ
STAFFANSBY

Suutarilantie

Peltokyläntie Siltakyläntie

Yrttimaantie
Örtagårdsvägen

Tapaninlankaar

Tapaninkyläntie

SUURMETSÄ
STORSKOG

Tapaninvainio
Staffansslätten

Kirkonkyläntie

Pk

Tapanila
Mosabacka

Suurmetsäntie

Päivölänkaari

Tapanila
Mosabacka

Tattarisu
Tattarmos

Vanha Tapanilantie
Gamla Staffansbyvägen

Malminkaari Malmbågen

Tattarisuont

naranta
dstrand

Kyrkobyvägen
Staffansby

Höstvägen

Ylä-Malmi
Övre Malm

Pk

Malmin lentokenttä
Malms flygfält

Bocksbackabågen
Tapanilantie

Syystie

5
PK

7 8
6 9

Niinimäentie

Filipusvägen

10

PUKINMÄKI
BOCKSBACKA

Björnkärrsvägen

Malmi
Malm

Vilppulantie

Ala-Malmi
Nedre Malm

Tuulivuorentie

Sepänmäki
Smedsbacka

Tattariharjuntie

Tatt

MALMI
MALM

Latokartanontie

Seppämestarintie
Smedsmästarsvägen

Pukinmäki
Bocksbacka

Rapakiventie

Ladugårdsvägen

Malmin hautausmaa
Malms kyrkogård

Kivikko
Stensbö

Savela
Lerstrand

11

Malmin
ampuma
Mal
skju

12

Oulunkylän
siirtolapuutarha
Äggelby
koloniträdgård

Pihlajamäki
Rönnbacka

13

Pihlajisto

Lahtisvägen

My

H4

Pekka Helin, Tuomo Siitonen: Ylätuvanpolku Residential Area, 1981. (H4/1)

Nurmela, Raimoranta, Tasa: The Malmi Post Office, 1986. (H4/6)

3

4

1

Ylätuvanpolku Residential Area 1981
Kotitorpantie 3, Ylätuvanpolku 2

Pekka Helin, Tuomo Siitonen

This group of houses was a part of an experimental construction project for single-family housing initiated by the City of Helsinki. The group was also an exhibit at a residential exhibition held in the summer of 1981 whose main theme was urban living. The group consists of eight semi-detached houses with units of from three to four rooms, a kitchen and sauna. Each unit has a sizable glass verandah. Two units have solar panels for waterheating. The houses are primarily made of prefabricated elements. The façade elements are covered with ceramic tiles, and some of the stone walls are clad with thin stucco. Finished board complements the light general appearance of the façades.

The Ylätuvanpolku experimental project was an attempt to combine the scale characteristics of traditional Finnish urban construction with modern production techniques to form an architectural entity in harmony with contemporary lifestyles.

2

Tuomarinkylä Manor 1790
Kartanomuseontie

The military treasurer Johannes Weckström bought Domarby Manor in 1781. The current manor house was completed in 1790. Later on four annexes were added around a square-shaped yard. The building in the northwest corner has been demolished, but there are plans to replace it with a new one. The manor was bought by agricultural councilor Jakob Kavaleff in 1845. The City of Helsinki acquired the manor in 1917 and has been its occupant since 1957. The manor house was restored in 1960 to its 18th-century form. Renovation of the interiors was completed in 1986. There are plans to restore the overgrown manor park to its original Gustavian form.

3

Kyläsuutarinpuisto and Kyläsuutarinpuistikko Residential Buildings 1983
Vanha Suutarinkyläntie 4–8

Timo Vormala

These government-financed apartment buildings are situated on both sides of Kyläsuutarinpuisto Park. In both developments two-story terraced houses frame a parkland, and consist, in addition to the apartment buildings, of a maintenance building with a sauna and laundry room. The basic apartment size is three rooms and a kitchen. The smaller apartments are in one-story sections between the two-story buildings. These one-story sections can also contain extra bedrooms that expand the three-room-and-kitchen units. The vertical terracing of the units gives the area its distinguishing character. The pale board-clad façades and the slope of the roofs harmonize with the single-family dwellings in the area.

4

Vaskihuhdantie Residential Buildings 1983
Vaskihuhdantie 1–3 and 4–6

Pekka Helin,
Tuomo Siitonen

The group of government-financed small apartment buildings is situated on both sides of Vaskihuhdantie. The two-story lamellas with from four to five apartments are joined with one-story unheated storage spaces. The oblique joints curve the buildings around a communal court.

The vast majority of the apartments, each of which has direct access, have from two to three rooms and a kitchen. The larger apartments are either in the ground floor or, rather in the mode of terraced houses, in the second floor and extend partially into the garret. The composition of the building blocks, the partial use of wooden materials, and the pastel colors harmonize with the single-family houses in the area.

5

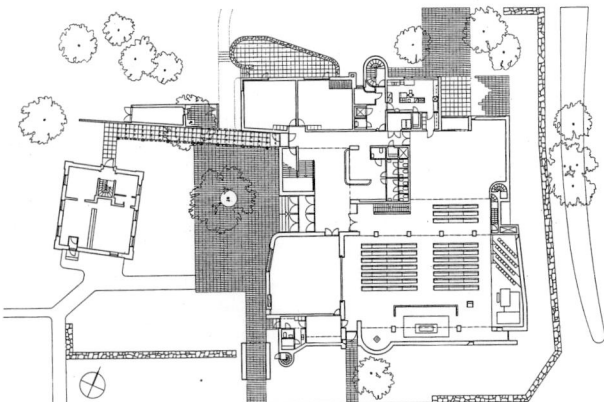

6

Malmi Church 1980
Kunnantie 1–5

Kristian Gullichsen

Plans for a church in Malmi had already been made in the 1950s, and a public competition for the church was held in the 1960's. The present church, completed in 1980, is based on the winning entry of an invitational competition held in the 1970s.

The church is situated along a busy street that runs through the suburb of Malmi. The building is closed toward the street, and its entrance opens on a court enclosed by stone walls, with access through the belfry portal.

The church hall has a broad space along the altar wall and a low arcade-type vestibule. The altar wall is top-lit along its entire length, with focus on the baptismal font. The church hall has an adjoining parish hall and music hall. The second story contains social facilities. These spaces are drawn together by a two-story-high vestibule hall.

The façades of malmi Church are traditional brick. The medieval allusion of the brick façade ornamentation, along with other references, tie the church to the architectural traditions of both the past and our own century.

A health-care centre by Sakari Laitinen (1988) is located next door, in Talvelantie 3.

The Malmi Post Office 1986
Hietakummuntie 19, Pekanraitti 20

Matti Nurmela,
Kari Raimoranta,
Jyrki Tasa

The Post Office Building is located on the southeast side of Ala- Malmi Square, in a fairly low row of public buildings along Pekanraitti. A tall entrance canopy and glass entrance hall front the square. A tall glazed cylindral hall joins the different floors. A small customer-service area with curving counters and back wall is adjacent to the cylindral hall. In addition to the actual Post Office the building contains a staff cafeteria, an occupational health facility, and the custodian's residence. The façade materials are plaster and ceramic tile in white, red and brown stripes.

A new interpretation of 1920s Scandinavian classicism is evident in the Malmi Post Office Building's architectural approach.

A public architectural competition for the Malmi Building on the neghboring site was held in 1987, and the winning entry was submitted by Reino Huhtiniemi and Kimmo Söderholm.

5

8

10

7

Malmi Swimming Hall 1983
Pekanraitti 14

Risto Kauria,
Risto Turtola

The swimming hall is located near the centre of the suburb of Malmi. To the south it borders the Ala-Malmi Park and to the north fronts Pekanraitti, which unites the swimming hall with the other public buildings in the area – the Post Office and the planned Malmi Building.

The entrance hall and ticket booth, the pools, and the swimming hall proper, have been elevated to the second floor, mainly due to the high water table level. The hall with the main pool, training pool and children's pool, opens on to a sun terrace. The dressing rooms and showers are placed symmetrically on both sides of the hall. A cafeteria is on the same level as the pools, separated from them by the lofty entrance hall. The façades are sandlime brick.

8

Soidintie 12 Residential Buildings 1986
Soidintie 12

Kalle-Heikki Narinen

The group of buildings near the Malmi area centre consists of four three-story buildings with one staircase and one four-story building with two staircases. The large building is along the street and the four others enclose a sheltered courtyard.

The partial fourth story in the street-side building contains the upstairs space of the largest apartments. A roof terrace, balconies and their supporting structures, together with varied materials, enliven the façades fronting Soidintie.

9

Ampujantie Residential Buildings 1986
Soidintie

Esko Kahri

One of the residential buildings is along the main street and the other borders the courtyard, accessible from the street through a forecourt and gate.

The architectural solution and basic composition of the street façade resemble the neighboring buildings at Soidintie 12. As with the neighbors, the four-story building requires no elevator, because part of the top floor is incorporated in the third-floor apartments. The building joins the street through an arcade. The curved bay in the gable is an interesting detail.

10

Helsinki-Malmi Airport 1938
Tattariharjuntie

Dag Englund,
Vera Rosendahl

The Helsinki-Malmi Airport is the oldest functioning airport in Finland. When the building was completed in 1938 Finnish civilian air traffic was fifteen years old. The airport buildings consist of the administrative building and a large hangar with space for six Junkers Ju-52 planes. The three-story, circular administration and restaurant building has one-story office wings that extend south-east and south-west. The tall top-lit central hall contained ticket sales and customs facilities on the ground floor. The restaurant is in the second floor, and the top floor contains office space. The cylindral shape of the airport is functionally and visually justified, and the building is a worthy representative of the functionalism of its era. The Helsinki-Malmi Airport is still in operation, mainly as an airfield for small propeller aircraft.

11

13

11

Liusketie Residential Buildings 1987
Liusketie 19

Veli-Pekka Tuominen

The residential area, located on a gradual slope, consists of a long three-story building that cuts off the traffic, and three small two-story apartment houses that enclose a courtyard. The wooden storage sheds in front of the staircases have been carefully planned to act as part of the whole and the pleasant scale of the courtyard. The irregular composition of the façade materials and colors, and the occasional exceptions in roof form provide the residential area with a character all its own.

12

Liuskekuja 1 Residential Buildings 1985
Liuskekuja 1

Sakari Laitinen

The hilltop block contains 79 residential units and a children's day-care centre. The buildings closely frame a semi-enclosed courtyard, enlivened with an comprehensive façade composition with vertical and horisontal terracing and materials and colors that depart from the basic structure of the prefabricated concrete element building.

13

Residential Area in Pihlajamäki 1961
Rapakiventie

Lauri Silvennoinen (the Sato area), Esko Korhonen (the Haka area)

The planning of the different divisions of this residential area on both sides of Rapakiventie is based on the disposition plan by Olli Kivinen. A public competition for the Sato area on the southwest side of the road was held in 1960. The area was constructed on the basis of the winning entry by Lauri Silvennoinen. It consists of longish, four-story lamellar buildings and eight-story tower blocks, which have been placed in two groups of five towers. The whole forms a controlled silhuette in the landscape. The Haka area consists of similar oblong lamellar buildings and groups of tower blocks.

Pihlajamäki was a dress rehearsal for the extensive suburban construction of the 1960s. It was the first instance in Finland of the use of prefabricated concrete elements in a large residential area.

13

Ladugård

oritie

Viikintie
Viikin puhdistamo
Viks reningsanläggning

Viikin opetus- ja koetila
Viks försöksgård

Myllypuro
Kvarnbäcken

Viikintie

15

Viikintie

Myllärintie Myllärit

Myllypadontie

Retasmyllyntie

16

Säynäslahti
Idviken

VIIKKI
VIK

Viksvägen

Fillarvägen

Hjulkvarnsvägen

äki
cka

Hyppyrimäki
Hoppbacke

Siirtie Igelkottsv

Roihupellon teollisuusalue
Kasaäkers industriområde

seo
eet

Luonnonsuojelualue
Naturskyddsområde

Loppi
Klobben

Länsi-Herttoniemi
Västra Hertonäs

Lammassaari
Fårholmen

Ryönälahti
Brakviken

Marjanie
siirtolapu

Kuusiluoto
Granholmen

Renut Rarv

Skridbacksvägen

Sågaregatan

Sahaajankatu

Kasbergsvägen

Marudc
kolonitråd

14
Roihuvuori
Kasberget

Tulis

nkaupunginselkä
nelstadsfjärden

Saunalahti
Bastuviken

HERTTONIEMI
HERTONÄS

Roihuvuorentie

Str
St

Kivinokka
Stenudden

Herttoniemen siirtolapuutarha
Hertonäs koloniträdgård

Hiihtomäentie

Laivalahdenkatu

Herttoniemen teollisuusalue
Hertonäs industriområde

7

Abraham Wetterint Abraham Wetters v

Porolahti
Poroviken

10

Leposaari
Vilan

Revholmssundet

Naurissalmi

Kulosaaren puistot Brändö parkväg

Hitsaajank Svetsarg

Linnanrakentajantie

Abraham Wetterint

TAMMISALO
TAMMELUND

9

11

1

Itäväylä Osterleden

2 KULOSAARI
BRÄNDÖ

Gsk

Kulosaarent Brändöv

Pk

6

Kaivolahdenkatu

8

Borgbyggarvägen

Tiiliruukinlahti
Tegelbruksviken

Reposalmi Rävsundet

opeasalmi

Silverstundet

5

4

Herttoniemen satama
Hertonäs hamn

Tullisaarenselkä
Turholmsfjärden

Yliskylänlahti
Uppbyviken

Yliskylä
Uppby

IKKAMAA
RSLANDET

12

Uimaranta
Badstrand

Tullisaari
Turholm

Huvudv Henrik Borgströmin

Reposalment

13

Uimara
Badstra

ASAARI
LMEN

© Kaupunkimittausosasto, Helsinki 1989
Julkaistu kaupungingeodeetin luvalla

Raimo Teränne: Myllärintanhua Residential Area, 1987. (H5/15)

H5

Heikki Saarela: Tammiväylä Residential Buildings, 1985. (H5/9)

1
2

1

The Jaatinen Private Residence 1939
Soutajankuja 5

Jarl Jaatinen

The building is on a shorefront site among pines, with a view over Vanhankaupunginlahti Bay. Placed on a hillside, the house is mainly two-storied. The entrance floor contains a livingroom, dining room and library in a loosely connecting series of spaces with outdoor terraces. The bedrooms in the second floor are grouped around a hall. There is a sizable roof terrace fronting the sea. The façade material is stuccoed brick, complemented by the wood-clad terrace and balcony.

2

The Kulosaari Secondary School 1955
Ståhlberginkuja 1

Jorma Järvi

The Kulosaari Coeducational School is a compact building without corridors, as the classrooms are grouped around a versatile central hall. The hillside site has been utilized to raize the seating in the central hall. One half of the gymnasium complements it as a stage. The school is based on a subject-orientated classroom curriculum, and the students store there personal belongings in the seats of the central hall. Staircases and galleries that lead to the classrooms circle the hall. The wooden trusswork supporting the roof slab forms an architectonic motif. The dominant material in both the façades and the interiors is red brick.

In 1967 an annex by Osmo Lappo was constructed further uphill.

3

The Stenros Experimental Residence 1981
Bertel Jungin tie 12 C

Helmer Stenros

The architect's residence and studio form one end of a terraced three-family house built on a hillside. Utilizing both active and passive solar energy, the external glass prisms of the experimental building mask the actual collectors behind. The building has a steel structure, with hollow slab intermediate floors.

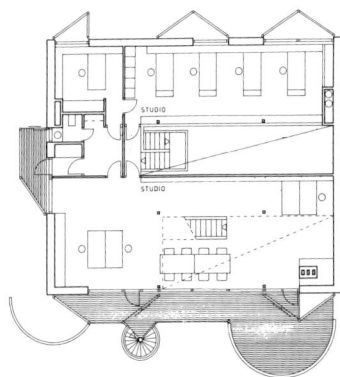

4

The Kulosaari Casino 1915
Hopeasalmenpolku

Armas Lindgren

The seaside restaurant on Valasluoto was originally called the Brändö Pavilion. Alterations were made by Bertel Jung (1929) and Niilo Kokko (1950). The summer restaurant was planned by Jaakko Laapotti (1985).

5

6

5

Wihuri Company Building 1917
Wihurinaukio 2

Lars Sonck

The building was originally a sea-side hotel. Together with the sea-side pavilion built a few years earlier, it was intended as part of a larger seaside tourist centre. The hotel had some forty rooms plus a restaurant and lounge in the first story. The entire topmost floor was a dormitory. The building is symmetric, it narrows towards the top and has balconies and ter-races. There is a magnificent view from the towers over the Kruunu-vuorenselkä bay toward Helsinki. The façades, except for the first story of natural stone, are of white-painted brick. The building was renovated in 1964 as the head office of Wihuri, and the open top floor was turned into a covered space.

6

The Ribbinghovi Terraced Houses 1917
Kulosaarentie 21–25

Armas Lindgren

The terraced houses between Ku-losaarentie and Vanha Kelkkamäki are among the first in Finland. The two rows of houses on the hillside contain thirteen residential units. The terracing and the powerful gable motifs on the long sides en-liven the houses.

On the other side of the street (Kulosaarentie 44) is the former Kulosaari Fire Station by Lars Sonck (1915), flanked by the Tele-phone Exhange and a residential building.

7

Marimekko Factory 1974
Sorvaajankatu 10–14

Erkki Kairamo,
Reijo Lahtinen

The first phase of construction consisted among other things, of the printing hall, warehouse, and power plant. The bearing structure of the building is steel. The space frame structure of the roof slab has produced a free area measuring 9 by 18 meters. The façades are artic-ulated by carefully composed de-tails such as stairs, exhaust ventila-tion blowers, and awning appara-tus.

An extension of the building was completed in 1983, to plans by Ilkka Salo.

8

Herttoniemi Manor 1820
Linnanrakentajantie 12

Pehr Granstedt

The manor, commissioned by Carl Olof Gronstedt, was built in 1814–20 according to a plan by Pehr Granstedt. The core of the building was Finland's first porce-lain factory (founded in 1762 by, among others, Augustin Ehren-svärd and Johan Sederholm). The 40-acre park was laid out concur-rently with the manor. The park before the manor house was de-signed in the French style. Both of the follies in the park are by C.L. Engel.

Herttoniemi Manor has been a museum since the 1920s. The 18th century Knudsbacka Farmhouse from the village of Box in Sibbo and a windmill from Bromarv have been moved to the manor grounds. There is a restaurant in the estate manager's house.

10

12

9

Tammiväylä Residential Buildings 1985
Vanhaväylä 22

Heikki Saarela

The whole consists of four identical single-family dwellings. The site has handsome trees, and borders a park on one side. The cube-like red-brick houses skirt the trees but still form a tight geometric pattern. The entrances are toward a fenced rectangular communal court. The living rooms and dining rooms in the first floors and the second-floor bedrooms, saunas and terraces are placed to ensure privacy, but contact with the courtyard is maintained. The total form and the details of the buildings embrace the spirit of brick architecture.

10

Three-family House 1966
Pellonperäntie 9

Timo Penttilä

The building is located on a westward slope among handsome pines. Its rich composition is set on the gradient, gracefully circumventing the trees.

The two-story terraced house consists of three nearly identical units. The plan of the dwelling unit is a cross: each arm is formed of a room or pair of rooms. In the ground floor the arms are the living room, dining room and kitchen, the stair hall, entrance hall and toilet. On the top floor each of the three bedrooms form one arm, and the stair hall, bathroom and toilet are in the fourth one.

There is access from both downhill and up-hill sides. The basement of each dwelling unit contains a room with a fireplace, sauna, and storage space; because of the slope it also has natural lighting. The apartments measure 120 square meters in area. The bearing frame is brick. The façades are red brick, and in part façade glass.

11

The Enarvi Duplex 1973
Leppisaarenkuja 1

Juhani Pallasmaa

The enviromental relationship, materials, colors and structures of this duplex have many features that suggest aesthetic experimentation and, on the other hand, industrial construction. The bright colors and plastic façades make no attempt to harmonize with the disparate shapes or colors of the surrounding buildings.

The actual residential space has been elevated to the second story. The 120-square-meter apartments have four rooms, a kitchen and dining room. The bottom floor contains leisure rooms and sauna facilities, with a swimming pool, and garages.

The bearing pillars are steel pipe, and the horisontal structures are beamless conctere slabs. The exterior walls have wood frames. The large balconies have steel frames, with protective plywood walls and glass railings.

12

Aino Ackté's Villa 1877
Tullisaari

Theodor Decker

Aino Ackté's villa, originally Villa Lindfors, is one of two extant villas of the three Theodor Decker planned. Commercial Councilor Henrik Borgström commissioned them for his children. The Finnish singer Aino Ackté bought the villa in 1904 as her summer residence and used it until her death in 1944.

The two-story villa is located in spacious, park-like surroundings near the sea. The vertical timber structure is an unusual feature. The façade of this ornamental neo-renaissance house is enlivened with extensions, towers, and wooden ornamentation familiar from vernacular architecture.

The City of Helsinki bought the villa in 1929. Long neglected, it was renovated in 1986–87. The board façade was painted, with dubious authenticity, in alternating brown and yellow. The villa is used for music rehearsals and other small-scale cultural activities.

13

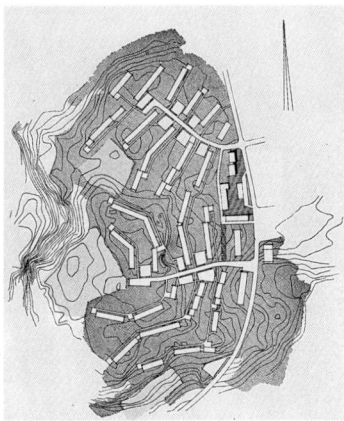

14

13

Laitatuulenkaari Residential Buildings 1984
Laitatuulenkaari

Jan Söderlund

This group of residential buildings consists of semi-detatched houses and terraced houses set in uneven terrain among older single-family dwellings. The block is framed by a circular street, with rows of semi-detatched houses on both sides of a bisecting pedestrians way. The semi-stepped composition of the terraced houses complements the whole.

The hillside residential units utilize a split-level solution, which gives added height to the living rooms. In some units the living room is extended with a gallery-type dining space. The façades are clad with pale painted board.

14

Residential Area in Roihuvuori 1954–60
Roihuvuorentie 18–32

Esko Korhonen

The area is located to the north of the eastern residential area in Herttoniemi, west of Roihuvuorentie. The streets in the area have been limited to two distributor roads ascending Roihuvuori Hill. The three-story and four-story residential buildings follow the contours of the terrain in longish bands of houses. The shopping and day-care centres are placed near Roihuvuorentie.

There is a separate building with one-room apartments at the shopping centre. It contains most of the small apartments in the area. Most of the apartments in the lamellar buildings have from two to four rooms and a kitchen. The façades are primarily plastered, with occasional light, panelled elements.

The elementary school at the end of Vuorenpeikontie, completed in 1972, is by Aarno Ruusuvuori.

15

Myllärintie Residential Area 1987
Myllärintie, Myllärintanhua

Raimo Teränne (Myllärintanhua)
Reijo Jallinoja (Kolsinkuja)

The area is based on the entries that were awarded first and second prizes in a competition held in 1981–82. The aim of the competition was to develop Finnish single-family housing environments.

The plan of the Myllärintanhua area is based on a hierarchic spatial composition of mixed-use street, communal court and private yard. The residential buildings consist of units in which the smaller apartments are placed in lamellas, and the large apartments in terraced sections in the ends of the buildings.

The Kolsinkuja Residential Buildings are built on a hillside. The general form of the area is more fragmented than the Myllärintanhua area. The apartments are in two and three-story buildings.

The dominant material in the whole area is red brick, complemented by painted board and concrete.

16

Artists' Studios 1974
Myllypadontie 5

Jan Söderlund, Erkki Valovirta

The Helsinki Artists' Society studio project was funded with government housing loans. The site is located in an existing residential area in Myllypuro. The studio-cum-residences are in four terraced houses around a courtyard. The communal spaces are in a maintenance building, which also contains a fairly large exhibition space. The studio section of the apartments is two stories high.

In addition to the studio the apartments have between one and three rooms and a kitchen. The bearing walls of the terraced houses are concrete, and the exterior walls have wood frames. The façades are clad in board with a dark finish.

Kontula
Gårdsbacka

Vesala
Årvings

Mustavuori
Svarta backe

Mellunmäentie

Mellunmäki
Mellungsbacka

MELLUNKYLÄ
MELLUNGSBY

Gårdsbackavägen

Aatteenetsijäntie

Slädv

Rekitie

Naulakalliontie

Mellungsbackav

Itäväylä

Keinutie

Kontulantie Porttt Porti

Humikkalantie

Humikkalankaari

Borghargev Linnanherjarti

Riskutie

Briskvägen

Broända

Niinisaarentie

Kangas-
lampi

Stenportsvägen

Vartioharju
Botbyåsen

Kviporrintie

Porslahdentie

Kallvikintie

Keski-Vuosaari
Mellersta Nordsjö

VARTIOKYLÄ
BOTBY

Venkalahdentie

mästarvägen

Kvanbacksvägen

Puotinharju
Botbyhöjden

Österleden

Rusthollarint Rusthållary

Puotilantie

Vartio-
kylän-
lahti
Botby-
viken

Rastböley Rastböle Lofit Loggv

Rastila
Rastböle

Kallviksvägen

VUOSA
NORDS

Vuosaarentie Nordsjö

Turunlinnantie

Itäväylä

Meripellontie

Puotila
Botby gård

Uimaranta
Badstrand

Leirintäalue
Camping

Itäkeskus
Östra centrum

Sjöåkersvägen

Vuotie

Norvägen

emen
utarha
dds
dgård

Marjaniementie Maruddsv

suontie

Marjaniemi
Marudd

Iso Koivusaari
Stora Björkholmen

Halkaisijant

Kallandenharju
Kallviksåsen

romsinlahti
trömsviken

Ramsöuddsvägen

Luonnonsuojelualue
Naturskyddsområde

Iso-Kallahti
Stora-Kallahti

Hepolahti
Hästviken

Ramsinniementie

Vasikkaluoto
Kalvholmen

Kallahti

© Kaupunkimittausosasto, Helsinki 1988
Julkaistu kaupungingeodeetin luvalla

Käpy and Simo Paavilainen: The Mellunkylä Parish Church of St. Michael, 1988. (H6/1)

H6

Erkki Kairamo: Itäkeskus Landmark, 1987. (H6/4)

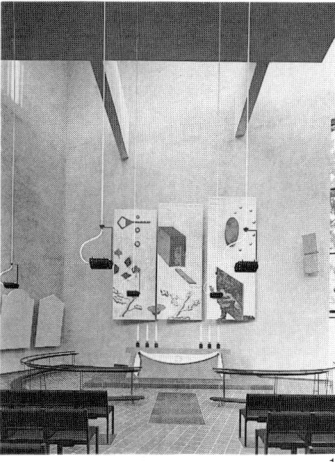

1

2

The Mellunkylä Parish Church of St. Michael 1988
Emännänpolku 1

Käpy and Simo Paavilainen

The Mellunkylä Parish Church of St. Michael is located in the Kontula suburb. It is based on the entry that was awarded second prize in a public architectural competition held in 1980. The longish, angular building with a church hall and other congregational facilities inclines against a rocky hillside. On the side fronting Emännänpolku it forms an entrance forecourt and on the side fronting the hill, functional courtyards for the interiors. The belfry occupies a landmark position in the forecourt. Its red-brick façade with yellow stripes is repeated in the church hall, providing a cube-like impression. An angel by Kari Juva perches on the eaves. The façade fronting the hillside continues the stripe theme in reverse.

The church hall seats 300, the adjacent parish hall 250, and the two halls may be combined. The pink interior walls of the church hall are lit with overhead skylights. A large glass door connects the hall to the forecourt. The lofty church hall contains many symbolic allusions, and the more everyday interiors have also been designed with an insight. Their details and colors make them an interesting functional space.

Itäkeskus Shopping Centre 1984
Tallinnanaukio

Erkki Kairamo

The Shopping Centre on the southern side of Tallinanaukio Square is the largest building in the Itäkeskus metro block. A smaller wing containing shops on the eastern side of the square is also a part of the centre. The façade fronting the Metro Square is two stories high, and consists of a steel frame with glazed and glass brick surfaces, canopies, stairways and advertising displays. The side fronting the Itäväylä Highway is four stories high, and its scale and materials blend in with the Itäkeskus environment.

The building contains mostly shops on four floors. From Tallinnanaukio Squre there is an entrance to a long glazed-roofed enclosed street with two large department stores at both ends, and smaller shops and services between. The architectural composition of the street is clear and avoids excessive commercialism. Both the structures and the well planned details have captured the spirit of the old market halls and shopping arcades.

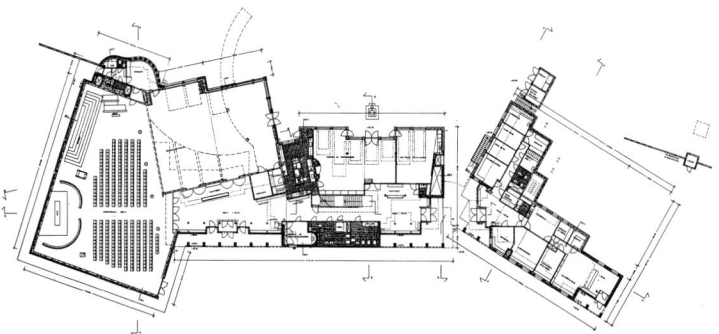

1

3

3

4

The Helsinki Itäkeskus Multipurpose Building and St. Matthew's Church 1979–84
Turunlinnantie 1–3

Björn Krogius,
Veli-Pekka Tuominen

A public architectural competition for the Multipurpose Building and Congregational Centre was held in 1977. The pair of buildings based on the winning entry turn their backs to the adjacent highway and shopping centre and front their own Stoa Square. The entrance halls of both buildings open onto the square and form an visual extension of it.

The Multipurpose Building contains a central hall and two halls that seat 400 and 200. The building also houses the Workers' Academy, a branch library, and facilities for youth activities. A cafeteria and exhibition space adjoin the central hall.

As the first Finnish example of this successful building type, the Multipurpose Building has served as the prototype for several similar buildings in various parts of the country.

The parish centre contains a church hall that seats 200, and an adjacent parish hall that can be joined with it, club rooms and the parish office.

Itäkeskus Landmark 1987
Kauppakartanonkatu,
Lyypekinaukio

Erkki Kairamo

This sixteen-story office block is a part of a whole consisting of the four-story Helsinki Eastern Social Services Centre at the base of the tower, and an adjacent building with restaurants and shops. The building is based on the winning entry of an invitational competition held in 1977. Because much of the permitted building volume was employed in the base, the tower was made as narrow and spike-like as possible. Its diameter is some twenty meters, and its vertical character is emphasized by slanted corners, the glazed staircase that rises over the office floors, external vertical vent stacks and advertisement surfaces. There is a cafeteria at the base of the tower and a two-story entrance hall. In the office floors the working space winds around a core, consisting of the elevators, reserve staircase, and auxiliary space. The sixteenth floor contains meeting rooms, training rooms and a sauna. The façade materials are white and green ceramic tiles. The steel parts have been painted blue-green and gray-green.

4

5

5

6

Vuosaari Church 1980
Satamasaarentie 7

Pirkko and Arvi Ilonen

The church was constructed in 1980, based for the most part on the winning entry of an invitational competition held in 1976. It is situated in the vicinity of a 1960s residential area and placed on the site to skirt the handsome trees that grow there. The church hall and other meeting rooms form an independent part of the building entity, and the parish office and apartments form another. The entrances to the different parts of the building are from a passage between the two parts, except for the parish office, which has access directly from the street. The church part is low where it fronts the passage and other pedestrian areas, with the scale increasing on the side facing the pine-covered slope, where the terrain is more imposing.

The church hall seats 270. Both parish halls and part of the vestibule can be joined with the church proper, making a 500-seat-space available for special occasions. The walls of the larger halls are painted white. The other walls are red brick worked fair. The floors are polished red brick.

The Unitas Training Centre 1964
Ramsinniementie

Martta and Ragnar Ypyä

The Union Bank's training centre is situated in seven different buildings connected by glazed passageways. The interaction of the generally horizontal buildings and the surrounding natural setting is the principal architectural theme of the training centre. The façade materials are burnt red brick and Lapland pine, which is also the main material of the interiors.

7

The Alko (State Alcohol Monopoly) Training Centre 1970
Ramsinniementie

Helmer Stenros

The Alko Staff Training Centre is near the sea and consists of the main building and two separate dormitories, the staff apartment building and a gymnasium building. The lowish buildings are terraced on a slope, and the interiors offer views of the sea.

The main building contains two lecture halls, a dining room and leisure facilities. During the summer months the training centre serves as a recreational center for the Alko staff. The façade materials in the group of buildings are dark red brick, concrete, and pressure-impregnated wood.

Käpy and Simo Paavilainen: Olari Church and Parish Centre, 1981. (E1/27)

Heikki Koskelo, Simo Järvinen: Amfi Residential Buildings, 1982–86. (E2/3)

Arto Sipinen: Espoo Cultural Centre, 1989. (E1/1)

Eliel Saarinen: Villa Miniato, 1904. (E2/4)

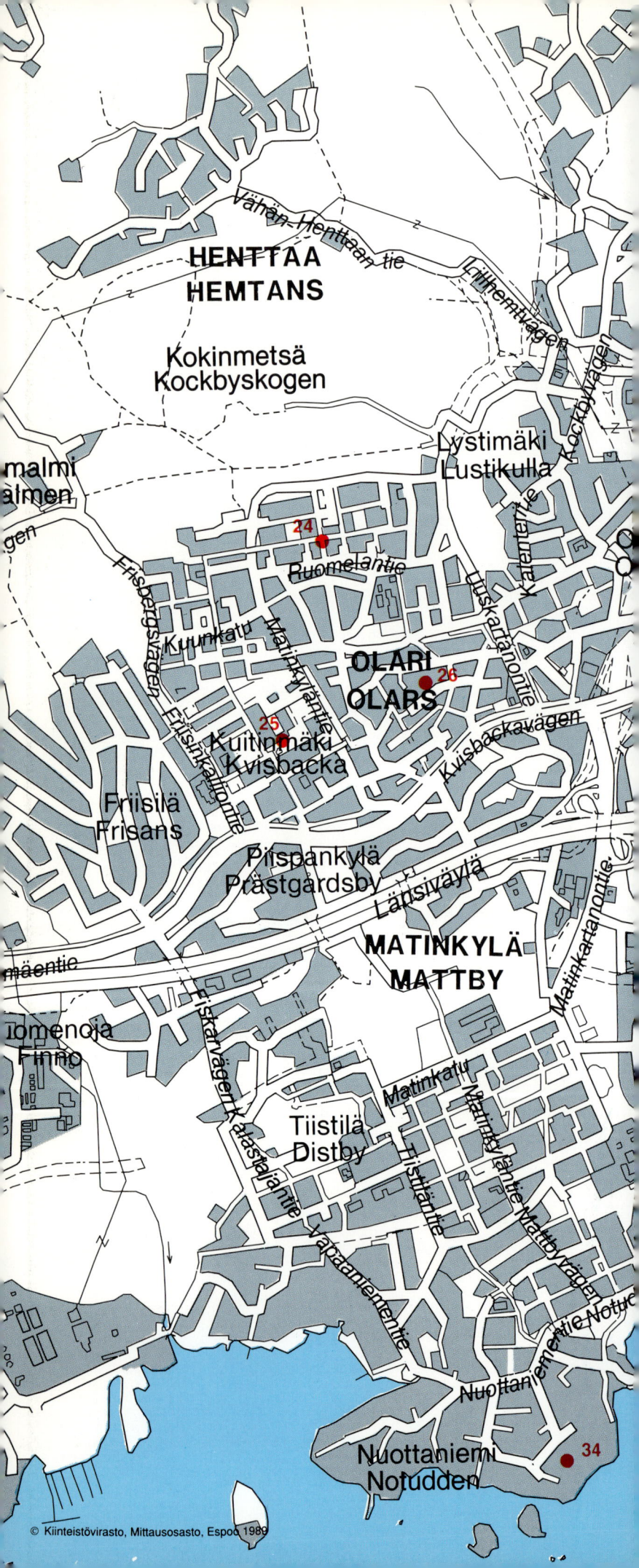

HENTTAA
HEMTANS

Kokinmetsä
Kockbyskogen

Vähän-Henttaan tie

Lillhemtvägen

Lystimäki
Lustikulla

malmi
almen

gen

Kockbyvägen

Friisbergsvägen

24

Ruomelantie

Kuunkatu

Matinkylä tie

Kaitatie

Uuskartanontie

OLARI
OLARS
26

Friisinkalliontie

25

Kuitinmäki
Kvisbacka

Kvisbackavägen

Friisilä
Frisans

Piispankylä
Prästgårdsby

Länsiväylä

MATINKYLÄ
MATTBY

Matinkartanontie

mäentie

Fiskarvägen/K atastajantie

omenoja
Finno

Matinkatu

Matinkylä tie Mattbyvägen

Tiistilä
Distby

Tiistiläntie

Valkjärventie Nuottaniementie

Nuottaniementie Notud

Nuottaniemi
Notudden

34

© Kiinteistövirasto, Mittausosasto, Espoo 1989

Etelä-Laajalahti
Södra Bredvik

Gamla
Mankans
Vanha
Mankkaa

POHJOIS-TAPIOLA
NORRA HAGALUND

OTANIEMI
OTNÄS

18

19

17

20

21

Lukupuro
Lukubäcken

Kalevalantie

Kalevalavägen

15

16

Otaniementie

Hagalundsvägen

Björnholms

14

5

22

13

4

6

Tapiolavägen

1

2

6

7

A

3

8

Keilaniemi
Kägeludden

11

12

Otsolahti

Tontunmäki
Tomtekulla

28

Havsvindsvägen

TAPIOLA
HAGALUND

joma
äcken

27

NIITTYKUMPU
ÄNGSKULLA

10

9

Västerleden

Karhusaari
Björnholm

23

29

Hanasaari
Hanaholm

WESTEND

Linholmsfjärden

Gäddviksvägen

HAUKILAHTI
GÄDDVIK

30

Haukilahdentie

Korkeasaari
Högholm

Stora Ängsholm

Tvijälp

31

32

Koukkuniemi
Krokudden

Varsasaari
Fölisholmen

33

Vehkasaari
Mössenholm

Miessaarenselkä
Karlöfjärden

Käärmesaari

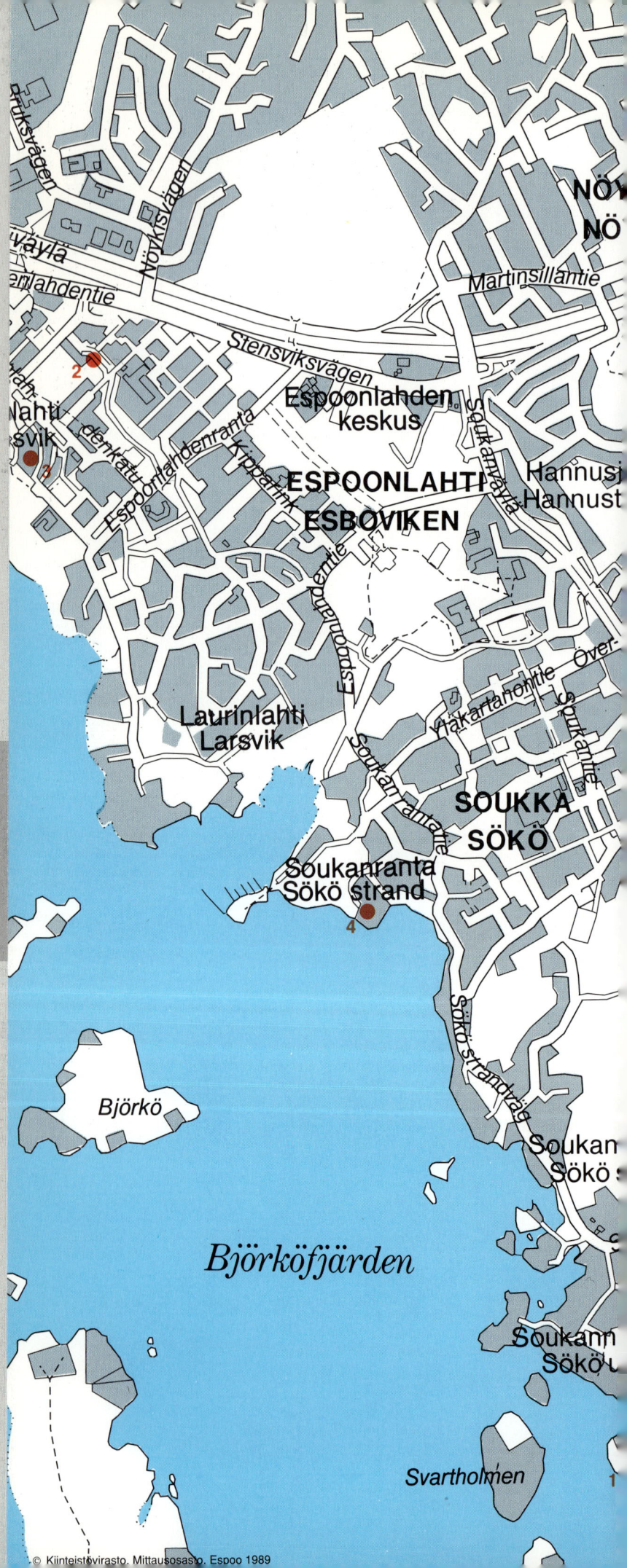

E1
E2

NÖ
NÖ

Martinsillantie

Stensviksvägen

Espoonlahden
keskus

ESPOONLAHTI
ESBOVIKEN

Hannusi
Hannust

Laurinlahti
Larsvik

Över

SOUKKA
SÖKÖ

Soukanranta
Sökö strand

4

Soukan
Sökö

Björkö

Björköfjärden

Soukann
Sökö u

Svartholmen

K   Downtown Tapiola

Downtown Tapiola is a large entity of public and commercial buildings based on the winning entry by Aarne Ervi in a public architectural competition held in 1954. The last part of the area was completed in 1989, when The Espoo Cultural Centre was constructed by the Central Basin. Other buildings along the basin are the swimming hall, church and a hotel.

The thirteen-story central tower (Ervi, 1961), a symbol of Tapiola, dominates the area. At the foot of the tower a U-shaped two-story business centre (1961) is composed around Tapiontori Sqaure. The tower is mostly office space. A shopping mall and the Heikintori Activity Centre are located behind the business centre, separated from it by a small square.

Since the end of the 1970s, a new business centre on a much larger scale has been constructed on both sides of Merituulentie. The whole also contains residential point blocks. The new, massive commercial centre gives a new expression to the earlier open and lush character of the garden city.

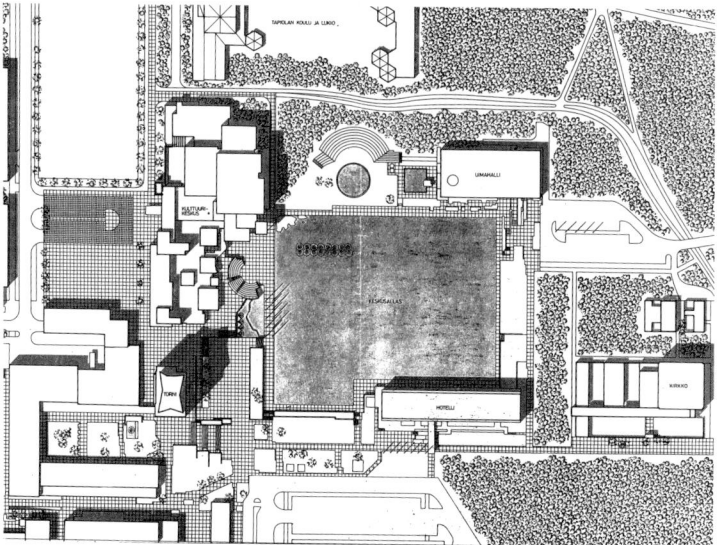

1

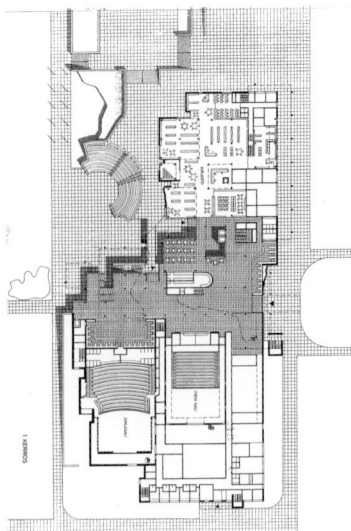

3

1

Espoo Cultural Centre 1989
Kaupinkalliontie 10

Arto Sipinen

The Cultural Centre is situated near the central basin, on a site Aarne Ervi had suggested for a theatre in his Tapiole Centre plan of 1954. The Cultural centre is based on the winning entry of a public competition held in 1979–80.

The lighter and more transparent parts of the building are reflected in the basin, whereas the heavier halls are drawn back from the basin. Access to the Cultural Centre is from the sides fronting the central basin and Kaupinkalliontie. The entrance fronting the basin links with waterfalls and an outdoor auditorium. The entrance hall serves partly as an exhibition space, and forms an impressive entity together with the second floor foyer, which has a view toward the central basin. The series of spaces culminates in a glazed pavilion, part of the gallery foyer of the Tapiola Hall. The building contains an 800-seat concert hall and 400-seat theatre, the Tapiola Branch Library, Music Institute and Workers' Institute.

The façade materials are sand-lime brick and travertine, which has also been used in the floors of the entrance halls and foyers.

2

Tapiola Swimming Hall 1968
Kirkkopolku 3

Aarne Ervi

The site of the Swimming Hall was placed north of the central basin even as early as in Ervi's Tapiola plan from 1954. The building was completed in 1968, and together with its vast outdoor spaces it occupies the entire northern side of the central basin. One of the outdoor pools is a diving pool, and the other a circular children's pool placed as the stage of an amphitheater-like sun terrace. The main entrance of the swimming hall opens to the balcony level, which commands a view of the entire hall. This level contains the ticket office, and a small cafeteria with direct access to the spectators' stands of the large pool. There is an expansive light cupola above the large diving pool. Vast glazed walls provide the pool area with a view of downtown Tapiola.

3

Tapiola Church 1965
Tapionraitti

Aarno Ruusuvuori

An invitational competition was held in 1961, and the church is based on the winning entry. It is situated behind concealing walls along a pedestrian throughway between downtown Tapiola and its eastern parts. Only the tall cube-like church hall can be discerned among the trees. The parish office, social facilities and parish hall are in their own wings along courtyards. A broad passageway links the spaces.

The church hall is lit principally through a field of windows at the back of the hall. A reflecting grid disperses the light in the hall, which has walls of gray concrete blocks. A characteristic feature of the Tapiola Church interiors is its spatial clarity, which is sustained by the refined asceticism of its materials and unpretentious details.

12

13

The building frame bends in horizontal steps, circumventing the white birches, and gradually increases from two to nine stories. A variable frame diameter facilitates several types of apartments.

Suvikumpu was constructed with traditional methods. Suvituuli used prefabricated elements in the intermediate floors and exterior walls. Both have the same basic façade material: horizontally profiled concrete and board together with white plaster or concrete.

11

Jousenkaari School 1960
Jousenkaari 10

Osmo Sipari

The lower story of this hillside school building contains the special classrooms, administrative facilities, dining room and gymnasium. The classrooms in the top floor are in four groups. Each four-classroom group has its own yard, rain shelter, entrance hall, cloak racks, and a staircase to the common rooms downstairs.

12

Riistapolku Residential Buildings 1961
Riistapolku 1

Aulis Blomstedt

The Riistapolku Residential Buildings are variations of Blomstedt's earlier apartment buildings in Tapiola (Kolmirinne Bld., 1954; Karhunpojat Bld., 1957). The slightly projecting staircases, recessed balconies, and the narrow top floor are characteristic features.

In the Riistapolku Buildings the balconies are only partially recessed and the façade is a more plastic entity than in the earlier buildings.

In the Riistapoku Buildings the red-brick façades of Kolmirinne have been replaced with white plastered surfaces.

The Riistapolku Buildings reflect an attempt, present in all works by Blomstedt, at harmony through weighed relations.

13

Weilin+Göös Printing Works 1966
Ahertajantie 5

Aarno Ruusuvuori

The two-story printing works building is on a gently sloping site located in the Tapiola light industry zone. Significant features in the exterior form of the building are the towers and projecting structures supporting the roof slab. This structural solution reduces the number of obstructing pillars in the production area of the second-story printing hall. The area supported by one pillar measures 27 by 27 meters. The first phase of construction consisted of four sub-areas. Each pillar tower, three meters in diameter, also serves as the ventilation centre for its area. The bottom floor contains offices, the staff cafeteria, restrooms and other staff facilities, and storage space. It has a normal pillar and beam structure.

The building was subsequently enlarged in a manner that differed decisively from the first phase of construction.

14

Kaskenkaatajantie Residential Buildings 1958
Kaskenkaatajantie 5, 8 and 10

Viljo Revell

The group consists of three residential buildings, in which Revell further developed the experimental themes of Mäntyviita and Sufika, completed four years earlier. Horizontal corrugated aluminum sheeting was at the time an unconventional and bold architectural solution.

The Kaskenpaja and Allakka residential buildings (Aulis Blomstedt; 1965) are in the same street, at Kaskenkaatajantie 16–18.

17

15

Tietäjäntaival Residential Building 1987
Kalevanvainio 4

Heikki Koskelo

The apartment building is situated on a central site in the Hopealehto residential area, on the axis of Tietä-jäntie. It is distinguished in both form and concept from the other lamellar houses in the area. The apartments in the four to-six story building are grouped in a wedge- shaped formation around a glazed courtyard. The staircase and sauna compartment in the third to fifth floors closes the courtyard on the northern side. There is a two-story high recessed entranceway below them.

The façades are yellow brick. The balconies are partially glazed.

16

Aarnivalkea School 1957
Aarnivalkeantie 9

Kaija and Heikki Siren

The low one-story school is based on an invitational competition held in 1956, and at the time it was an experimental solution. The classroom wings utilize the central corridor principle and they are joined by a section containing the special classrooms, gymnasium and dining room. The rear part of the deeper classrooms is lit by skylights. The façades are of wooden prefabricated elements. A terraced house with apartments for the teachers is a part of the unit.

17

Technical University Main Building 1964
Otakaari 1

Elissa and Alvar Aalto

The Technical University Main Building had already assumed its place and basic form in Alvar Aalto's winning entry in the planning competition held in 1949. The Main Building is set atop a central hill that dominates the area. A park joins it to the Teekkarikylä Student Village and the Student Union buildings.

The large auditorium is the dominant part of the university, its roof forming an amphitheater-like outdoor space. The actual teaching areas have been grouped in wings around small courtyards. The Main Building houses the Department of General Sciences, the Department of Architecture, and the Department of Surveying. The principal façade material is red brick, with some black granite, and marble as a collection of architectural fragments in the façades of the Department of Architecture.

The University Library was built in 1965–69. Bordering a tree-lined lane that dates from the time of Otaniemi Manor, it complements the park-side composition of the main building.

18

Otaniemi Chapel 1957
Jämeräntaival 8

Kaija and Heikki Siren

A public architectural competition for the chapel was held in 1954, and the purchased entry by Kaija and Heikki Siren provided the basis for the work. The chapel consists of a concise series of spaces, beginning at a fenced in forecourt, continuing with a low entrance hall to the tall chapel hall, and terminating at the glazed altar wall and the surrounding natural setting. The altarpiece is a wooded Otaniemi out-

cropping on which a cross has been erected.

The chapel hall, set between two brick walls, is defined by the high wooden roof trusses. The unprocessed brick floor and walls, and the wood-clad upper walls and ceiling impart warmth to the space.

Arson destroyed the chapel in 1976, but it was rebuilt to the original plans.

19

Polytechnic Campus 1950–54, 1970–73
Jämeräntaival

Heikki Siren, Martti Melakari

The plan and basic grouping of the Polytechnic campus are based on Alvar Aalto's winning entry to the competition for the town plan of the Otaniemi University Area, held in 1949. The first construction phase consisted of three groups terraced to the terrain, with three four-to-five story point blocks. The compact tower solution is based on a central staircase and efficient landing access to the dormitory units, each accommodating from six to eight students.

Servin Mökki, a building with a student restaurant and meeting rooms, was built in 1952, during the first phase of construction. Wooden clustered columns and rough-cut board roof beams create the basic architectural tone of the restaurant.

The Teekkarikylä campus was expanded in 1970–73 with four-story lamellar houses. Both phases of the Polytechnic campus had red brick as the façade material.

20

Dipoli Polytechnic Student Union Building 1966
Luolamiehentie

Raili and Reima Pietilä

The building is based on the winning entry to the competition held after the general planning competition in 1961. During terms it is used as a student union building, and in the summer as a hotel and conference centre.

The Student Union Building consists of two parts separated in the ground floor by the Teekkari Hall. The area with an irregular plan contains the large interiors, and the rectangular part the office and administrative space and the restaurant kitchen.

The upper foyer, auditorium, restaurant and cafeteria can be used separately or as one large whole.

The façades of the Student Union Building are copper and concrete, and occasional cyclopean walls made of large undressed stones. The interiors repeat the concrete and stone walls, with wood in the ceilings and walls.

The Swedish-speaking student union building, the Urdsgjallar, by Kurt Moberg, was completed the same year on an adjacent site.

E1

23

24

21

Residential Area, Otaniemi 1952–62
Otaniementie

Kaija and Heikki Siren

This apartment building development was built by the University of Technology Students Union for newly graduated engineers and architects. It was constructed over a period of ten years in the so-called »Retuperä» area. Penthouse apartments in the top, fifth floor provide unity to the different phases of construction. The balcony solutions and materials lend variety to the buildings. The Otalaakso Buildings from 1956 are the first example of large-scale use of light wooden façades.

22

Miestenmetsä Office Building 1987
Miestenmetsä 1

Juhani Junttila,
Mika Penttinen

The Finnoil Building is situated in the corner of Karhusaarentie and Hagalundintie. Its red-brick material complements an area of red-brick buildings: The Firemen's Academy on the other side of Miestentie, and the large group of VTT Technical Research Centre buildings. An invitational competition for the building was held in 1983.

The partially five-story office building consists of two wings and a central hall that joins them. The office wing fronting Hagalundintie is accompanied by a parallel one-story wing with training and service facilities.

The office floors use both the one and two-corridor principles. The ends of the corridors offer a view of the vicinity. The cafeteria, sauna area, and most of the meeting rooms are in the fifth floor. The central hall is as tall as the building, with gallery bridges that combine the office wings. Vast glass surfaces provide views in two directions.

23

Villa Sinebrychoff 1892
Karhusaari

Karl August Wrede

Karhusaari Island is one of the most valuable architectural and environmental entities in Espoo. The Neo-Renaissance villa built for Commercial Councilor Nicholas Sinebrychoff served as the farmhouse for a miniature farm, also consisting of a still extant barn and dairy building, servants quarters, woodshed, and pleasure pavilion, as well as a boat house, pier, and bathing cabin which were razed to make way for the highway.

The board-clad villa has a very gently sloped roof and an extremely broad eaves supported by cassette-based consoles. A balustrade runs around the roof. Horizontal moldings separate the floors. The foundation of the villa is a granite wall, which continues as terracing and joins the building to the terrain. The glazed verandas, balconies and terraces give the building its own character.

The City of Espoo acquired the deed to Karhusaari in 1980.

24

Olari Residential Area 1969–73
Ruomelanraitti

Simo Järvinen,
Eero Valjakka

The Olari Residential Area is located on top of a high hill. The apartment buildings are placed along a pedestrian street running east to west, with alternating blocks and park areas. Access to services and work spaces is also along the road, to create a bustling pedestrian milieu.

A high standard residential environment has been achieved in Olari through careful planning of the vicinity and expressive residential construction. The use of warm red brick provides a strong unifying touch. The structures are pillar slabs poured on site, facilitating flexible apartment floor plans.

E1

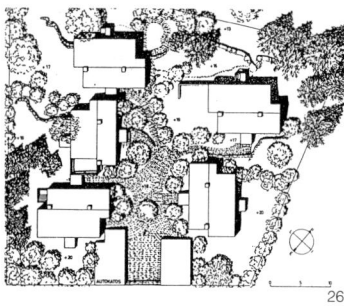

26

27

25

Piispankoti Residential Building 1984
Ellipsikuja

Simo Järvinen

The Piispankoti Apartment Building combines large terrace balconies with features from single-family dwellings. Each terrace contains glazed or walled-in and covered space. The free rhythm of the terraces and balconies, and the slender supporting pillars contribute to the powerful plastic character of the façades.

Some of the apartments in the top floor have two stories, with the sauna, leisure room, greenhouse and roof terrace on the topmost floor. There is a small school and day-care centre in the street-level floor.

26

Rajakatri Residential Houses 1980
Aamuyöntie 11

Reijo Jallinoja

This group of five buildings is located in an old residential area which is being gradually built up. The fundamentally similar houses form a courtyard milieu on a gently sloping hillside facing north. The carport and maintenance building form a gateway to the courtyard. The private gardens of the houses are either on the side opposite the entrance or at the gable, depending on the point of the compass. The living space is in two stories and each house has a full size basement. In some of the houses the living room is two stories high, in others there is a large second-story terrace in the same space.

The houses were constructed on the site, partly of brick and partly of wood. The façades are red brick. The small window openings impart the feeling of a castle wall. Some corner windows have been used to lighten the general expression.

27

Olari Church and Parish Centre 1981
Olarinluoma 4

Käpy and Simo Paavilainen

A public architectural competition for the church was held in 1976. The site is surrounded by a collection of industrial facilities, auto repair shops and traffic zones. The actual site is Gräsa Manor Hill with its old garden. The group of three buildings and the belfry turn their backs to the discordant vicinity, forming a semi-closed courtyard on the hill-top. Differences in elevation have been utilized in the placement of the church hall and entrance, which are on the same level as the upper courtyard; whereas entrance to the parish office is from the lower courtyard, near the parking area. The social rooms of the Finnish and Swedish-speaking congregations frame the churchyard on two sides. The church hall, which seats 500, is a typical long church. The parish hall can be joined to the church to provide 100 extra seats. The ceiling in the hall rises gradually towards the south wall, which has narrow vertical band windows. The main illumination of the hall is from large windows facing north. The façade material is red brick.

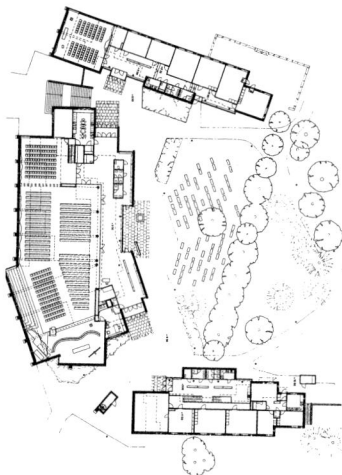

E1

29

30

28

Tonttukallio Residential Buildings 1959
Tonttumäentie 17–23

Toivo Korhonen,
Jaakko Laapotti

This compact residential area consists of three rows of atrium houses. Two are traditional terraced houses, with high walls separating the yards. The third row is formed of two-story quadruple house, which are rare in Finland.

Tonttukallio is an interesting area of single-family dwellings of the period. The privacy of the apartments was effectively ensured but the lane milieu is harsh and lacks a hierarchal spatial composition.

30

Hiiralankaari Residential Building 1983
Hiiralankaari

Erkki Kairamo

The five-staircase lamellar house has apartments in three stories, and auxiliary space in part of the ground floor. The living rooms and dining rooms are on the side facing the street and the seaview. The façade on this side has a composition of several open and glazed balconies. The side fronting the yard is completely different in nature, with narrow band windows and vertical staircase windows. The façade material is small white ceramic tiles complemented by larger green ones.

29

Liinasaarenkuja 3–5 Residential Area 1982
Liinasaarenkuja 3–5

Erkki Kairamo

The area consists of ten two-story semi-detached houses placed along a pedestrian walk that runs through an oblong site. The considered placement of the buildings and the varied alignment of the terraces and balconies bring life and an excellent hierarchical spatial composition to the views from the street and pedestrian lane. The buildings are simple basic white houses, embellished by the colored steel details of the hand-rails, stairs and canopies.

31

Iirisranta Residential Buildings 1984
Iirislahdentie 42

Harto Helpinen

The four chain houses in the residential area border a central courtyard, which opens onto a private marina. With its Central European gable house motifs, the group of dwellings is an exception in the general picture of Finnish residential architecture. There are 13 dwellings in the area, varying in size between 115 and 155 square meters. The façade material is thin white stucco.

31

33

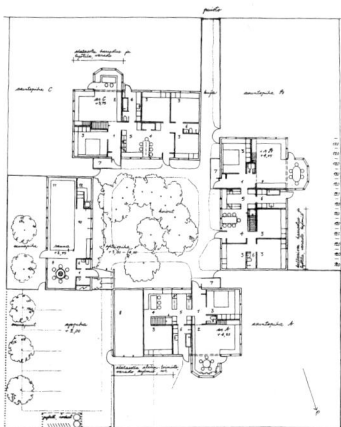
32

34

32

Grouped Dwellings 1973
Iirislahdentie 33

Erkki Kuoppamäki

This group of houses for three families is based in spirit on the vernacular Finnish central courtyard. The houses frame the courtyard on three sides and a building with a sauna and swimming pool completes the frame on the fourth.

The successful composition of hierarchical spaces – street, drive, communal court, private yard, sauna yard, park lane – is emphasized by the joining gates. A handsome stand of birches on the site was preserved to enhance the communal court, and a row of apple trees, the drive and sauna area. Two of the houses have five rooms and a kitchen, and one has four rooms and a kitchen plus a studio. All three houses have leisure rooms, workrooms and storage space in the basement.

The buildings are of wood and were constructed on the site, with a loadbearing structure of glued wood pillars and latticed trusses as the roof frame. The façades are vertical board.

33

Villa Kolikari 1916
Palosaarentie

Wivi Lönn

Villa Kolikari was built in 1914–1916 as a summer residence for Archiater Juho Jaakko Karvonen. The fairly large, two-story villa on Cape Koukkuniemi, in the village of Matinkylä, is a representative of the more classical and rational architecture that followed the Jugendstil. The building has a mansard roof which is folded at the gables. The basic symmetry of the villa is broken by a semicircular glazed veranda on one long side, and an open veranda on the opposite side.

In 1985 Villa Kolikari underwent renovations planned by Ilkka Pajamies, and it is now a leisure and training facility for a construction company.

34

Villa Carlstedt 1915
Itäinen Rantatie 14

Lars Sonck

The villa was built for the artist Birger Carlstedt. Its most prominent feature is the powerful mansard roof, which consists of curved parts. The villa has two verandas on the long side and one in the gable. The façades are partly rounded log with a dark finish, and partly vertical board cladding.

Carlstedt himself planned the studio building on the same site in 1930. Today the buildings are administered by the Konstsamfundet Foundation.

1

3

1

Villa Frosterus 1913
Amiraalinkuja

Sigurd Frosterus

This seaside villa is a two-story timber structure clad with board. The façade scale and apertures in this small, hip-roofed villa are controlled. The semicircular, covered open veranda is particularly beautiful.

The yacht club pavilion »Paven» on nearby Pentala Island is also designed by Frosterus (1914).

2

Merisilta Residential Buildings 1987
Aallonhuippu 13 and 16

Timo Vormala

This group of eight apartment buildings forms part of a projected larger whole. The buildings are compactly terraced on the hillside along a light traffic route that circles the area. They are connected to the road with stairs, pergolas and supporting walls, which border a playground and outdoor communal area immediately accesible from the road. Shopping and social facilities front the pedestrian path. The minimized mien of the residential buildings has been enlivened by the placing of the balconies, the use of colors and by other details.

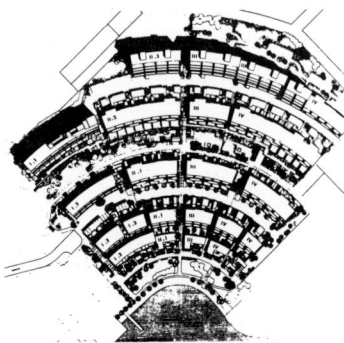

3

Amfi Residential Buildings 1982–86
Aallokko

Heikki Koskelo
(first phase, western side),
Simo Järvinen
(second phase, eastern side)

The Meritori Square and some of the Amfi Residential Buildings are the phases of the new Kivenlahti Centre that have been completed thus far. A tall residential or office tower has been planned as the vertical element in the composition and a landmark in the area. The amphitheater-shaped residential area on a fairly steep hillside by the sea is an urban composition rare in Finland. Amfi indicates clearly what new solutions geometry can bring to a hillside village. The deft choice of the number of stories, and the recessing of the buildings into the hillside has provided every apartment with a seaview.

4

Villa Miniato 1904
Miniatontie

Eliel Saarinen

Villa Miniato was built in 1903–04 for engineer Knut Voldemar Selin, according to plans by Eliel Saarinen. It is an important example of Gesellius-Lindgren-Saarinen villa architecture, albeit less well known than the contemporary studio-residence the architectural trio had on the shores of Lake Vitträsk in Kirkkonummi.

Miniato, as well as Hvitträsk, grows from the surrounding landscape, and is joined to it with native stone walls, and vast, steep roofs. A massive tower, irregular projections and balconies, lattice windows, and exquisite doors are characteristic elements of the buildings. The façades are plastered and the roof clad with tile.

The central interior is the two-story hall. The building contains several Jugendstil tiled stoves. Renovations and repairs were carried out in 1981–83.

Miniato is privately owned.

Kristian Gullichsen: Kauniainen Church, 1983. (E3/9)

Pekka Helin, Tuomo Siitonen: Unic Office Building, 1987. (E4/6)

Hanaja
Hanabäck

Oittaa
Oitans

Gunnarsvägen

uro
äck

Ristimäki
Korsbacka

Kummarlantie

Miilukorpi
Milkärr

Bemböle

Turuntie

Nupurbolevägen

Karv

Lommila
Gloms

Ring II

KARVASMÄKI
KARVASBACKA

Kasavuori
Kasaberget

Muuralantie

Turunväylä

Espoonjoki

1

Kirkkokatu

Kirkkojärvi
Kyrkträsk

2

ESPOON KESKUS

Pappilantie

Kyrkogatan

Kirkkojärventie

Södrikvägen

Suvelantie

ESBO CENTRUM

Siltakatu

Kiltakallio
Gillesberget

Kirstintie

Suvela
Södrik

Kirstinmäki

Tuomi
Dom

Sokrinpuistie

Saarniraivio
Åskrödjan

Hösmärintie

3

© Kiinteistövirasto, Mittausosasto, Espoo 1989

JÄRVENPERÄ
TRÄSKÄNDA

LÄHDERANTA
KÄLLSTRAND

LAAKSOLAHTI
DALSVIK

Kolkekannas
Klappedet

Järvenperä

Rastaala
Trastmossen

Pihlajarinne
Rönnebacka

4

Järvenperäntie

Klappedsvägen

Piikäjärventie

LIPPAJÄRVI
KLAPPTRÄSK

Kolkekannaksentie

5

Lippajärvi
Klappträsk

Kolkejärventie

Myllykylä
Kvarnby

VIHERLAAKSO
GRÖNDAL

Karakalliontie

7

KARAKALLIO

orvi
Jörv
ttie

6

Abovägen

Kavallinmäki
Kavall-en-backen

Karamalmi
Karamalmen

Bemböläntie

Gallträsk

KAUNIAINEN
GRANKULLA

Helsingforsvägen

8

Lansa

Bembölveg

Stationsvägen

Asemantie

Kasavuorentie

Bredantie

10

9

11

Helsingintie

Nihtisilta
Knektbro

Tunnelintie

Lansantie

Bredavägen

Kauniaistentie

Grankullavägen

Nihtisillantie

Ymmersta

12

Kauppalantie

Köpingsvägen

SEPÄNKYLÄ
SMEDSBY

Klovi
Klovis

Sinimäentie

Kuurinmä-
-entie

Jerkki
Gerk

Taavinkylä
Dåvitsby

Mankeantie

Mankeansvägen

KUURINNIITTY
KURÄNGEN

Kuurinniityntie

MANKKAA
MANKANS

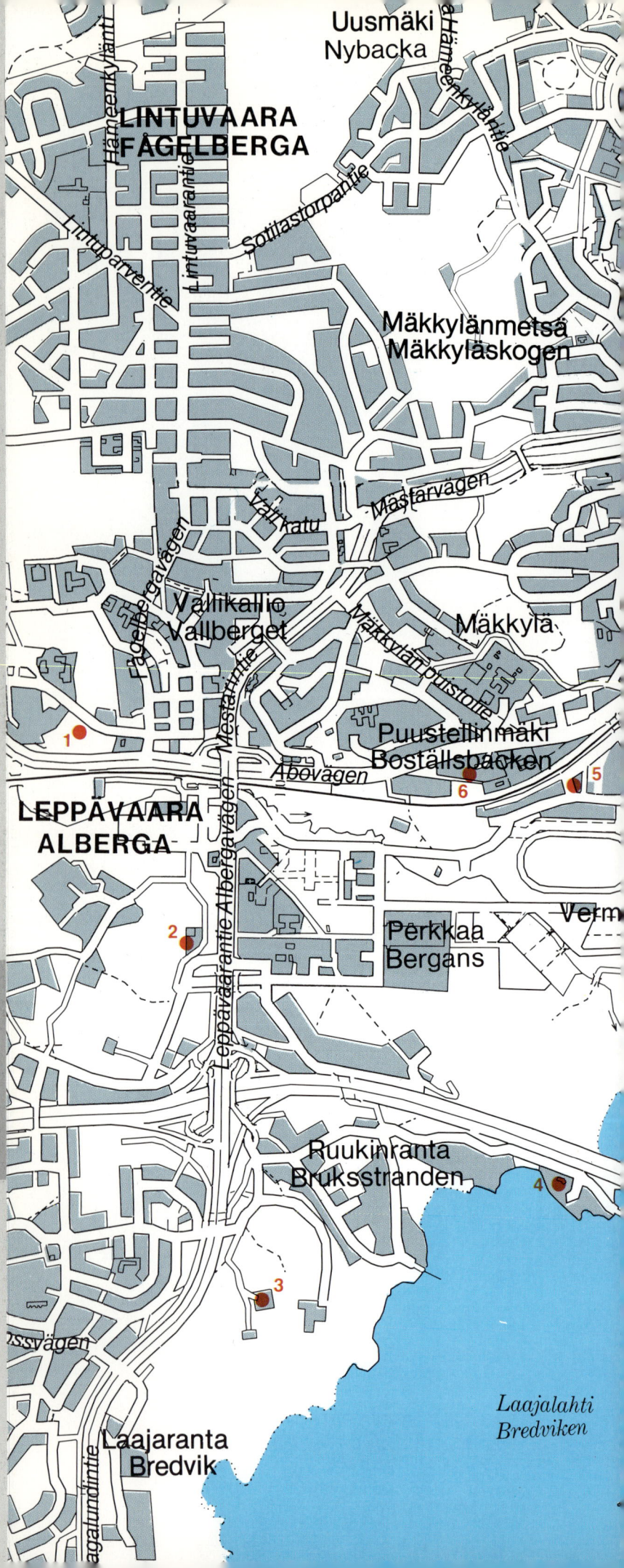

Uusmäki
Nybacka

LINTUVAARA
FÅGELBERGA

Hämeenkyläntie

Lintuvaarantie

Sotilastorpantie

Mäkkylänmetsä
Mäkkyläskogen

Lintuparventie

Mästarvägen

Valli katu

Fågelbergavägen

Vallikallio
Vallberget

Mäkkylän puistotie

Mäkkylä

Mestarintie

1

Puustellinmäki
Boställsbacken

Åbovägen

6

5

LEPPÄVAARA
ALBERGA

Leppäväärantie Albergavägen

2

Perkkaa
Bergans

Verm

E3
E4

Ruukinranta
Bruksstranden

4

3

ssvägen

Laajaranta
Bredvik

Laajalahti
Bredviken

1

2

Espoonkartano Manor
1797–1801
Kuninkaankartanontie

The present manor house was originally a part of a manor Provincial Governor Anders Henrik Ramsay planned, but only two red-brick wings were constructed. The western wing was completed in 1797, and the eastern wing in 1801.

The western wing underwent thorough alterations in 1914–15 according to plans by W.G. Palmqvist. The building was lenghtened and a large columned veranda was built on the side fronting the courtyard. The building, now a manor house, was given plaster façades and adorned with rich Baroque ornamentation. The Manor Park was also expanded according to plans by Paul Olsson.

The grounds of the manor are a valuable historic milieau, containing, among other things, an extant stretch of the King's Road (between Turku and Vyborg) and, beside the Espoonkartano Manor mill, the oldest stone-vault bridge in Finland.

Espoo Church Late 15th century
Kirkkotie

The oldest parts of Espoo Church probably date from the 15th century. In its late medieval form it was a typical gray stone church with a rectangular frame hall, an armory in the south and the sachristry in the north. The ornaments in the brick tympanum are an indication that the church is of the eastern Uusimaa type. The church has three aisles. The broader central aisle has star vaults and the narrow side aisles cross vaults.

The church retained its nearly medieval form until the early 19th century, when it was expanded as a cross church according to plans by Pehr Granstedt. The gray stone wing facing south was completed in 1821. Initially the northern wing was slightly longer than the southern one. The central pair of pillars and its vault was dismantled and replaced with a barrel vault.

In 1929–31 the church was renovated according to plans by Armas Lindgren. The Empire-period barrel vault was removed and the centre of the church was covered with a concrete cupola shaped like a ribbed star vault. The late medieval wall and vault paintings were revealed.

The second renovation of Espoo church was completed in 1982, according to plans by Olof Hansson. Some renovations that Lindgren had planned but not executed were also undertaken – among them the shifting of the altar to the central part of the church.

The belfry from 1767 is attributed to Samuel Berner.

3

Suna School 1985
Solisevantie 10

Kari Järvinen,
Timo Airas

The primary school for three hundred pupils is located on a wooded hill surrounded by a housing area. The building is placed on the northern edge of the site, offering the schoolyards the sunniest areas.

The building is divided into one part containing the gymnasium and dining room, and a longer wing for the classrooms. The latter is split lengthwise by a two-story corridor and entrance-hall space. The slanted entrance-hall roof has slash-like skylights, providing character to the interiors and exterior form of the building. The façades are red brick, stuccoed here and there in white.

4

Träskända Manor 1921
Kuninkaantie 43

I.G. Clason,
Armas Lindgren,
Bertel Liljeqvist

The present manor house is the fourth in a succession. The previous one, built in 1899–1900 was planned by the Gesellius-Lindgren-Saarinen firm for summer use only.

Armas Lindgren and Bertel Liljeqvist based their plans for the Träskända Manor House, constructed in 1921, on preliminary plans by I.G. Clason of Stockholm. Its strictly classical façades are adorned with a native stone Baroque portal. The heavy tile roof is steep. Espoo Municipality bought the manor in 1922 and from 1923 on it has been the Aurora Home for the Elderly.

A large Neo-Classical pleasure pavilion from the 1820s, with a circular plan and cupolaed roof, has been preserved in the southern part of the large Träskända Manor Park. It, and the Neo-Gothic warehouse, are attributed to C.L. Engel. Also extant is the imperial latrine by G.Th. Chiewitz, which dates from the early 1860s.

5

Lippajärvi Day-Care Centre 1984
Tammihaantie 6

Matti Nurmela,
Kari Raimoranta,
Jyrki Tasa

The day-care centre is located on the western shore of Lake Lippajärvi, on a birch covered hill. The building frames the playground on two sides. The separate areas and entrances for three groups of children are suggested by the façade fronting the playground and the glazed lanterns on the roof ridge. The entrance halls are cut obliquely through the building frame, and are visible on the façade opposite as balconies. The wooden façades are painted yellow, the roofs are red sheet metal.

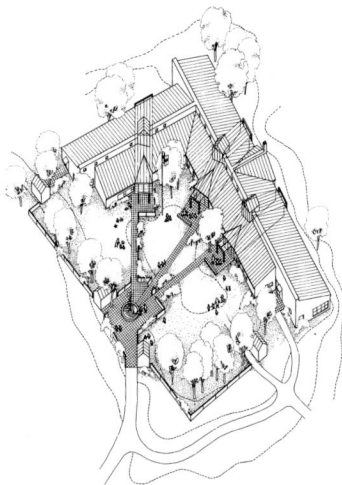

6

6

Villa Dalkulla 1922–23
Turuntie 167, Viherlaakso

Lars Sonck

Lars Sonck designed this round-log villa, atop a tall steep hill, for his private use. The log villa is placed around an atrium courtyard. The building was given its present form in 1938, when a tall tower was added, and the villa was enlarged according to plans by Sonck. It later underwent considerable alterations. Today it is used by the Espoo Bureau of Mental Health.

7

Karakallio Multipurpose Building 1987
Kotkatie 4

Matti Nurmela,
Kari Raimoranta,
Jyrki Tasa

The multipurpose building is located on a hillside between Kotkatie and the track and field grounds. Streetward it displays a low façade and strongly curved roof, which is cut by the stepped glazed lantern of the canopied extension of the lobby. The lobby continues through the building, and its glazed-field motif is repeated on the side fronting the track and field grounds. Its open and spirited character stands in contrast to the severe introversion of the opposite side of the street.

The building has a fairly large multipurpose hall for music, theatre and cinema performances, rehearsal rooms for music, leisure and youth work facilities, and a maternity and child welfare clinic.

The surface of the red-brick façade has been enhanced by the exceptional way the bricks are laid, with the mortar partially covering the surface of the brick.

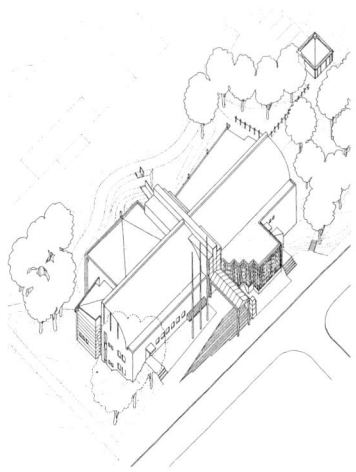

7

8

Villa Eka 1905
Edelfeltinkuja, Lansantie

Eliel Saarinen

The villa was built at the beginning of the century for the artist Albert Edelfelt. The modest villa and artist's studio has a two-story part with a mansard roof, and a perpendicular low wing with a pitched roof. The original tile roof was later replaced with tarred felt.

The building was long in private use, until the City of Espoo bought it in 1981 for a training, meeting and exhibition space for visual artists. In 1984–86 the villa was renovated according to plans by Pirkko and Pekka Piirta.

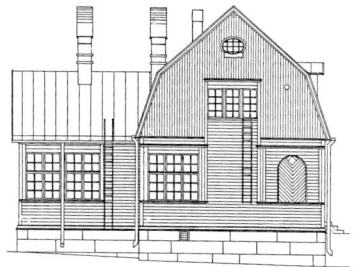

9

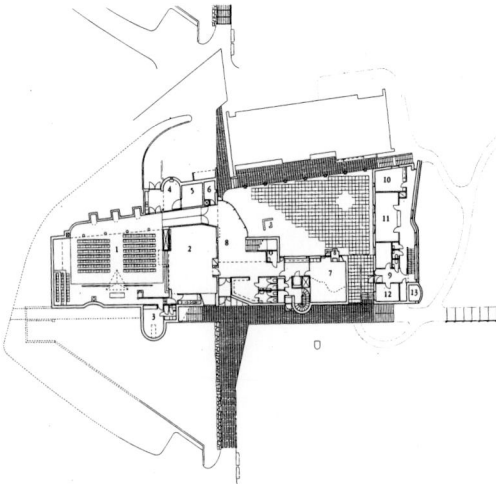
10

9

Kauniainen Church 1983
Kavallintie 3

Kristian Gullichsen

An invitational competition for the church was held in 1979, and the ideas and solutions expressed in the winning entry were carried out in the completed church in near accordance with the preliminary sketches.

Entrance to the church is through the wall-like west façade. Curving glazed walls connect the spacious entrance hall to a closed courtyard which is bordered on one side by the Parish Hall (Keijo Petäjä, 1960). A passageway descends gradually to the church hall, whose floor is considerably below ground level. The altar is on the long wall of the church hall, which is lit naturally with a lantern above the altar and a large skylight above the choir and organ. The building consists of the church hall, two parish halls, social rooms, and the parish office.

The façades are plastered brick walls painted white. The curved southern wall of the parish office is red brick covered with wooden trellicing.

The formal expression and details of Kauniainen Church include several levels of symbolism and allusions to both classical and modern architectural tradition.

10

Villa Vallmogård 1907
Valmukuja 3

Lars Sonck

The villa was built for the writer Mikael Lybeck in 1907. The building has a high fieldstone ground floor and two other stories. The façades are plastered and the roof tiled.

The villa was in private use until 1948, when it was taken over by a hospital for disabled veterans. The Kauniainen Municipality bought it in 1956 and it became Town Office. The villa was renovated in 1980–82 and has since then served as the Town Cultural Centre. The renovations were planned by Rurik Packalen.

9

11

12

11

12

Kauniainen Railway Station 1908
Gresantie

Bruno F. Granholm

The station house has been attributed to Bruno F. Granholm, because it bears such a strong resemblance to other station houses, particularly that in Punkaharju, he planned as an architect in the Department of Railways.

The Kauniainen Railway Station is related to National Romantic wooden architecture through its general form and forceful roof. The simple façades have lattice windows and painted borders. In 1911 an annex for the stationmaster's quarters was added to the building.

Villa Junghans 1916
Leankuja 4

Villa Junghans was probably built for the owner of the Helsinki Seurahuone Hotel and Restaurant, Wilhelm Noschis, who for a period of time was also the manager of Bad Grankulla Spa. When Noschis owned the villa it was called Villa Le.

The fairly small two-story villa has plastered walls and a tiled mansard roof. A one-story wing was added in the 1920s. The German businessman Constantin Junghans bought the villa in 1923. After the Second World War the villa was appropriated by the Soviet Union, which owned it for 25 years.

Renovations were completed in 1986, and the villa serves as a recreational facility for pensioners. The renovations and extension were planned by Karl-Erik Hagner.

1

3

1

Espoo-Vantaa Technical Institute, Espoo Unit 1988
Vanha maantie 10

Hannu Jaakkola

A public architectural competition for the Institute was held in 1985, and the building is based on the winning entry. The Institute is located in the Leppävaara area centre north of the old Turku Highway. The principally two-story building consists of common space constructed around a semi-open entrance forecourt, and the actual teaching facilities which frame a more enclosed inner courtyard.

There is a crenelated staircase tower at the end of the forecourt. A similar formal theme appears in the corners of the classroom building. The consierge's and superintendent's residences have also been squeezed into the same form.

The group of buildings opposite the Institute (Vanha maantie 9–11) was planned by Timo and Tuomo Suomalainen and constructed in 1968–72. It consists of the Commercial Institute, The Worker's Institute, the Municipal and Province Library, and Family Welfare Clinic.

2

Alberga Manor 1874
Leppävaarantie

The present Alberga Manor House was built in 1874 for Feodor Kiseleff, owner of a sugar factory. The house is U-shaped in plan, with the central part between the two-story wings having one story. The building has a full-height vaulted cellar. The building is attributed to Konstantin Kiseleff, a relative of the sugar factory owner.

The Manor House, also known as the »Sugar Castle,» was constructed using an interesting technique. Inch thick, half-meter-wide mahogany boards obtained from imported raw sugar crates were nailed on both sides of the timber frame of the exterior walls, which were then plastered on the outside. The character of the Manor House was altered when the volute gables of the wings were dismantled in the 1950s. There are plans to use the Alberga Manor House as a part of the Espoo Centre for the Visual Arts.

3

Villa Elfvik 1904
Elfvikintie

Mauritz Gripenberg

Villa Elfvik was built for Baroness Elvira Standertskjöld in 1904, at the head of Laajalahti Bay. The timber-frame plastered building has two stories. The tall hip roof is clad in red tile. The plan is multifaceted and the building has several balconies, projections, chimneys, and windows freely grouped and in various sizes. The exterior form and interiors have affinities with late-19th century English residential architecture, particularly the works of Philip Webb and C.F.A. Voysey.

The villa passed from private use to the Svenska Litteratursällskapet (the Swedish Literary Society in Finland) and later the Otaniemi Administrative Body and the City of Espoo. In 1985 Anna Brunow and Juhani Maunula drafted plans for converting the villa into a centre for environmental information.

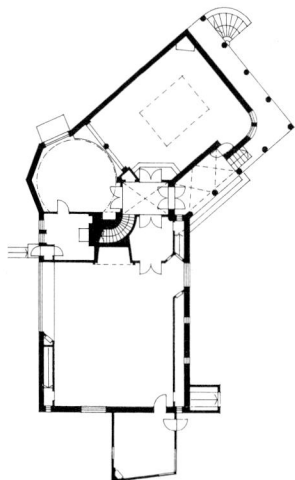

5

4

5

Gallen-Kallela Museum 1913
Gallen-Kallelantie 27

Akseli Gallen-Kallela

Akseli Gallen-Kallela's second studio and residence, Tarvaspää, was built in 1911-13 on the rocky Cape Linudd. Eliel Saarinen drafted a rough plan for the house, but Gallen-Kallela saw to it that the house matched his own views down to the very last detail.

The building consists of the studio, gallery, and a tower between them, and is a combination of medieval church, the tower of Vyborg Castle, and Florentine loggia. The studio was expanded in 1930. When the building was converted to the Gallen Kallela Museum, renovations and repairs were carried out according to plans by Kirsti and Erkki Helamaa. The Museum was opened to the public in 1961.

The museum cafeteria is in the 1850s Linudden Villa, which was enlarged to its present size in the 1860s and 1870s, when the building also received its gingerbread-style ornamentation. In 1988 Markku Komonen and Juhani Pallasmaa drafted a plan for renovations to the entire museum area.

Vermonhovi Residential Area 1986
Vermonpolku 3

Matti Nurmela, Kari Raimoranta, Jyrki Tasa

This residential area was financed by the National Board of Housing and consists of one-story terraced houses and two-story low-rise apartment buildings. Apartment size varies between one room and a kitchen and three rooms and a kitchen. The façade materials are red brick, sandlime brick and board; the roofing is machine-seamed sheet metal. The irregular composition of the materials, and the atypical roof forms in particular bring a new, cheerful look to this rental accommodation area.

6

Unic Office Building 1987
Kalkkipellontie 6

Pekka Helin,
Tuomo Siitonen

The Unic Computer Software Company held an invitational competition between three architectural offices for the planning of its office building, located on a site between the Turku Motorway and railway line. The two-part building is based on the winning entry. One part is clearly defined for the company's own use; the other forms a reserve space for future expansion, and is more general and conventional in its solutions. The starting point for the spatial concept was the special features of the organization, with the emphasis on teamwork. The working space is divided in normal offices, teamwork rooms and landscape cells. A smallish atrium serves as a unifying central space, distributing natural lighting to the core of the deep-framed structure. The delicate façades consciously seek an antithesis to the user's field of operations.

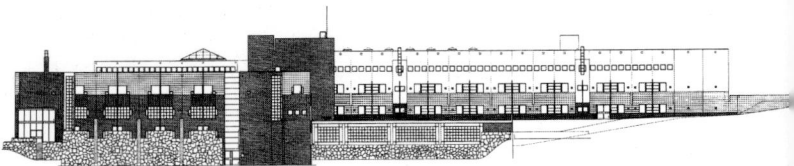

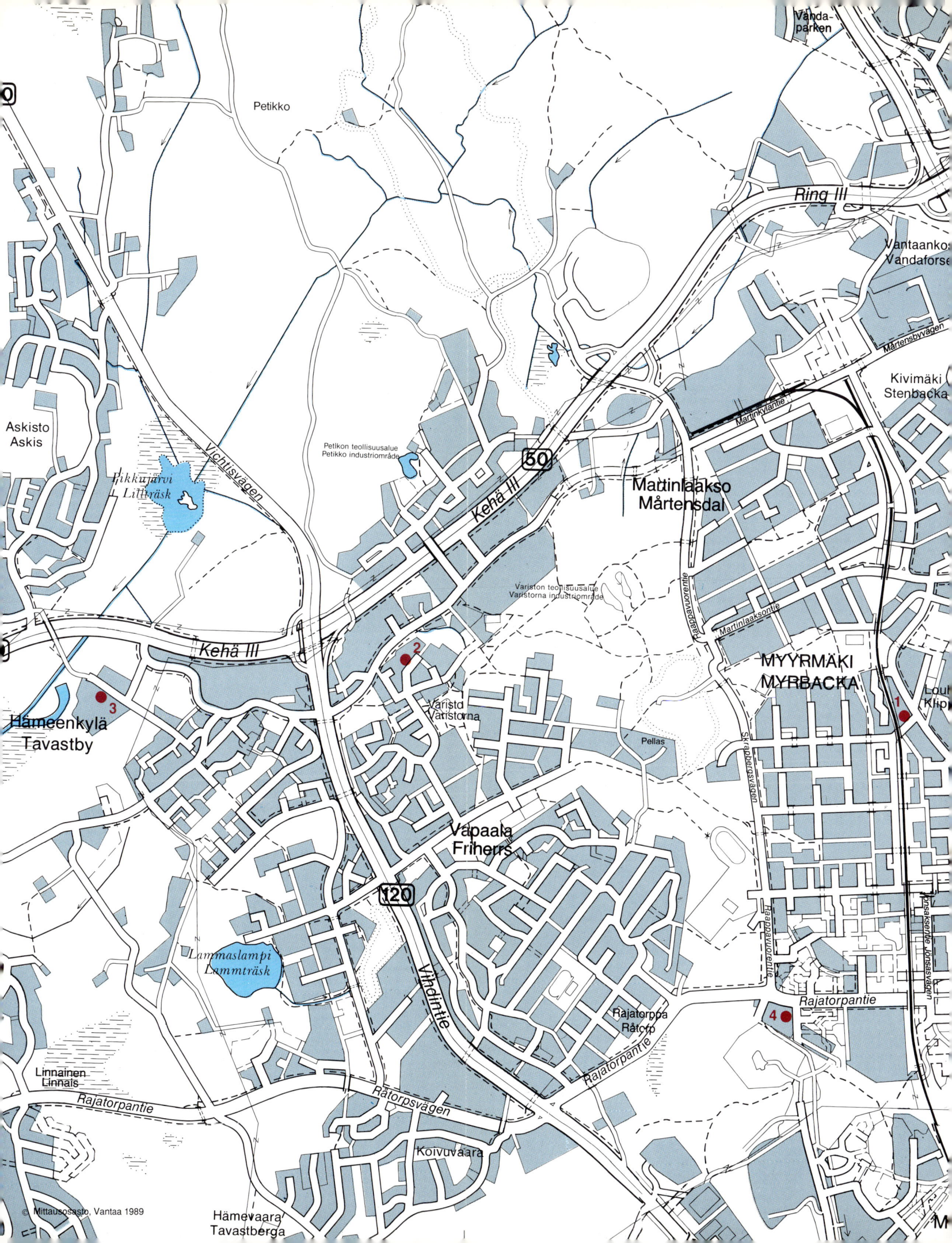

Vanda-
parken

Ring III

Petikko

Vantaankos
Vandaforse

Mårtensbyvägen

Kivimäki
Stenbacka

Askisto
Askis

Petikon teollisuusalue
Petikko industriområde

Martinkylantie

50

Mattinlaakso
Mårtensdal

Pikkujärvi
Lillträsk

Vichtisvägen

Kehä III

Variston teollisuusalue
Varistorna industriområde

Raappavuorentie

Martinlaaksontie

Kehä III

2

MYYRMÄKI
MYRBACKA

Varisto
Varistorna

1

3

Hämeenkylä
Tavastby

Pellas

Skrapbergsvägen

Raappavuorentie

Jonsaksentie Jonsasvägen

Vapaala
Friherrs

120

Lammaslampi
Lammträsk

Vihdintie

Rajatorppa
Råtorp

4

Rajatorpantie

Rajatorpantie

Linnainen
Linnais

Rajatorpantie

Råtorpsvägen

© Mittausosasto, Vantaa 1989

Hämevaara
Tavastberga

Koivuvaara

Juha Leiviskä: Myyrmäki Church and Parish Centre, 1984. (V1/1)

V1

1

2

1

2

Myyrmäki Church and Parish Centre 1984
Uomatie 1

Juha Leiviskä

The church is based on the winning entry in a public planning competition held in 1980. The site is near the embankment of the local railway line. The building and parking lots have been placed immediately beside the railway embankment, leaving most of the site as a cohesive park. A brick wall of varying height fronts the railway and forms the main theme of the composition and the spine of the building, to which the church hall, parish halls, and social rooms are joined in a free-flowing rhythm.

The functional-acoustic solution of the church hall is a most coherent implementation of recent tendencies to make church halls shallow in the direction of speech and deep in the direction of music. Light falls from above the broad, high altar wall, and together with that from reflectors it creates ever-changing ripples of light in the church hall, and a sense of spatiality approaching weightlessness.

The strongly articulated façade facing the park provides a contrast to the closed wall fronting the railway embankment. Narrow windows harmonize the light yellow brick, painted board, and the white trunks of the birches growing on the site.

Heinäkuja 10 Residential Buildings 1980
Heinäkuja 10

Timo Vormala

The group of two-story low-rise apartment buildings is located on a steep northern hillside. The 45 apartments are in eight low-rise buildings grouped in pairs around a unifying thoroughfare. The external staircases are on the eastern sides of the buildings, and the large steel-framed hanging balconies on the western sides. The terraced building frames enable the apartments to open in various directions. The façades are sandlime brick, the balconies and exterior stairs are steel and pressure-impregnated wood.

1/200

1

4

3

4

Hämeenkylä Manor 1830
Vanhankyläntie

The group of buildings is a part of a manor planned by C.L. Engel in 1820–23. Only the cellars, foundation and wings of the manor house were completed. The east wing was completed in 1830 and served as the manor house. It is a two-story plastered brick and mortar building with a hip roof. The west wing, built ten years earlier, is externally almost identical with the east wing. A Neo-Classical latrine and a barn from the 1830s are also extant.

Espoo-Vantaa Technical Institute, Vantaa Unit 1988
Leiritie 1

Pekka Salminen

A public architectural competition for the Technical Institute was held in 1985. The unit in Vantaa is largely based on the winning entry. The theory classrooms are grouped as a ring and form the largest part of the two-story building. The laboratory wing joins it from the side. A separate gymnasium hall is connected to the Institute building with a canopy. The curved roof of the hall is repeated in the curved roofs of the laboratory wing and rain shelter.

The common rooms are placed between the section with the theory classrooms and the laboratory wing parallel with the main entrance hall. The tall dining room and adjacent gallery library open to the courtyard through a curved glazed wall. The most interesting interior in the building is the tall glazed-roof square hall bordered by the theory classrooms. A cylindral auditorium rises from its center. For larger functions the hall and auditorium can be combined by opening the front wall of the auditorium. The façade material is yellow fired brick.

Mikko Heikkinen, Markku Komonen: Heureka, the Finnish Science Centre, 1988. (V2/8).

Helsinki — Vantaan lentoasema
Helsingfors — Vanda flygstation

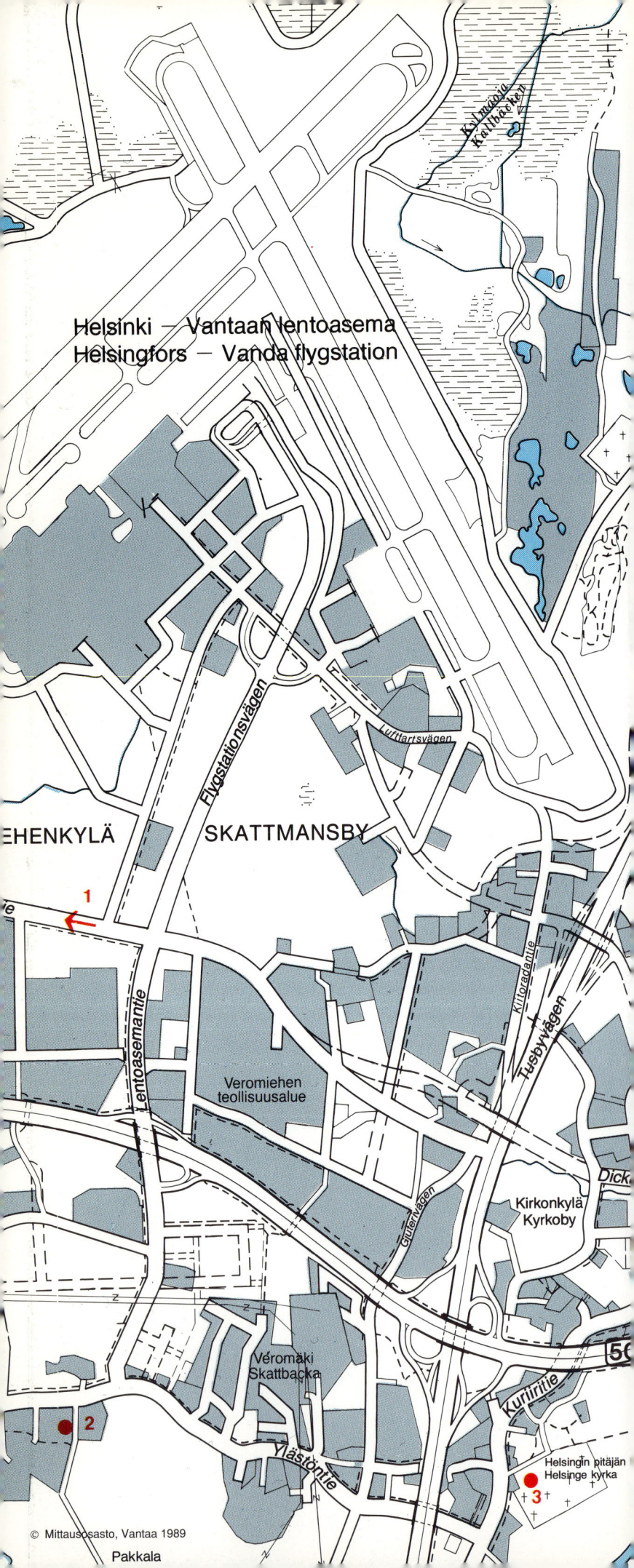

EHENKYLÄ   SKATTMANSBY

1

Veromiehen
teollisuusalue

Kirkonkylä
Kyrkoby

Dick

Veromäki
Skattbacka

50

2

Kuriiritie

Ylästöntie

Helsingin pitäjän
Helsinge kyrka

3

Lentoasemantie

Flygstationsvägen

Luftfartsvägen

Kiitoradantie

Tusbyvägen

Gjuterivägen

Kylmäoja
Kallbäcken

Pakkala

Laurintie

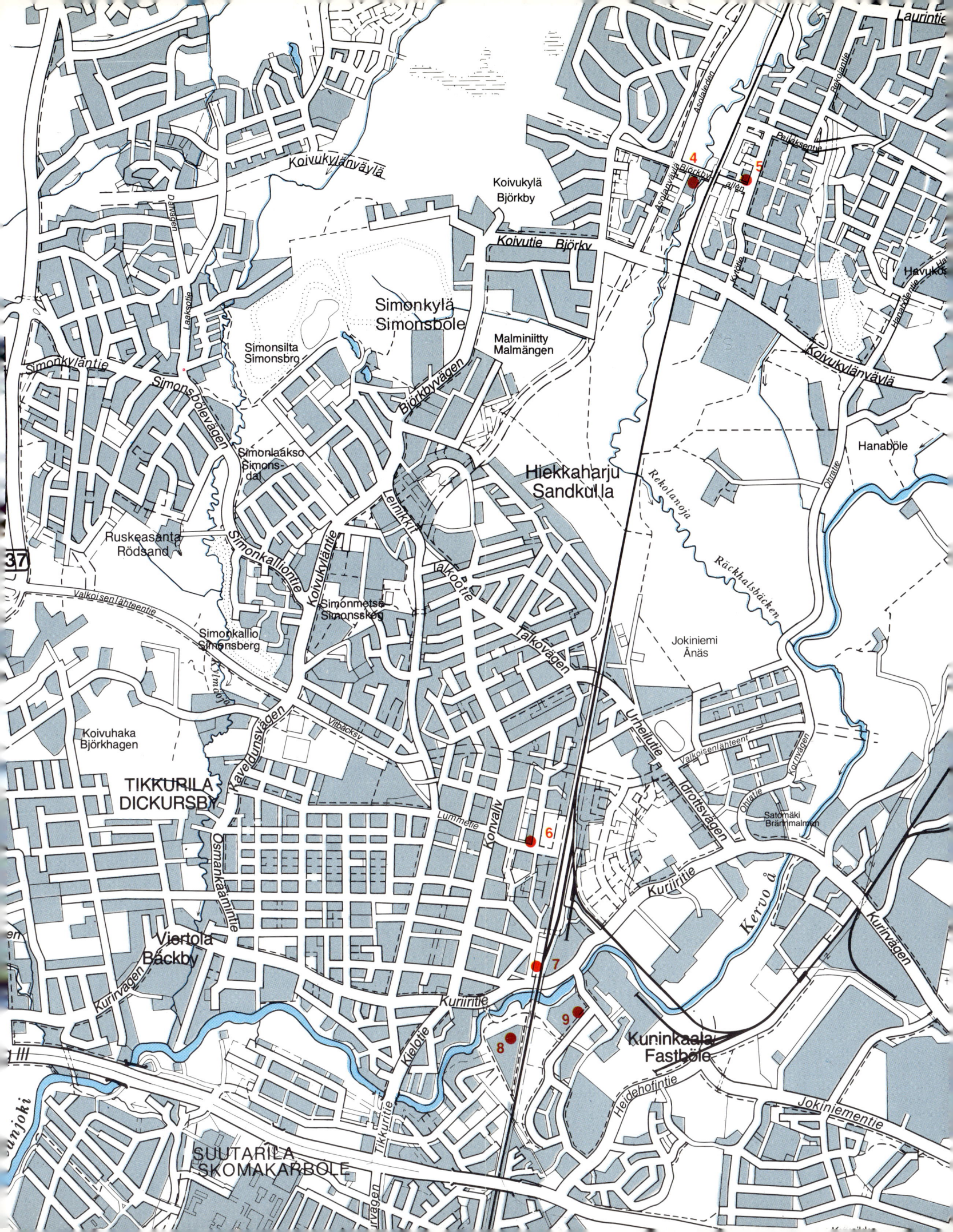

Koivukylänväylä

Koivukylä
Björkby

Koivutie Björk

4

5

Havuko

Koivukylänväylä

Simonkylä
Simonsböle

Simonsilta
Simonsbrg

Malminiitty
Malmängen

Hanaböle

Hiekkaharju
Sandkulla

Rekolanoja

Räckhalsbäcken

Simonkyläntie

Simonsbölevägen

Simonlaakso
Simons-
dal

Jokiniemi
Änäs

Björkbyvägen

Lemikki

37

Ruskeasanta
Rödsand

Simonkalliontie

Koivukyläntie

Talkootie

Valkoisenlähteentie

Simonmetsä
Simonsskog

Talkovägen

Simonkallio
Simonsberg

Kylmäoja

Urheilutie Idrottsvägen

Koivuhaka
Björkhagen

Viitbacksv.

Valkoisenlähteent.

Ontatie

Satomäki
Brännmalmen

Käyrdunsvägen

TIKKURILA
DICKURSBY

Lummetie

Konvaliv.

6

Kuriirintie

Kervo å

Kotivägen

Osmankäämintie

Viertola
Bäckby

Kuririvägen

7

Kurirvägen

Kielotie

9

8

Kuriirintie

Kuninkaala
Fastböle

Kunirvägen

Jokiniementie

Heidehofintie

njoki

SUUTARILA
SKOMAKARBÖLE

Tikkuritie

Jokiniementie

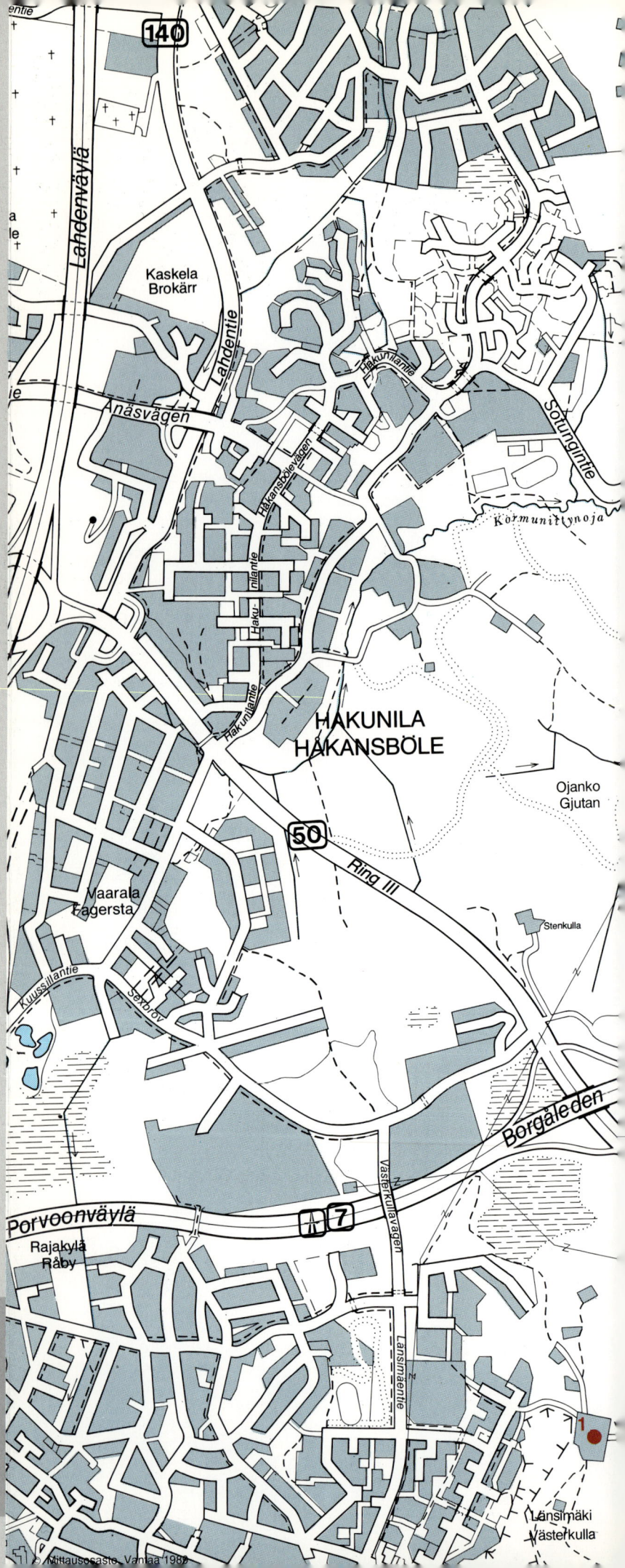

140

Kaskela
Brokärr

Lahdenväylä

Lahdentie

Anäsvägen

Hakunilantie

Håkansbölevägen

Sotungintie

Kormunitlynoja

HAKUNILA
HÅKANSBÖLE

Hakunilantie

Ojanko
Gjutan

50

Ring III

Stenkulla

Maarala
Fagersta

Kuussillantie

Sexbiöv

Borgäleden

Västerkullavägen

Porvoonväylä

7

Rajakylä
Råby

Länsimäentie

V2
V3

Länsimäki
Västerkulla

1

3

2

1

Königstedt Manor 1816
Solbackantie

The Königstedt Manor and the Linna Manor on the opposite side of the Vantaa River constitute an important milieu.

The present Engelian Empire-style manor house was completed in 1816. In 1915–16 the building underwent thorough renovations planned by Jarl Eklund, and the entrance porch with Ionic columns was built. The Ionic columns and tympanum fronting the park were designed by Eklund and constructed in 1937–38.

The state bought Königstedt Manor in 1961, and it is used for receptions and entertaining.

2

Backas Manor 1818
Ylästöntie

The main part of the wooden manor house was constructed in 1818 and the two protruding wings in 1844. The large steep-roofed brick barn visible from Ylästöntie was built by expanding and repairing an old barn in 1920 according to plans by Urho Åberg. The employees houses are located on the northern side of Ylästöntie. The red-brick buildings are attributed to Väinö Vähäkallio.

3

Helsinki Parish Church 1494
Kirkkotie 45

The Helsink Parish Church is dedicated to St. Laurence and is a late medieval Uusimaa stone church with the typical three aisles and ornate brick gables.

The western end of the church has retained its medieval appearance. The windows were altered in 1811, when the galleries were constructed. The church was severely damaged by fire in 1893. Repairs and renovations in 1893–94 were planned by Theodor Höijer.

The wooden houses and yards in the area to the west of the church and graveyard offer a good example of the traditional village. In the mid-1960s three new buildings were added to the Olofs House, the westernmost dwelling in the village. A day-care centre, child welfare clinic and a dormitory by Marjatta and Martti Jaatinen acknowledge the milieu in their scale and materials.

4

5

4

Seljapolku Day-Care Centre 1984
Seljapolku

Kari Järvinen, Timo Airas

The day-care centre is in Koivukylä, on a field to the west of the Helsinki-Hämeenlinna railway line. The lively rhythm of the roof is a noticable feature in the exterior form of the red-brick building, its steep oblique faces in an otherwise simple basic structure indicating the area of each group of children. The departments are also differentiated by the oblique skylight lanterns of the corridors. The slanting roof theme is repeated in the playrooms and playground canopies.

5

Hakopolku Commercial and Public Services Building 1981
Hakopolku 2

Eero Valjakka, Aarno Passoja

The building is located near the Koivukylä Residential Area and provides a route between there and the railway station for pedestrian traffic, which is directed through the building to the top level of the terraced Koivutori Square.

A library, youth activities facilities and restaurant are on the top level, and office space is in the first floor. A separate home for the elderly is a part of the whole. The façade material of the Commercial and Public Services building is red brick, and the same material, together with profiled concrete, has been used in the landscaping between the building and the railway station.

6

Lummetie Residential Buildings 1984
Lummetie

Eero Valjakka

The group of five three-story point blocks borders Tikkurila Central Park to the east. A split-level solution provides a partial gallery floor in the ground floor apartments. These apartments have a private walled-in courtyard. The façade material is sandlime brick.

7

Old Tikkurila Railway Station 1861
Haukipurontie

Carl Albert Edelfelt

The Tikkurila Railway Station is the oldest station building in Finland. It is also the only example of brick railway station architecture on the Helsinki-Hämeenlinna line to have retained its original appearance.

The façades of the three-story building are articulated with moldings between the floors and central projections on the long sides. The semicircular windows are singular, or they have been grouped as pairs or series of three windows. The building is framed by an eaves supported by wooden consoles.

The building was renovated in 1989 according to plans by Risto Mäkelä and now houses the Vantaa City Museum.

The Tikkurilan Raha-asema Building (Egil Nordin, 1979), the structure terminating the southern part of downtown Tikkurila, is cater-cornered to the Railway Station on the other side of the street.

7

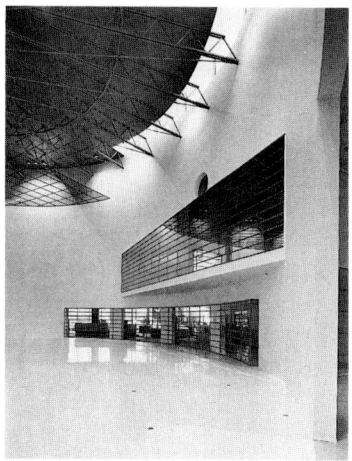

8

8

Heureka, the Finnish Science Centre 1988
Tiedepuisto

Mikko Heikkinen,
Markku Komonen

A public architectural competition for the science centre was held in 1985, and a divided first prize was awarded to Mikko Heikkinen and Markku Komonen. The competition was also significant because its object was a completely new type of building, both in its function and contents. This centre for cultural and leisure activities has no actual models or prototypes abroad.

The Heureka Science Centre was opened to the public in 1989. It is located between the heavily trafficked main railway line and the winding Keravanjoki River. Access to the building is through pedestrian bridges from Tikkurila or a tunnel, »The Black Hole,» from the parking area on the other side of the tracks. The entrance canopy fronts Tikkurila. The view of Heureka from a train window is of the long slanting, mirrored office-wing façade, with its network of steel bars, reflecting the sunlight in every color of the spectrum.

In its exterior form, geometric shapes intersect one another dynamically. In the interiors this creates a sense of a new kind of harmony. The central space for basic exhibitions is a large cylindral hall with Pantheon windows and a Foucalt pendelum. The structure supporting its roof resembles the spokes of a bicycle wheel, and is one of the several features in the building that illuminate science and technology. The spherical segment of the steel mirror-surfaced planetarium intersects the semicircular hall for temporary exhibitions, thus forming a new spatial boundary.

The production units of the Tikkurilan Silkki Textile Mill are opposite the science centre, on the other side of Keravanjoki River. The consistent and uniform industrial milieu dates from 1934–64 and was planned by Matti Finell.

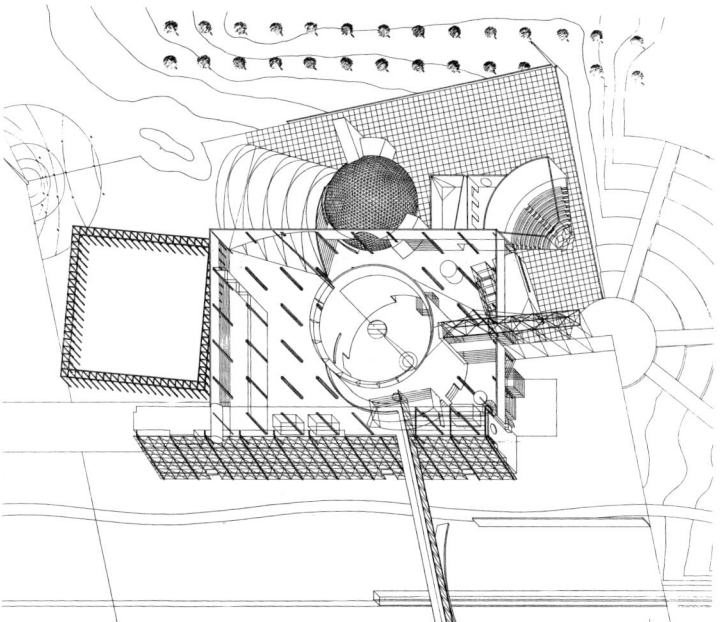

1

9

Tikkurila Research Centre 1985–88
Kuninkaalantie 1

Kaarina Löfström

An invitational competition for the laboratory building and a subsequent extension of the factory area was held in 1983. The three-story research centre is based on the winning entry. The two top floors contain laboratories and offices, separated by the staircase. The laboratory area is divided in six units. The research centre occupies a prominent site on Kuninkaanmäki Hill along the Keravanjoki rapids, and its external form is enhanced by strong vertical heating and ventilation elements, which also express the function of the building, and the metal sun screens in the windows.

The nearest of the old production units of the Tikkurila Company, is the former turn-of-the-century varnish factory on the other side of Keravanjoki River. In 1937 a cube-shaped annex by J. Fabritius was added atop the three-story factory building. The varnish factory is administered by the City of Vantaa, and it is to be transformed into a cultural and multipurpose building for young people. The renovations and alterations, planned by Risto Mäkelä, are scheduled for completion in 1990. Most of the space will be youth facilities, with an industrial museum in the varnish cooking room.

Westerkulla Manor 1827
Länsimäki

The nucleus of the present manor house was built in 1826–27. In 1875 an annex was added to the east side of the log-built mansard-roofed building. The two parts were joined with a gallery room in 1915 to plans by Jarl Eklund. The connecting part has an open entrance hall fronting the courtyard, with a pair of Doric columns and a tympanum. The resulting, fairly long building has a mansard roof. There is a barn, stables and employees residence in the courtyard area.

CHRONOLOGICAL INDEX

HELSINKI

ESPOO

KAUNIAINEN

VANTAA

INDEX OF BUILDING TYPES

INDEX OF ARCHITECTS

193

ABOUT THE AUTHORS

Otto-Iivari Meurman (b. 1890)
Architect, pioneer of Finnish town planning. Professor emeritus of town planning at Helsinki University of Technology. He is the author of the first Finnish textbook of town planning (Town planning 1947).

Kirmo Mikkola (1934–1986)
Architect, Doctor of Technology. Through his writings, teaching and various activities he had a great influence on the architectural discourse in Finland. He edited several publications and was the chief editor of Arkkitehti – Finnish Architectural Review 1967–68.

Marja-Riitta Norri
Architect. She has also designed exhibitions and edited several publications. Chief editor of Arkkitehti – Finnish Architectural Review 1981–87. Head of the Museum of Finnish Architecture since 1988.

Arvi Ilonen
Architect. In addition to his practical work he has been teaching at Helsinki University of Technology and at the University of Industrial Arts. Senior lecturer of the history of modern architecture 1979–85 and acting professor of architectural design at Tampere University of Technology 1986–88.

Pia Ilonen
Architect. She has designed exhibitions and worked as a graphic designer, for example as lay-out designer for Arkkitehti – Finnish Architectural Review for several years.

PHOTO CREDITS